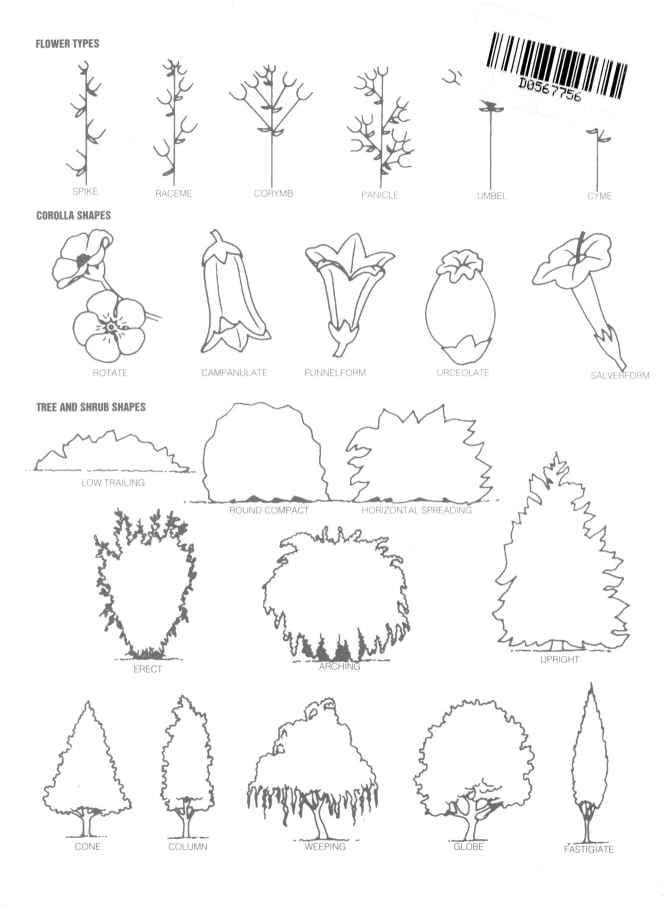

FLOWER TYPES

SPIKE RACEME CORYMB PANICLE UMBEL CYME

COROLLA SHAPES

ROTATE CAMPANULATE FUNNELFORM URCEOLATE SALVERFORM

TREE AND SHRUB SHAPES

LOW TRAILING ROUND COMPACT HORIZONTAL SPREADING

ERECT ARCHING UPRIGHT

CONE COLUMN WEEPING GLOBE FASTIGIATE

THE AMERICAN GARDEN GUIDES

perennial gardening

General Consultants:
Robert Bowden, Atlanta
Donald Buma, Botanica, The Wichita Gardens
Galen Gates, Chicago Botanic Garden
Jim Heinrich, Denver Botanical Garden
Mary Irish, Desert Botanical Garden
Richard Isaacson, Minnesota Landscape Arboretum
Kim Johnson and Nelson Sterner, Old Westbury Gardens, New York
Dr. Linda McMahon, Berry Botanical Garden, Portland, Oregon
Kathy Musial, Huntington Botanical Gardens
Susan Nolde, Brookside Gardens, Wheaton, Maryland

Daylily Consultant: Greg Piotrowski
Fern Consultant: Mobee Weinstein

Historical Consultant: Frank J. Anderson, former curator, The New York
Botanical Garden Library
Botany Consultant: Dr. Lucile McCook, former taxonomist, Missouri
Botanical Garden
Enabling Garden Consultant: Eugene Rothert, Chicago Botanic Garden

Design Consultant: Lynden B. Miller

perennial gardening

The New York Botanical Garden

By Michael Ruggiero
Senior Curator

With Ruth Rogers Clausen
Series Editor: Elvin McDonald
Principal Photographer: Albert Squillace
Preface: Gregory Long

Pantheon Books,
Knopf Publishing Group
New York
1995

Acknowledgments
This book was created with the help, expertise, and encouragement of a great many people. We would like to thank all the consultants who contributed so much to it, and Albert Squillace who took magnificent photographs. We appreciate the help of Liz Innvar and other members of The New York Botanical Garden horticulture department: Andrew Block, Theresa Broglio, Lisa Cady, Wayne Cahilly, Ashley Christopher, Margaret Falk, Chris Gioia, Joan Gori, Milie Dal Pino, Susan Keiser, Bob Lehman, Ken Molinari, Ralph Padilla, Robert Russo, Patti Scheuring, Elaina Schott, Noah Schwartz, Doris Straus, Kathy Venezia, Janet Whippo, and Terry Zahairades. Thanks are also due to Karl Lauby, Marilyn Ratner, Richard Schnall, Kenneth Roman, Sydney Eddison, Ken Druse, Bob Bartolomei, Jimmy Martucci, Brad Roeller, Claire's Nursery, Joseph Blank, Daphne White, Susan Ralston, Jennifer Bernstein, Jennifer Parkinson, Ellen McNeilly, David Prior, Alan Kellock, Jay Hyams, Eric Marshall, Chani Yammer, Etti Yammer, Jane Gil, Stephen and Cathy Weinroth, Michelle Stein, and Deena Stein.

Project Director: Lori Stein
Book Design Consultant: Albert Squillace
Editorial Director: Jay Hyams
Associate Art Director: Eric Marshall

Library of Congress Cataloging-in-Publication Data
Ruggiero, Michael,
Perennial gardening / by Michael Ruggiero, with Ruth Rogers Clausen; preface by Gregory Long; principal photography by Albert Squillace.
—1st ed.
p. cm. -- (The American garden guides)
Includes indexes
ISBN 0-679-41431-2
1. Perennials –United States. 2. Perennials –Canada.
3. Perennials–Pictorial works. I. Clausen, Ruth Rogers
II. Title III. Series
SB434.R83 1994
635.9'32'097–dc20   93-11358
                                     CIP

Manufactured in Singapore

9 8 7 6 5 4 3

Opposite: **The New York Botanical Garden perennial garden.**

contents

Balloon flower.

Daylilies and Balloon flowers

the american garden guides

The network of botanical gardens and arboreta in the United States and Canada constitutes a great treasure chest of knowledge about plants and what they need. Some of the most talented, experienced, and dedicated plantspeople in the world work full-time at these institutions; they are the people who actually grow plants, make gardens, and teach others about the process. They are the gardeners who are responsible for the gardens in which millions of visitors exclaim, "Why won't that plant grow that way for me?"

Over thirty of the most respected and beautiful gardens on the continent are participating in the creation of *The American Garden Guides*. The books in the series originate with manuscripts generated by gardeners in one or several of the gardens. Drawing on their decades of experience, these originating gardeners write down the techniques they use in their own gardens, recommend and describe the plants that grow best for them, and discuss their successes and failures. The manuscripts are then passed to several other participating gardens; in each, the specialist in that area adds recommended plants and other suggestions based on regional differences and different opinions.

The series has three major philosophical points carried throughout:

1) Successful gardens are by nature user-friendly toward the gardener and the environment. We advocate water conservation through the precepts of Xeriscaping and garden health care through Integrated Pest Management (IPM). Simply put, one does not set into motion any garden that is going to require undue irrigation during normal levels of rainfall, nor apply any pesticide or other treatment without first assessing its impact on all other life—plant, animal, and soil.

2) Gardening is an inexact science, learned by observation and by doing. Even the most experienced gardeners often develop markedly dissimilar ways of doing the same thing, or have completely divergent views of what any plant requires in order to thrive. Gardeners are an opinionated lot, and we have encouraged all participants to air and share their differences–and so, to make it clear that everyone who gardens will find his or her own way of dealing with plants. Although it is important to know the rules and the most accepted practices, it is also important to recognize that whatever works in the long run for you is the right way.

3) Part of the fun of gardening lies in finding new plants, not necessarily using over and over the same ones in the same old color schemes. In this book and others in the series, we have purposely included some lesser-known or underused plants, some of them native to our vast and wonderful continent. Wherever we can, we call attention to endangered species and suggest ways to nurture them back to their natural state of plenty.

This book was originated at The New York Botanical Garden. Mike Ruggiero, senior curator, was the principal author; the sections of daylilies and ferns were provided by his colleagues at The New York Botanical Garden, Greg Piotrowski and Mobee Weinstein, respectively. Lynden Miller provided information for the design chapter. The manuscript was then passed to other gardens, where changes were made to include other opinions and regional information. Ruth Rogers Clausen then completed the manuscript.

Elvin McDonald
Houston, Texas

president's preface

One of the special pleasures of visiting The New York Botanical Garden from May through October is the ever-changing display of blooms and foliage, colors, textures, and architecture in the Jane Watson Irwin Perennial Garden. Indeed, because of their vitality and vibrant beauty, perennials have increased enormously in popularity among gardeners as well as visitors to the Garden in recent years. In *Perennial Gardening,* Mike Ruggiero, Senior Curator at The New York Botanical Garden, along with Ruth Rogers Clausen and Albert Squillace, has captured perennials' vitality in a lively, resourceful guide for novice as well as experienced gardeners.

Of course, the professional gardeners here at The New York Botanical Garden devote hours each day to the care of the Perennial Garden. When weekend gardeners like me strive for similar effects in our back-yards, we are sometimes disappointed or frustrated with the results. For example, delphinium are one of my favorite perennials and a highlight of my own garden in upstate New York. *Perennial Gardening* tells me what professional gardeners already know about these stately plants: they need staking and they are "greedy feeders," requiring careful tending and attention. It's helpful to know their pitfalls and growing requirements and very useful to have a list of superior delphinium hybrids recommended by these demanding horticulturists.

This book places a special emphasis on the maintenance of perennials, culling the best hints from the authors' decades of gardening experience. In addition to the expert opinions and observations of the principal authors, this volume includes quotes from noted writers, gardeners, and garden designers from all over the nation. It also contains practical tips and step-by-step photographs in the "techniques" section and inspiring suggestions in the "garden design" section.

The New York Botanical Garden in the Bronx is pleased to be part of *The American Garden Guides* series. Many NYBG staff members, knowledgeable and passionate about perennials, ferns, daylilies, garden design, and gardening techniques, are contributing their expertise in these volumes. We hope the observations and advice in this volume will enlighten many who enjoy *Perennial Gardening*.

Gregory Long
President
The New York Botanical Garden
Bronx, New York
January, 1994

1. INTRODUCTION

Perennials can be enjoyed from the first hint of spring to the first frost of winter–and sometimes even peek their heads through the snow. *Above:* An iris bud, about to burst into bloom. *Opposite bottom:* The famous walled garden at Old Westbury Gardens is a riot of color in midsummer. *Opposite top:* In The New York Botanical Garden's fall border, asters, *Artemisia, Sedum,* and *Perilla* provide a striking display of deep color well into autumn.

Preceding pages: The Jane Watson Irwin Perennial Garden at The New York Botanical Garden.

Some people rely on calendars to inform them of the passage of time. Far more eloquent are the messages sent by nature through the flowers that arrive, year after year, in our gardens. Anyone who grows perennials is intimately connected to the wheel of the seasons, waiting for the coming of the old friends that spring up each year and then recede into the earth to await their next resurrection. The beauty of perennial flowers and the never-ceasing wonder of their miraculous reappearance combine to make them the favorite plants of gardeners around the world.

DEFINING PERENNIALS Perennials–the word comes from a Latin word meaning "enduring" or "perpetual"–are plants that survive for more than two growing seasons. A vast number of plants live for many years–all trees and shrubs are perennials, as are many ferns, vines, and bulbs–so perennials are further divided into two groups: woody perennials and herbaceous perennials. Woody perennials–trees, shrubs, and some vines–have bark-covered stems that do not die to the ground at the end of the growing season. Herbaceous perennials usually have green and pliant stems without woody tissue. At some point each year, due to environmental factors, such as changes in temperature, light, or water, herbaceous perennials die back to ground level. But their roots remain alive, and the plants "reawaken" when conditions are suitable for growth. For some perennials, the right conditions arrive in the spring; others come to life in the summer, still others in the fall. In this book, we use the term *perennials* to refer to herbaceous perennials.

In horticultural terms, the fact that perennials normally survive more than two full growing seasons separates them from annuals, which die after a single growing season, and biennials, which die at the end of two growing seasons. Some perennials, such as hostas, daylilies, and peonies, will bloom reliably for decades, while others, such as delphiniums and Shasta daisies, will die out after only a few seasons. Plants are often considered perennials even if they technically fall into another class–for example, *Digitalis* is a biennial that often seeds itself and exceeds two seasons; *Iberis sempervirens* (candytuft) is a subshrub, but is usually listed as a perennial.

USING PERENNIALS Perennials have enormous appeal for the gardener. Properly selected, they will bring bloom to a garden from the earliest spring irises to the asters and chrysanthemums that last until the first frost. When they are not in bloom, their foliage adds shape, texture, and color to the garden. It should also be admitted that perennials are attractive because they allow the gardener to avoid the once-a-year toil associated with annuals.

Perennials can be used in all types of gardens. Some gardeners prefer their perennial gardens to be composed mostly of perennials; some people even specialize in a single type of plant, such as irises or daylilies. But most good gardens use other types of plants–trees, shrubs, bulbs, annuals, and biennials–as companions to their perennials; these gardens are called mixed gardens.

Most perennial gardens are composed of flowerbeds and borders. A bed can be flanked by a structure like a wall or hedge, or it may form an island with walking space around it. A border is really just a long, narrow bed; borders are frequently backed by walls, hedges, or buildings and are sometimes used along driveways, paths, or property lines. These borders can consist of a single row of flowers–daylilies are often used this way–or an intricately designed mixture of foliage that is appealing through most of the year, accented by shrubs and enlivened by blooms as they occur.

Rock Gardens Following an old tradition, alpine or mountain plants were once the only flowers used in rock gardens, but today small or low-growing perennials, such as the moss pink (*Phlox subulata*)–which remain in scale and within bounds–are used. Perennials are ideal for rock gardens since their foliage creates the structure of the garden and adds color and texture even when the plants are not flowering.

Woodland Gardens With the increased tendency to naturalistic and low-maintenance shaded gardens, woodland gardens have become popular, and they are perfect for perennials. Subtle effects can be achieved by mixing plantings of native and introduced perennials with ferns, trees, and shrubs.

Native Plant Gardens If you decide to use only native flora–those plants originally found in the wild somewhere in North America–you will discover that perennials have a wealth to offer. Native-plant gardens are often referred to as wildflower gardens, particularly when they are limited to herbaceous perennials, but you can also use native plants to create a meadow, although that type of garden is seldom restricted to native plants and is usually planted with suitable plants from all over the world. Wildlife gardens, planted to attract birds

HISTORICAL NOTES

Anchored in the narrows that today bear his name, the Italian navigator Giovanni da Verrazzano, probably the first European to enter New York Bay, reported that the wind was full of the sweet smell of flowers. To our first generations of colonists and frontiersmen, the vastness of this land was a wilderness to be tamed: land to be broken by the plow and seeded to feed the growing republic.

Some of the people who ventured forth from the Old World brought with them seeds from their former homesteads, and they used those stocks to raise familiar crops and flowers in the new land. Those were the heirloom plants that established reminders of Europe outside the doorsteps of the newly built homes in that raw wilderness. Such grain crops as wheat, barley, and oats were set out in the kitchen garden, along with old-time blooms of hollyhock, calendula, canterbury bells, and that herald of English springtime, the primrose. Thus did the Old World mingle with the New, relieving some of the strangeness felt by those first settlers.

In accordance with the Puritan denial of beauty for its own sake–and reflecting the fact that Americans had little time for the pursuit of pleasurable hobbies–the first American gardens were vegetable or herb plots. Most of the plants were eaten or used in some way; even the flowers were usually used as medicines or dyes. Rarely was an effort made to design the garden for symmetry or beauty, and most colonial gardens were laid out to allow the most plants in the smallest amount of space, with the greatest access for ease of maintenance.

Though formal gardens were something of a rarity, they did exist, particularly on government property. There were extensive formal gardens at the governor's mansion in Williamsburg, Virginia, which contained many ornamental beds in addition to kitchen gardens. The garden of John Bartram (1699-1777), near Philadelphia, was famous for its ornamentals as well as for other rare plants that he collected and propagated. Bartram, a ploughman, devoted his life to collecting specimens of the wealth of new plants available in the New World, traveling from Lake Erie to Florida; he was appointed King's Botanist for his efforts. He conducted the first American experiments in hybridization, working with *lychnis,* and named his plants according to the Linnaean system. Among the plants he sent to England were lilies, dog-tooth violets, shooting stars, wild asters, gentians, and honeysuckle; from England, he imported iris, snapdragons, oriental poppies, carnations, and daffodils for distribution here.

Another important plantsman was our first president. In June 1797, Polish poet and patriot Julian Ursyn Niemcesicz visited Mount Vernon and wrote about George Washington's garden: "It is well cultivated and neatly kept . . . one sees there all the vegetables for the kitchen . . . one sees also in the garden lilies, roses, and pinks. . . . After seeing his house and his gardens, one would see that he had seen the most beautiful examples in England of this style."

Other early botanists included Benjamin Smith Barton, who held the first chair of botany at the University of Pennsylvania, and Benjamin Waterhouse, who lectured in botany at Harvard as early as 1768. New York Lieutenant Governor Cadwallader Colden wrote the first treatise on the flora of New York; Mrs. Martha Daniel Logan is credited with writing the first gardening book, *Gardener's Kalendar*, in this country. The New York Horticultural Society was founded in 1818, horticultural societies in Pennsylvania and Massachusetts followed in 1827 and 1829. Throughout the 19th century gardening and agriculture magazines abounded, including *Floral Magazine and Botanical Repository*, *Ladies Horticultural Magazine and Floral Register,* and the *Horticulturist*. The first American flower show was held in Philadelphia in 1829 and soon became an annual event; exhibits took place in Boston, New York, and other cities as well. Plant crazes swept the country periodically: chysanthemums in 1890, asters in 1900-10, sweet peas in 1912.

Until recently, Americans have been influenced by England in their choice of garden design. Until the end of the 19th century that meant following the stylized, enclosed gardens of Capability Brown and Humphrey Repten. In the 20th century, William Robinson and Gertrude Jekyll broke this tradition, placing an emphasis on perennial plants and striving for a more natural look. Jekyll, a British garden designer, is considered by many to be the most influential voice in perennial design; she placed great importance on juxtaposition of plants, studying each one for shape, texture, and color, and popularizing many new plants. Today, the "new American garden" style accepts many of Jekyll's ideas and extends them, incorporating the native plants that were found on this continent by the original settlers into gardens that echo the country's natural landscape.

and butterflies, are sometimes restricted to natives, but the emphasis in such gardens is on the ability of the plants to attract fauna, so the place of origin is of less importance.

Cut Flowers Like annuals and biennials, perennials make excellent cut flowers. Indeed, the perennials in a well-planned garden will provide you with cut flowers throughout the season, from spring irises and peonies to autumn's asters and mums. If you have the space, you can set aside part of your garden for this purpose; if not, you can cut flowers selectively from the beds. Some perennials, such as yarrow, feverfew, and baby's breath, may be used both fresh and dried.

WHAT PERENNIALS NEED The basic requirements of perennials are the same as those of other plants–soil, sun, water, and protection–but since your perennials will spend many seasons in your garden, it is best to plan ahead and make certain not only that their placement fits your garden's design but that you are putting them in the best place for their needs. Find out ahead of time precisely what each needs so that those with similar needs can be grown together.

Soil Matching the condition of the soil to the needs of the plant is an essential aspect of gardening and is always stressed at The New York Botanical Garden. In general, the better the structure of the soil at planting time, the greater the success you will have with perennials. Poor soil can be improved in several ways, such as by adding organic matter. The New York Botanical Garden frequently amends poor soil; see page 187 for a complete description of how this is done.

Most perennials grow best in soil that is well drained, not overly dry or waterlogged, but some, such as purple coneflowers, tolerate or even require such extremes. Many desert plants adapt well to dry soils, and some of the perennials that naturally grow in wet places are ideal for bog gardens. Sandy soils dry out rapidly, while those with a high clay content drain slowly. The addition of organic material helps retain moisture in dry soils and improves the draining of wet ones.

Also important is the alkalinity or acidity, known as the pH. Acid soils range from 0 to 6.9 while alkaline soils range from 7.1 to 14. The vast majority of perennials are at their best in soils from 6.0 to 7.0 but they tolerate a wide range. A few, such as pinks and baby's breath, prefer a slightly higher pH.

Sun or Shade The amount of sun or shade to which the plants are exposed is of great importance. The less sun available, the more restricted the plant palette, but here again perennials display a wide range of tolerance. Some plants, such as daylilies, grow reasonably well in shade, but they will have little in the way of flowers. The sun-versus-shade requirements provided in books and nursery catalogs are designed to serve as guides only, for such requirements differ across the country. For example, in northern climates Japanese anemones do well in full sun, but in a similar location in southern California the foliage would burn.

The type of shade and what creates it are also important. Shade cast by

At The New York Botanical Garden, perennials are grown for their foliage as well as for their flowers; the foliage remains in the garden for the full season, and the flowers are usually short-lived bonuses. Combinations of different textures, colors, and shapes of foliage can be more interesting than vivid blossoms. *Above,* ***Lamium,*** ***Artemisia,*** and ***Ceratostigma*** foliage.

A BRIEF LESSON IN BOTANY

Plants are living things and share many traits with animals. Plants are composed of millions of individual cells that are organized into complex organ systems. Plants breathe (take in and expel gases) and extract energy from food; to do this they require water, nutrients, and atmospheric gases. Like animals, plants reproduce sexually, and their offspring inherit characteristics through a genetic code passed along as DNA and, unlike animals, some plants reproduce asexually.

Plants, however, can do one thing that no animal can do. Through a process called photosynthesis, plants can capture energy from the sun and convert that energy into compounds such as proteins, fats, and carbohydrates. These energy-rich compounds are the source of the energy for all animal life, including humans.

THE IMPORTANCE OF PLANTS

Because no living animals can produce the energy they need to live, all their energy comes from plants. Like other animals, we eat green plants directly, in the form of fruits, vegetables, and grains (breads and cereals), or we eat animals and animal products that were fed green plants.

The oxygen we need to live on Earth is constantly pumped out of green plants as a byproduct of photosynthesis. Plants prevent the erosion of our precious soils and hinder water loss to the atmosphere.

Plants are also an important source of drugs. Fully one-quarter of all prescriptions contain at least one plant-derived product. Aspirin, one of the most commonly used drugs, was originally isolated from the bark of the willow tree. Today, scientists are screening plants from all over the world in search of new compounds to cure cancer, AIDS, and other diseases.

THE WHOLE PLANT

Basically, a plant is made up of leaves, stems, and roots; all these parts are connected by a vascular system, much like our circulatory system. The vascular system can be seen in the veins of a leaf, or in the rings in a tree.

LEAVES

Leaves are generally flattened and expanded tissues that are green due to the presence of chlorophyll, the pigment that is necessary for photosynthesis. Most leaves are connected to the stem by a stalk, or petiole, which allows the leaves to alter their position in relation to the sun and capture as much energy as possible. Plants that have leaves year-round are often called "evergreen," while plants that lose all their leaves at one time each year are termed "deciduous."

Leaves come in an astounding variety of shapes, textures, and sizes. Some leaves are composed of a single structure, or blade, and are termed simple. Other leaves are made up of many units, or leaflets, and are called compound (see endpapers).

STEMS

Technically, a stem is the tissue that supports leaves and that connects the leaves with the roots via a vascular system. Stems also bear the flowers on a plant. Therefore, a stem can be identified by the presence of buds, which are the unexpanded leaves, stems, or flowers that will develop at a later time.

Plants that send up leaves in a rosette or clump may have stems so short that they are difficult to distinguish. Other plants, like the iris, have a stem, called a rhizome, that travels horizontally underground. Many plants of arid regions have very reduced leaves or have lost their leaves altogether in order to avoid loss of water to the atmosphere. The barrel cactus is an example of a plant that is almost entirely stem.

ROOTS

Although out of sight, roots are extremely important to the life of the plant. Roots anchor a plant in the soil, absorb water and nutrients, and store excess food, such as starches, for the plants' future use. Basically, there are two types of roots: taproots and fibrous roots. Taproots are thickened, unbranched roots that grow straight down, taking advantage of moisture and nutrients far below the soil surface. Taproots, such as carrots, store carbohydrates. Fibrous roots are fine, branching, and generally more shallow. They often form dense mats of roots, making them excellent agents of soil stabilization. Fibrous roots absorb moisture and nutrients from a shallow zone of soil and may be more susceptible to drought.

Roots obviously need to come into contact with water, but they also need air in order to work properly. Except for those adapted to aquatic environments, most plants require well-drained soils that provide them air as well as water.

VASCULAR SYSTEMS

Plants have a well-developed vascular system that extends throughout the plant body and that allows movement of water and compounds from one part of a plant to another. Once the roots absorb water and minerals, the vascular system funnels them to the leaves, where they are used in photosynthesis. Likewise, energy-rich compounds that are produced in the leaves must travel to the stems and roots to provide nutrition for further growth. The vascular system also strengthens plant tissues. Although much of the vascular system is part of the internal anatomy of a plant, some parts can be seen.

PHOTOSYNTHESIS

A green plant is like a factory that takes raw materials available in the environment and converts them into other forms of energy. In a complex series of energy transfer and chemical conversion events called photosynthesis, plants take energy from the sun, minerals and water from the soil, and gases from the atmosphere; these raw materials are converted into chemical forms of energy that are used for plant growth. These same energy-rich compounds (proteins, sugars and starches, fats and oils) can be utilized by animals as a source of food and nutrition. All this is possible because of a green pigment, chlorophyll.

Photosynthesis is an extremely complex series of reactions that takes place in the cells of leaves, the byproducts of which are connected to other reactions throughout the cell. The most basic reactions of photosynthesis occurs like this. Energy from the sun strikes the leaf surface, and electrons in the chlorophyll molecule become "excited" and

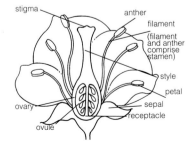

stigma — anther
filament
(filament and anther comprise stamen)
style
petal
ovary
sepal
receptacle
ovule

are boosted to a higher energy level. Excited electrons are routed through a chain of reactions that extracts and stores energy in the form of sugars. As a byproduct of electron loss, water molecules (H_2O) are split; hydrogen moves in to replenish the electrons lost from chlorophyll, and Oxygen is released, finding its way into our atmosphere. In another photosynthetic reaction, carbon dioxide from the atmosphere is "fixed," or converted into organic compounds within the plant cell. These first chemical compounds are the building blocks for more complex reactions and are the precursors for the formation of many elaborate chemical compounds.

PLANT NUTRITION

Plants require mineral nutrients from the soil, water, and the atmosphere in order to maintain healthy growth and reproduction. Macronutrients, those nutrients needed in large amounts, include hydrogen, oxygen, and carbon so essential for photosynthesis. Other macronutrients are nitrogen, phosphorus, potassium, sulfur, and calcium. Nitrogen is an important component of chlorophyll and of proteins, which are used to construct DNA, cell membranes, and other vital compounds in the cell. Phosphorus is also used in building DNA and is important in cell development. Potassium is important in the development of tubers, roots, and other storage organs. If macronutrients are in limited supply, growth and development in the plant will be strongly curtailed. Micronutrients, such as iron, copper and magnesium, are required in smaller amounts and are of variable importance to different kinds of plants.

LIFE CYCLE

Higher plants (except for ferns) begin life as a seed. Given the right set of conditions (temperature, moisture, light), a seed will germinate and develop its first roots and leaves using food stored in the seed (humans and other animals take advantage of the high-quality food in seeds when we eat wheat, rice, and corn, just to name a few). Because of the presence of chlorophyll in the leaves, the small plant is soon able to produce its own food, which is used immediately for further growth and development. As the seedling grows in size, it also grows in complexity. The first, simple root gives way to a complex root system that may include

underground storage organs. The stem is transformed into an intricate system of vascular tissue that moves water from the ground upward into the leafy part of the plant, while other tissues transport energy-rich compounds manufactured in the leaves downward to be stored in stem and root systems.

Once the plant reaches maturity, flower initiation begins. Flowers hold the sexual apparatus for the plant; their brilliant colors and glorious odors are advertisements to attract pollinators such as insects or birds. In a basic, complete flower, there are four different parts, given below. However, many plants have incomplete flowers with one or more of these parts missing, or the parts may be highly modified.

1. Sepals. The outermost part of the flower, the sepals cover the young floral buds. Although they are often green, they may be variously colored.

2. Petals. The next layer of parts in the flower, petals are often colorful and play an important role in attracting pollinators.

3. Stamens. Stamens are located next to the petals, or may even be basally fused to the petals. The stamens are the "male" reproductive parts of the flower; they produce the pollen. Pollen grains are fine, dustlike particles that will divide to form sperm cells. The tissue at the end of the stamen that holds pollen is called the anther.

4. Pistil. The innermost part of the flower holds the female reproductive apparatus for the plant. The stigma, located at the tip of the pistil, is often covered with a sticky substance and is the site where pollen is deposited. The stigma is held by a floral tube, call the style. At the base of the style, the ovary holds one to many ovules, which contain eggs that represent undeveloped seeds.

Pollination is the transfer of pollen from

an anther to a stigma and is the first step in the production of seeds. Pollen can be transferred by an insect visiting the flower, by the wind, or even by the splashing of raindrops. After being deposited on a compatible stigma, the pollen grains grow into tubes that travel from the stigma down the floral tube into the ovary, depositing sperm cells to the ovules. If all goes well, sperm cells unite with the eggs inside the ovules, and fertilization takes place.

After fertilization, the entire floral structure is transformed into a fruit. Fruit can be fleshy, like an apple, or dry like a pea pod. Within each fruit, fertilized eggs develop into seeds, complete with a cache of storage tissue and a seed coat.

ANNUALS AND PERENNIALS

An annual is a plant in which the life cycle is completed in a growing season; a biennial returns the following year and then dies; a perennial is a plant that persists and produces reproductive structures year after year. The seed of an annual might germinate in the spring, produce flowers in the summer, and drop their seeds a little later; the plant itself will wither and die completely by the time winter arrives. The following growing season, seeds are the only tissue available to begin another round of the life cycle of the annual plant. In contrast, a perennial plant may die back during the winter, but some part of the plant, usually a stem or root structure, remains alive all winter. When spring comes, perennials resprout new leaves or stems from last season's plants and may also have seeds from the previous year.

These definitions are based on the biology of the plant, but do not account for the many ways that humans cultivate plants. Many of the plants that we cultivate as annuals are actually perennials in their native habitate. For example, pampas grass is a perennial, but does not survive very cold weather; in colder climates, it is grown as an annual, or dug up and brought inside for the winter.

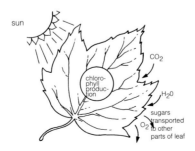

sun

CO_2

chlorophyll production

H_2O

sugars transported to other parts of leaf

O_2

THE JANE WATSON IRWIN PERENNIAL GARDEN is one of 27 specialty gardens and plant collections in the 250-acre New York Botanical Garden in the Bronx. In recent years, Lynden B. Miller and Mike Ruggiero have redesigned, replanted, and revitalized this garden, adding hundreds of outstanding perennials along with excellent shrubs and ornamental grasses, providing the visitor with exciting ideas for home gardens.

Here, the rich tones of purple smokebushes, red barberry, and shrubby red-stemmed dogwood enhance the beauty of phlox, meadow rue, Japanese anemones, geraniums, salvias, daylilies, and much more. The garden is divided into two sections, displaying flowering perennials on the "hot" and "cool" sides of the color spectrum. Shady areas under huge white pines are filled with an oustanding collection of luscious hostas as well as astilbes, ferns, ligularias, and hellebores. With an emphasis on foliage and form as well as bloom, this area looks captivating all year.

deciduous, high-branched and deep-rooted trees or by walls and high buildings is preferable to the all-year shade from evergreens.

Water Water availability is another factor to consider when growing perennials. The amount of available water is tied inextricably to the soil. In hot, dry areas of North America, it would be wise to select perennials that prefer dry conditions and plant them together, since those requiring more water would suffer in the same setting. Millions of gallons of water are wasted in trying to grow plants not adapted to the climate, a waste made even sadder when one considers the many other species to choose from. Even if you select your plants carefully, some will need additional water during times of drought.

Hardiness The hardiness of a particular plant is the final deciding factor in its selection. The hardiness to winter cold or summer heat determines whether a plant will be successful in a particular climatic zone. Ranges have been established for all plants, and they are given in this book, but such ranges can serve only as guides. Many plants on the market today are tolerant of a wider set of conditions than apparently thought, so experiment with various plants–you may find some that thrive against all expectations. Many professional gardeners try a particular species at least three times before concluding that it is not adapted to their zone. The system of zones is based on minimum winter temperatures and is thus somewhat vague. Summer hardiness refers to a plant's ability to perform during the hottest time of the year.

Perennials can be grown under a wide range of conditions, and there is a plant for every site and every climate. But don't let your enthusiasm to plant a new bed or border make you overlook the fact that each species has needs and optimum growing conditions. Don't try to force plants to adapt to adverse conditions; instead, select your plants based on their ability to thrive under the particular set of circumstances in your garden. Then, having planted your perennials, you can wait for the timely arrival of each season's colors.

Below: Michael Ruggiero. *Above:* a field of hostas, one of Ruggiero's specialties. Opposite page: Two views of The Jane Watson Irwin Perennial Garden at The New York Botanical Garden, showing usage of both flowering and foliage plants.

MICHAEL RUGGIERO, the Frederick and Patricia Summer Senior Curator of the Peggy Rockefeller Rose Garden and the Special Gardens, has been working at the New York Botanical Garden since he was fourteen years old. He is in charge of the planting and maintenance of the perennial garden, as well as the rose, demonstration, herb, and several other specialty gardens, and teaches in the School of Horticulture. He has taught and lectured in 27 different horticultural subjects, including the horticulture of woody plants at the University of Connecticut. He is also involved in the design of these gardens.

Mike believes that the success of a garden is determined mostly by the quality of its soil. Although plants can be found for any soil type, Mike believes in amending–or replacing–soil to provide the proper growing medium; once that is done, plants need much less care.

Although he knows and loves thousands of plants, Mike's specialties are daylilies, daffodils, tulips, and hostas; he has over 100 hosta plants in his own home garden, and has created hundreds of hybrid daylilies. His many years of experience have taught him that the flowers in a perennial garden are the icing on the cake; a successful perennial garden will also include interesting combinations of foliage plants, and flowering plants that have interesting foliage. He is married to Mobee Weinstein, fern consultant for this volume.

SCIENTIFIC NOMENCLATURE

Botanists and horticulturists use a binomial, or two-name, system to label the over 250,000 species of living plants. Because the names are in Latin form, this system crosses both time and language barriers and allows people all over the world to communicate about plants. Occasionally, a scientific name will be changed by scientists; these changes reflect additions to our knowledge about the plant.

A scientific name is made up of the genus (singular; genera is plural) and the species, as in *Achillea millefolium*. The genus is always first and is always capitalized. The species name follows the genus and is generally not capitalized. If another Latinized name follows the genus and species, it denotes a subspecies, such as a subset or variety.

Cultivated plants are often selected for a particular attribute, such as leaf or flower color or resistance to disease. These selections are given a cultivar, or cultivated variety, name in addition to the genus or species. Cultivar names are capitalized and in single quotations, such as 'Summer Pastels' or 'Rose Beauty'.

Hybrids are plants resulting from sexual reproduction between two different kinds of plants. A hybrid may be denoted by an "x" such as *Sedum* x 'Autumn Joy'.

Many plants have common names as well. In fact, most familiar plants have too many common names, creating a problem in communication–for example, *Monarda didyma* is called beebalm, bergamot, and Oswego tea. But it has ony one correct scientific name.

Gardeners don't always enjoy every part of the gardening process–but finding a great new plant is pure pleasure for just about everyone. Since thousands of different varieties and cultivars are currently being sold, and nurseries, botanists, and private gardeners all over the world are busy finding and creating more, there will never be a shortage of new plants to discover. Moreover, new methods of transportation and communication are making it easier for us to find and use perennials that are common in other parts of the world. The key is finding out which ones are right for you.

This plant selector chapter is designed to give you basic information about perennials to grow in your own garden. For information on techniques like how to plant or how to start seeds indoors, see Chapter 3; for information on how to design a garden, see Chapter 4. In this chapter, you will find portraits of individual perennials. Our gardening experts have selected about 200 varieties that work well for them; they mixed some common, easy-to-find selections with others that you might not know about, but should. Gardeners from other botanic gardens around the country added varieties that do well in their regions.

When deciding which perennials to grow, ask yourself:

1. Do I want flowers for cutting? For fragrance? For early spring? For winter interest?

2. What is my climate zone? Do I live in the right geographical region for this plant? If you live in a warm region, you may be able to grow pampas grass, but not delphinium, which do better in a cooler climate. If you are not sure about your climate zone, talk to your county extension service, local nursery, or botanic garden. But don't forget that your site is unique; it has its own "microclimate," and conditions may be different from those 2 blocks away let alone at the nursery 10 miles down the road. Even within your own yard, the climate in a sheltered spot near the house might be different from the site on the other side of a hill. (See page 182 for information on choosing a site, and Chapter 5 for information on growing perennials in difficult climates.)

3. How much care will this plant need? And how much time do I wish to spend caring for it? Is it susceptible to a disease that is rampant in my area? Will it need staking? Pruning? Extra watering? How much care is it worth? You can grow almost anything if you are willing to take the time to pamper it.

4. Can I find the plants and seeds I want in regional catalogs and local nurseries? Regionally grown plants are already acclimated to your climate and will be easier to care for.

5. What are the shade and sun conditions at my site?

Answer these questions honestly. It's easy to fudge–but the plant will know. Much heartache and wasted effort can be saved by putting the right plants in the right place right from the start.

CHOOSING PLANTS

When choosing plants, you will find dozens or even hundreds of varieties available for each plant. Every gardener has his or her personal favorites; one gardener's heaviest yielder is another's certain failure. A species that yields beautiful blooms for dried arrangements may not provide the foliage for a long season. We have listed varieties that have worked for our gardeners; the only way to find the ones that will work for you is to try them yourself. If you find a plant you love that seems only marginally suited to your climate, plant it–and see if it grows.

The U.S. Department of Agriculture has prepared the map below, which separates the country into climate zones; many seed companies use these zone numbers to indicate where a particular variety will survive the winter. Find out what zone you're in, and pay attention to the growers' recommendations–but remember that climate zone is only one part of the picture.

The plants in this section are arranged in alphabetical order by their Latin names; flowers are followed by ferns and grasses. Latin names of some common perennials:
Columbine: *Aquilegia*
Pink: *Dianthus*
Bleeding Heart: *Dicentra*
Purple Coneflower: *Echinacea*
Daylily: *Hemerocallis*
Coral Bells: *Heuchera*
Candytuft: *Iberis*
Baby's Breath: *Gypsophilia*
Poppy: *Papaver*
Balloon Flower: *Platycodon*
Primrose: *Primula*
Coneflower: *Rudbeckia*

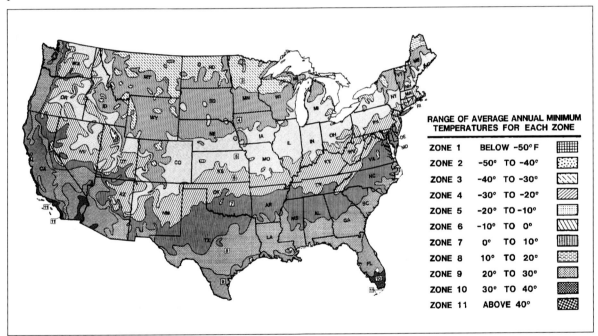

RANGE OF AVERAGE ANNUAL MINIMUM TEMPERATURES FOR EACH ZONE

ZONE 1	BELOW −50° F
ZONE 2	−50° TO −40°
ZONE 3	−40° TO −30°
ZONE 4	−30° TO −20°
ZONE 5	−20° TO −10°
ZONE 6	−10° TO 0°
ZONE 7	0° TO 10°
ZONE 8	10° TO 20°
ZONE 9	20° TO 30°
ZONE 10	30° TO 40°
ZONE 11	ABOVE 40°

PINK FLOWERS

Geranium (cranesbill), 78 (pictured above)
Achillea (yarrow), 26
Anemone (windflower), 32
Aquilegia (columbine), 34
Aster (aster), 40
Astilbe (false spirea), 44
Astrantia (masterwort), 49
Begonia grandis (hardy begonia), 50
Bergenia (pigsqueak), 51
Boltonia (boltonia), 52
Centaurea (knapweed), 55
Chelone (turtlehead), 59
Delphinium (larkspur), 65
Dianthus (pink), 66
Dicentra (bleeding heart), 68
Digitalis (foxglove), 71
Echinacea (purple coneflower), 72
Epimedium (barrenwort), 73
Eupatorium (boneset), 73
Filipendula (meadow sweet), 74
Gypsophila paniculata (baby's breath), 80
Helloborus (hellebore), 82
Hemerocallis (daylily), 85
Hibiscus moshatus (rose mallow), 88
Iberis (candytuft), 93
Iris bearded hybrids *(x germanica)* (bearded iris), 95
Lamium (dead nettle), 102
Lupinus (lupine), 109
Lythrum (loosestrife), 110
Monarda (wild bergamot), 112
Paeonia lactiflora (peony), 116
Penstemon (beard-tongue), 118
Phlox maculata (wild sweet William), 120
Phlox paniculata (garden phlox), 123
Phlox stolonifera (creeping phlox), 123
Phlox subulata (moss pink), 124
Physostegia (false dragonhead), 125
Primula (primrose), 128
Pulmonaria (lungwort), 130
Sedum (stonecrop), 133
Sidalcea (prairie mallow), 137
Stokesia laevis (Stokes' aster), 141
Tanacetum coccineum (painted daisy), 60

WHITE FLOWERS

Iberis (candytuft), 93 (pictured above)
Anemone (windflower), 32
Arabis (rock cress), 35
Aster (aster), 40
Astilbe (false spirea), 44
Astrantia (masterwort), 49
Bergenia (pigsqueak), 51
Boltonia (boltonia), 52
Cimicifuga (bugbane), 64
Dianthus (pink), 66
Dicentra (bleeding heart), 68
Dictamnus (gas plant), 68
Echinacea (purple coneflower), 72
Epimedium (barrenwort), 73
Eupatorium (boneset), 73
Filipendula (meadow sweet), 74
Galium (sweet woodruff), 77
Gaura lindheimeri (white gaura), 78
Gypsophila paniculata (baby's breath), 80
Helloborus (hellebore), 82
Hemerocallis (daylily), 85
Heuchera (coral bells), 88
Hibiscus moshatus (rose mallow), 88
Hosta (plantain lily), 90
Iris cristata (dwarf crested iris), 97
Iris ensata (Japanese iris), 97
Iris sibirica (Siberian iris), 98
Lamium (dead nettle), 102
Macleaya (plume poppy), 110
Oenothera (evening primrose), 114
Paeonia lactiflora (peony), 116
Papaver (poppy), 118
Penstemon (beard-tongue), 118
Phlox maculata (wild sweet William), 120
Phlox paniculata (garden phlox), 123
Polygonatum (Solomon's seal), 128
Primula (primrose), 128
Pulmonaria (lungwort), 130
Scabiosa (scabious), 133
Sedum (stonecrop), 133
Sidalcea (prarie mallow), 137
Tiarella (foam flower), 142
Verbascum (mullein), 144
Veronicastrum (bowman's root), 145
Yucca (Adam's needle), 146

RED/ORANGE FLOWERS

Asclepias (butterfly weed), 40 (pictured above)
Aquilegia (columbine), 34
Armeria (thrift), 35
Astilbe (false spirea), 44
Belamcanda (blackberry lily), 51
Coreopsis (tickseed), 64
Dianthus (pink), 66
Euphorbia (spurge), 74
Gaillardia (blanket flower), 77
Geranium (cranesbill), 78
Geum (avens), 80
Helenium (sneezeweed), 81
Hemerocallis (daylily), 85
Heuchera (coral bells), 88
Hibiscus moshatus (rose mallow), 88
Kniphofia (torch lily), 101
Ligularia (ligularia), 105
Lobelia (lobelia), 109
Lupinus (lupine), 109
Lychnis (campion), 109
Monarda (wild bergamot), 112
Oenothera (evening primrose), 114
Paeonia lactiflora (peony), 116
Papaver (poppy), 118
Persicaria [polygonum] (smartweed), 120
Phlox paniculata (garden phlox), 123
Primula (primrose), 128
Rudbeckia (coneflower), 130
Sedum (stonecrop), 133
Tanacetum coccineum (painted daisy), 60
Trollius (globeflower), 144

BLUE/PURPLE/LAVENDER FLOWERS
Phlox x 'Chattahoochee' (Chattahoochee phlox), 125 (pictured above)
Aconitum (monkshood), 28
Ajuga (bugleweed), 28
Amsonia (blue star), 31
Aquilegia (columbine), 34
Aster (aster), 40
Baptisia (false indigo), 50
Brunnera (Siberian bugloss), 52
Campanula (bellflower), 55
Ceratostigma (leadwort), 56
Delphinium (larkspur), 65
Echinacea (purple coneflower), 72
Echinops (globe thistle), 73
Eupatorium (boneset), 73
Geranium (cranesbill), 78
Hosta (plantain lily), 90
Iris, 95
Lavendula (lavender), 102
Liatris (blazing star), 104
Liriope (lilyturf), 106
Lobelia (lobelia), 109
Lupinus (lupine), 109
Nepeta (catmint), 114
Perovskia atriplicifolia (Russian sage), 119
Phlox maculata (wild sweet William), 120
Phlox paniculata (garden phlox), 123
Phlox stolonifera (creeping phlox), 123
Phlox subulata (moss pink), 124
Platycodon grandiflorus (balloon flower), 127
Primula (primrose), 128
Pulmonaria (lungwort), 130
Salvia (sage), 131
Scabiosa (scabious), 133
Sempervivum (hens-and-chicks), 137
Sidalcea (prairie mallow), 137
Stachys (betony), 139
Stokesia laevis (Stokes' aster), 141
Symphytum (comfrey), 141
Thalictrum (meadow rue), 142
Tricyrtis (toad-lily), 144
Verbascum (mullein), 144
Veronica (speedwell), 145
Viola (violet), 146

YELLOW/GOLD FLOWERS
Achillea (yarrow), 26 (pictured above)
Aconitum (monkshood), 28
Anthemis (dyer's marguerite), 32
Aquilegia (columbine), 34
Asclepias (butterfly weed), 40
Aurinia [Alyssum] (basket-of-gold), 49
Centaurea (knapweed), 55
Chrysogonum (goldenstar), 63
Chrysopsis (golden aster), 63
Coreopsis (tickseed), 64
Digitalis (foxglove), 71
Gaillardia (blanket flower), 77
Geum (avens), 80
Helenium (sneezeweed), 81
Helianthus (sunflower), 82
Hemerocallis (daylily), 85
Inula (inula), 93
Iris ensata (Japanese iris), 97
Iris pseudacorus (yellow flag), 98
Iris sibirica (Siberian iris), 98
Kirengeshoma palmata (yellow waxbell), 101
Kniphofia (torch lily), 101
Lupinus (lupine), 109
Oenothera (evening primrose), 114
Primula (primrose), 128
Rudbeckia (coneflower), 130
Solidago (goldenrod), 139
Symphytum (comfrey), 141
Trollius (globeflower), 144
Verbascum (mullein), 144

PURPLE/RED/BRONZE FOLIAGE
Heuchera (coral bells), 88 (pictured above)
Ajuga (bugleweed), 28
Amsonia (blue star), 31
Astilbe (false spirea), 44
Begonia grandis (hardy begonia), 50
Bergenia (pigsqueak), 51
Ceratostigma (leadwort), 56
Cimicifuga (bugbane), 64
Epimedium (barrenwort), 73
Eupatorium (boneset), 73
Euphorbia (spurge), 74
Iris bearded hybrids *(x germanica)* (bearded iris), 95
Kirengeshoma palmata (yellow waxbell), 101
Ligularia (ligularia), 105
Penstemon (beard-tongue), 118
Persicaria [polygonum] (smartweed), 120
Sedum (stonecrop), 133
Sempervivum (hens-and-chicks), 137

BLUE/GRAY/SILVER FOLIAGE
Achillea (yarrow), 26
Ajuga (bugleweed), 28
Arabis (rock cress), 35
Artemisia (wormwood), 36
Baptisia (false indigo), 50
Brunnera (Siberian bugloss), 52
Chrysopsis (golden aster), 63
Dicentra (bleeding heart), 68
Echinops (globe thistle), 73
Euphorbia (spurge), 74
Hosta (plantain lily), 90
Lamium (dead nettle), 102
Lavendula (lavender), 102
Lysimachia (loosestrife), 110
Nepeta (catmint), 114
Perovskia atriplicifolia (Russian sage), 119
Platycodon grandiflorus (balloon flower), 127
Pulmonaria (lungwort), 130
Salvia (sage), 131
Sedum (stonecrop), 133
Stachys (betony), 139
Symphytum (comfrey), 141
Veronica (speedwell), 145

ACHILLEA YARROW *Asteraceae (Daisy family)*

Most of the yarrow species are from the Old World. In this country, they are often found growing wild on roadsides and in other open areas where the soil is poor and dry. They even thrive at the Desert Botanical Garden in Phoenix; at Huntington Botanical Gardens in San Marino, California, they need some watering until they are established. These conditions are most favorable for yarrows in the garden too. Even in seasons of drought, they will not need watering or mulching, which makes them perfect companions for bulbs. Avoid both rich and damp soils; the resulting growth will be soft and floppy, may be susceptible to fungal problems, and may need staking. Grown well, yarrows are considered to be reliable, pest-free perennials (some gardeners find they are attacked by spider mites). The fernlike green or silvery leaves of most species are aromatic and provide an interesting contrast to bolder foliage in sunny mixed or perennial beds and herb gardens. As a cut flower they are superb, both fresh during the summertime or dried for winter arrangements. Young plants from spring or summer sowings or divisions may be planted in spring or fall. At the Chicago Botanic Garden, they are planted before September 15, so that they can become established before winter. For fast stock buildup, soft cuttings may be taken in summer, and these make strong plants for fall planting. After flowering, cut the plants back almost to ground level to avoid straggliness. This will promote healthy new foliage and sometimes a second crop of flowers. Expect that the plants will need division every few years to avoid weakness. The best flowers are borne on vigorous young plants.

A. millefolium 'Rose Beauty' is one of the most popular pink cultivars, although 'Cerise Queen' has stronger color. The exciting Galaxy hybrids, such as pink 'Appleblossom', dusty red 'Paprika' (which turns orange), and the 'Summer Pastels Mix' open up a new color palette and should gain popularity, particularly in the relative coolness of northern summers. *A.* x 'Coronation

Achillea x 'Moonshine' with *Salvia nemorosa* 'Ostfriesland'.

ACHILLEA MILLEFOLIUM 'ROSE KING' (YARROW) 2-2½ feet tall, space 2 feet apart. Flat 2-inch heads of bright pink flowers. Full sun. Blooms in summer-early fall. Zones 3-10, heat-tolerant.

ACHILLEA 'CORONATION GOLD' (YARROW) 3 feet tall, space 1½ feet apart. Fine, gray-green foliage, bright gold flowerheads, 3 inches wide. Full sun. Blooms in summer. Zones 3-10, heat-tolerant.

ACHILLEA X 'MOONSHINE' (YARROW) 2 feet tall, space 1½ feet apart. Deeply dissected gray-green foliage, 2- to 3-inch pale yellow flowerheads. Full sun. Blooms in summer. Zones 3-10, heat-tolerant.

ACHILLEA PTARMICA 'BOULE DE NEIGE' (SNEEZEWORT, 'THE PEARL') 1½-2 feet tall, space 2 feet apart. Green undissected leaves, buttonlike pure white double flowers. Full sun. Blooms in summer. Zones 3-10, heat-tolerant.

Aconitum carmichaeli.

Gold' is one of the best yellows, with large heads of brilliant gold flowers held above gray-green leaves. *A.* x 'Moonshine' has dense, pale yellow 2- to 3-inch flowerheads and deeply dissected gray-green leaves–most satisfactory in northern climates. *A.* x Hoffnung, grown at Brookside Gardens in Maryland, is a lovely creamy yellow. *A. ptarmica* 'Boule de Neige' ('The Pearl'), commonly called sneezewort, has green, undissected leaves and buttonlike pure white double flowers. Regrettably it tends to romp through the garden and easily becomes straggly.

ACONITUM MONKSHOOD *Ranunculaceae (Buttercup family)*
This genus of elegant but poisonous plants is found throughout the north temperate regions of the world. Although some species have yellow or pink flowers, the blue-flowering ones are most popular, providing the garden with a splash of blue in the late summer and fall. The monkshoods make fine cut flowers, but care should be taken to protect your hands and eyes from the poisonous sap. Never plant near a vegetable garden or children's play area. These clump-forming, tuberous-rooted perennials are best planted in the fall, although containerized plants will usually succeed with spring planting. Monkshoods are not difficult to grow given a fertile, moist soil enriched with plenty of organic material; they do not thrive in southern California. Fertilize annually in early spring. They resent drying out, and although best in an open position must be protected from intense noonday or early afternoon sun. Mulch in summer to help retain moisture; in cold regions, protect the plants with a winter mulch (they do well without a winter mulch at the Denver Botanic Garden). Propagation is by division in early spring or late fall, but disturb the plants only when really necessary. Seed may be sown out of doors in the autumn to germinate the following spring. Stem and crown rots may sometimes become a nuisance, as well as some insect pests, but generally monkshoods are relatively free of problems. Common monkshood, *Aconitum napellus,* is readily available, but the newer cultivars 'Bressingham Spire', 'Newry Blue', and 'Sparks' Variety' are also becoming popular.

AJUGA BUGLEWEED *Lamiaceae (Mint family)*
These low, mostly creeping plants are invaluable as ground covers, although sometimes the ease with which they colonize an area can only be described as invasive. *Ajuga reptans* and its cultivars are commonly available, and these display a striking range of foliage colors and textures. 'Catlin's Giant', a semi-evergreen, has large, bronze-green leaves and 8-inch spikes of blue flowers in spring. 'Bronze Beauty' has metallic bronze foliage, particularly effective in a sunny area, and 'Burgundy Glow' has multicolored foliage of pink, cream, rose, and green. Both the latter have violet flowers in spring. 'Silver Beauty' and 'Gray Lady' have gray-green leaves. *A. genevensis, A. pyramidalis,* and their cultivars are more clump-forming. A sunny or partially shaded position is ideal for bugleweeds, especially where the soil is well drained but slightly moist and high in organic content. Watering is seldom required except in

ACONITUM CARMICHAELII (AZURE MONKSHOOD) 4 feet tall, space 2 feet apart. Erect plant with glossy dark green foliage, purple flowers. Full sun or partial shade. Blooms in late summer to early fall. Zones 2-9, not heat-tolerant.

AJUGA REPTANS 'BRONZE BEAUTY' (BUGLEWEED) 4-8 inches tall, space 8 inches apart. Low creeping plant with metallic bronze foliage, purple flowers. Full sun to full shade. Blooms in late spring to early summer. Zones 3-10, not heat-tolerant.

AJUGA REPTANS 'CATLIN'S GIANT' (BUGLEWEED) 4-8 inches tall, space 8 inches apart. Large, bronze-green leaves, spikes of purple flowers. Full sun to full shade. Blooms in late spring to early summer. Zones 3-10, not heat-tolerant.

ALCHEMILLA MOLLIS (LADY'S MANTLE) 1-2 feet tall, space 1½ feet apart. Scalloped leaves, chartreuse flowers. Full sun to partial shade. Blooms in late spring to early summer. Zones 3-9, not heat-tolerant.

AMSONIA TABERNAEMONTANA (BLUE STAR) 2-3 feet tall, space 2-3 feet apart. Pale blue star-shaped flowers, glossy foliage turns gold in fall. Full sun to partial shade. Blooms in early summer. Zones 3-9.

ANEMONE TOMENTOSA (WINDFLOWER) 3-4 feet tall, space 2 feet apart. Pale rose flowers, dark green foliage. Full sun to partial shade. Blooms in mid to late summer. Zones 4-10.

ANEMONE X HYBRIDA 'HONORINE JOBERT' (JAPANESE ANEMONE) 3-5 feet tall, space 2 feet apart. Pure white flowers, large leaves. Full sun to partial shade. Blooms in late summer to early fall. Zones 6-10.

ANTHEMIS TINCTORIA (DYER'S MARGUERITE) 1½-3 feet tall, space 2½ feet apart. Finely dissected leaves, 1½-inch-wide bright yellow ray flowers. Full sun. Blooms in late spring to early fall. Zones 3-10, not heat-tolerant.

severe droughts; it needs to be watered every 2-3 weeks at Huntington Botanical Gardens in southern California. A light annual dressing of complete fertilizer in early spring is sufficient to assure healthy growth. After blooming, remove the spent flowers to reduce spreading by seed. Sporadic flowers will appear throughout the season. Crown rot is sometimes a problem, particularly in the South, and mildew in the Northwest, but general hygiene and removal of plant debris in fall and winter will reduce the likelihood of disease. Aphids may become a nuisance. Either spring or fall planting is successful (ideally by September 15 in cold climates), and stocks may be increased by division at these times too. Seed is seldom used for propagation except for the species.

ALCHEMILLA LADY'S MANTLE *Rosaceae (Rose family)*

The nomenclature of lady's mantles is much confused because of their habit of producing seed without first being pollinated. In the garden, however, the slight variations found in nursery stock are seldom a problem. The best-known is *Alchemilla mollis*, sometimes listed as *A. vulgaris*. This clump-former is at home grouped in perennial or mixed borders and beds, or may be used as a ground cover or even low hedge to separate different parts of the garden. Both the velvety, scalloped leaves and frothy chartreuse flowers are highly regarded by flower arrangers. A well-drained, partly shaded position, where the soil remains moist, but not wet, is ideal for lady's mantles; they will be successful in full sun only if the soil is adequately supplied with moisture-holding organic matter. A summer mulch is recommended, but extra water will still be needed during dry spells. After flowering, cut the plants back to ground level to encourage fresh new leaves and to eliminate self-seeding, which may become a nuisance. Planting may be done in spring or fall. To propagate, divide healthy plants before they flower in early spring; this plant is very easy to propagate. Few diseases or pests bother lady's mantles, although if the plants are severely stressed during drought, the foliage may be attacked by red spider mites.

AMSONIA BLUE STAR *Apocynaceae (Dogbane family)*

The best-known member of this North American genus is *Amsonia tabernae-montana*. It is a fine, low-maintenance perennial that deserves to be more widely grown, particularly by those who are attracted to native plants. Not only are the pale blue, star-shaped flowers excellent for cutting, as well as in the spring garden, but in the fall the foliage turns golden yellow. Massed in the border or used as specimen plants, the blue stars earn their place; they add needed height and color in early May. These taprooted plants grow best in slightly moist, but well-drained soil in a partially shaded place (full sun is better in cold climates). Regular fertilizing is seldom necessary, particularly if an organic mulch is applied for the summer. This will help keep the soil evenly moist as well, although extra water is appreciated during dry times. Divide the plants to increase stock, preferably in spring, although it can be delayed until fall. Young seedlings should be in place by late summer or early fall.

I spend my summer going through the catalogues, making notes of what I want to plant in the fall. I make lists and then tear them up and start over again. I want everything I see, and it is so hard to choose. I used to try a hundred or so new things each year, but as I grow older the days seem to get shorter . . . and the garden gets fuller.
FROM *Through the Garden Gate*, by Elizabeth Lawrence

'McKana Giant' hybrid columbines come in a range of color combinations including lilac, pink, yellow, white, and purple. As with most hybrids, planting seeds will result in offspring that are not identical to the parent, making it difficult to recreate specific colors.

New plants are best purchased when dormant in early spring. After flowering, it is advisable to remove the spent flowers to avoid seed production. Blue stars are usually free of pests and diseases.

ANEMONE WINDFLOWER *Ranunculaceae (Buttercup family)*

This large genus is mostly confined to north temperate regions of the world. The flowers bloom on stems from 6 inches to 3-5 feet in height, either in the spring or in the fall. Most windflowers do best in partially shaded parts of the garden, although the spring-blooming, tuberous-rooted types, such as *A. blanda,* will tolerate sunnier spots. They make charming additions to informal woodland gardens or rock gardens. For best results, soak the tubers overnight prior to planting. The Japanese group (sometimes listed incorrectly as *A. japonica*) blooms in the late summer and fall, and of these *A. hupehensis, A. tomentosa* 'Robustissima' [*A. vitifolia* 'Robustissima'], and *A.* x *hybrida* are most widely grown; 'Robustissima' is the most coldhardy. Of particular beauty are the *A.* x *hybrida* cultivars 'September Charm' [*A. hupehensis* 'September Charm'] (silvery pink), 'Honorine Jobert' (white), 'Pamina' (deep pink), and 'Margarete' (double deep pink). Japanese anemones form an integral part of most late-summer and fall perennial gardens and are possibly at their best seen in large groups dramatized by a dark background of trees or shrubs. Cultivars of *A. coronaria,* poppy anemone, are hardy only in warm zones, but may be container-grown with protection elsewhere. All require deep, fertile soils, high in water-holding organic matter, which should also be applied regularly as a light summer mulch. Protect the fall bloomers with a light mulch in winter in cold areas. Extra fertilization is unnecessary. Propagation is usually by division in early spring, although root cuttings may be taken then also. Leaf spot, leaf nematodes, and rust occasionally become problems, and cut worms may need controls.

ANTHEMIS DYER'S MARGUERITE *Asteraceae (Daisy family)*

Anthemis is also known as golden marguerite and yellow or dyer's chamomile–"chamomile" because it's related to the perennial form of that herb, *A. nobilis* and "dyer's" because its flowers yield a distinctive yellow dye, and its foliage a pale green dye. Its large, solitary flowers display in many shades of yellow, and its finely divided leaves have an unusual acrid odor. The plant is native to Europe. Dyer's marguerite is an excellent ornamental, covered with richly colored flowers, well-suited for cutting from June through late October. *A. tinctoria* grows best in full sun, in any well-drained, fertile, moist soil. While this is a perennial herb, the center of the plant tends to die out as it becomes increasingly mature. To maintain best appearance, treat this as an annual, allowing it to self-sow or dividing it yearly. Purchase young, well-branched plants free from any center dying out, and set out in spring. Or start from seed sown in late summer or early fall. If you wish to select for a certain color, propagate by cuttings. The plants will get fairly large and bushy, so space 1-2 feet apart. A mulch will keep out weeds, and a fertilizer applied

AQUILEGIA CANADENSIS (WILD COLUMBINE) 1-2 feet tall, space 1 foot apart. Nodding red and yellow flowers, deeply lobed leaflets. Full sun to partial shade. Blooms in late spring to early summer. Zones 3-10.

AQUILEGIA X HYBRIDA 'MCKANA GIANTS' (COLUMBINE) 2-3 feet tall, space 1½ feet apart. Long-spurred bicolored flowers in a range of colors. Full sun to partial shade. Blooms late spring to early summer. Zones 5-10.

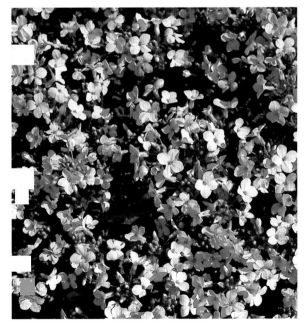

ARABIS CAUCASICA (ROCK CRESS) 6-12 inches tall, space 1 foot apart. Gray-green foliage, small white flowers. Full sun. Blooms in spring. Zones 4-10, not heat-tolerant.

ARMERIA MARITIMA 'DUSSELDORF PRIDE' (THRIFT, SEA PINK) 6-12 inches tall, space 1 foot apart. Carmine red flowers, compact plant. Full sun. Blooms late spring to early summer. Zones 3-10.

In early spring, The New York Botanic Garden's Rodney White Garden blooms with *Aquilegia, Dicentra,* and *Polemonium.*

at regular intervals during the growing season will keep the plant flowering over a longer period. If you allow plants to dry out to the point of wilting, they will look ragged and unsightly. Although dyer's marguerite is very resistant to disease, it is sometimes susceptible to aphids. At The New York Botanical Garden gardeners find that it keeps a stronger, less floppy shape and reflowers more abundantly when deadheaded and grows to about 2½ feet tall and wide after a few years.

AQUILEGIA COLUMBINE *Ranunculaceae (Buttercup family)*

One of our most popular garden perennials, the columbines are as much at home in cottage and woodland gardens as they are in the more formal settings of mixed and perennial beds and borders. The smaller species such as *A. flabellata* and its cultivars are well-suited to rock gardens. The hybrid columbines, *A.* x *hybrida*, are the most showy of the group and include such strains as 'McKana Giants', noted for its long-spurred, bicolored flowers in a wide range of pastel colors. *A. chrysantha* is the best species for dry climates; grown in partial to deep shade at the Desert Botanical Garden in Phoenix, it is a short-lived perennial that reseeds freely and does not like wet feet in summer. Our native wild columbine *A. canadensis* makes up in charm what it lacks in glamor. A colony in bloom in a woodland clearing presents an unforgettable sight. Columbines are mostly short-lived and will need replacement every 2-3 years, though the species will reseed itself. In the hottest parts of the country, they may be treated as annuals, though they do well as perennials in coastal California. Propagation is easy from fresh seed sown in early spring, although seed collected from the hybrids probably will not come true to the parents. Plant the seedlings in the fall for bloom the following spring. Self-sown seedlings should be weeded out if a particular selection is to be maintained. Deadheading after bloom curtails reseeding. All columbines require well-drained soil, enriched with organic matter. They will not tolerate wet feet, but respond well to deep watering during periods of drought. A summer mulch helps to keep the soil evenly moist, while a light winter covering provides insulation from alternate freezing and thawing. A partially, but not deeply shaded place in the garden is ideal; columbines are seldom successful where they are exposed to the full glare of noonday sun (though they do thrive in full sun at Oregon's Berry Botanic Garden. Leaf miner is the most serious pest found on columbines, and while it seldom kills the plants, the foliage is severely disfigured. Early control is essential. Badly affected leaves should be removed and destroyed promptly; new ones will carry the plant through the season. Pay strict attention to hygiene and burn all infected plant remains.

ARABIS ROCK CRESS *Brassicaceae (Mustard family)*

Members of this large genus are found in the wild mostly in rocky parts of Eurasia, but only a few are important horticulturally. *A. caucasica* [*A. albida*] and its cultivars are widely available in nurseries. The double form *A. c.* 'Floro Plena' [*A. c.* 'Plena'] is particularly attractive, and the double flowers are longer lasting than those of the single form. *A. c.* 'Variegata' has single flowers, but provides winter interest with its cream-variegated leaves. Although rock cresses lend themselves well to rock-garden settings and wall plantings, they are equally attractive as edgings for paths, driveways, or even borders and look especially attractive contrasted with some of the minor spring bulbs, such as squills and glory-of-the-snow. They will not tolerate wet feet, and a well-drained, gravelly or sandy soil is essential. A gravel mulch round the crowns of the plants facilitates the run-off of surface water, which may cause the mats of foliage to rot. Additional fertilizing is unnecessary since these are plants of lean soils. Rock cresses grow best in the cooler parts of the country, in full sun, although they will survive under less than ideal conditions. They resent the high humidity of some southern zones. Drought-tolerant, they do well in southern California, but are short-lived in heavy soils. New plants may be set out in spring or early fall, and established plants may be divided at the same time. Cuttings of soft young growth are taken soon after flowering. Sometimes older plants become straggly and untidy, but severe cutting back after flowering keeps the plants neat and shapely. Given good growing conditions, pests and diseases are seldom a problem.

ARMERIA THRIFT, SEA PINK *Plumbaginaceae (Leadwort family)*

Sea pinks are native to coastal regions of the world, where they are found growing in fully exposed positions, in lean and very porous soil. In the garden, they thrive in full sun with well-drained and even poor soil. In the hottest parts of the country, they require light shade from the noonday sun; they also tolerate partial shade at the Chicago Botanic Garden. A light application of

The silvery gray foliage of *Artemisia* x 'Powis Castle' is an excellent foil for brightly colored flowers like *Aster* 'Purple Dome'.

complete fertilizer in the spring promotes strong growth where the soil is very poor. Free drainage is essential to their well-being, as the tussocks of grassy foliage tend to rot if water does not drain away readily. Although thrifts are invaluable in seaside gardens where salt spray is prevalent, inland gardeners also use them to good effect. Such cultivars of *A. maritima* as 'Dusseldorf Pride' and 'Vindictive' are admirable plants for rock gardens and make fine edging and front-of-the-border plants. The taller species such as *A. plantaginea* are excellent as cut flowers. All can be planted in spring or fall, at which time established plants may be divided. A light covering of hay or evergreen boughs is advisable where winters are cold, particularly for recently planted stock. Otherwise maintenance is minimal, since few pests or diseases attack these tough plants; they may, however, be short-lived. Removal of spent flowers keeps the plants looking neat.

ARTEMISIA WORMWOOD *Asteraceae (Daisy family)*

In the garden, most of the wormwoods are grown for their strongly aromatic, silvery-gray foliage, which is used to introduce important contrast to the brightly colored flowers and predominantly green leaves of the flower border. Some of the most readily available include *A. ludoviciana* 'Silver Queen' (an Arizona native), *A. schmidtiana* 'Silver Mound', and *A. stellerana,* beach-wormwood, also known as dusty miller or old woman. *A.* x 'Powis Castle' has recently become popular and although sold as a perennial is more properly a small shrub; older plants of some other species become woody also. Wormwood foliage is sometimes used fresh with cut flowers, but is more widely used in dried arrangements and herbal wreaths. Common to most silver-leaved plants, wormwoods succeed best in full sun where the soil is low in fertility and drains freely. Richer soils, as well as the addition of high-nitrogen fertilizers, produce soft, spindly growth prone to flopping. *A. schmidtiana* 'Silver Mound' loses its compact rounded shape under hot, humid conditions and high fertility and is a poor choice for southern gardens, as it often melts in extreme heat. It does not do well as far north as Brookside Gardens in Wheaton, Maryland, and is short-lived in southern California; it tends to rot if overwatered. Except during severe droughts additional water is not required. *A. lactiflora,* white mugwort, is the only species grown for its flowers. Its dark green foliage and elegant plumes of tiny flowers make it well suited to the back of the border and as a cut flower. Plant in sun or partial shade, where the soil is fertile and moisture-retentive; in very dry areas they do best in partial shade. To build stock, the plants may be divided in spring or fall, at which time new plants may be set out. Other species of artemisia are propagated by division, or cuttings may be taken in spring or early summer. Woody plants age with little grace and should be pruned severely in the spring to encourage fresh new growth; avoid hard pruning before the onset of cold weather, since the plants may not recover. Wormwoods are pest-free, but are sometimes subject to rust attack.

ARTEMISIA X 'POWIS CASTLE' (WORMWOOD) 2-4 feet tall, space 2-3 feet apart. Bushy plant with feathery, silvery foliage; rarely flowers. Full sun. Zones 4-10, not heat-tolerant.

ARTEMISIA LUDOVICIANA 'SILVER KING' (WORMWOOD) 2-3½ feet tall, space 2-3 feet apart. Simple erect stems, silvery white foliage. Full sun. Zones 5-10, not heat-tolerant.

ARTEMISIA SCHMIDTIANA 'SILVER MOUND' (WORMWOOD) 1-2 feet tall, space 1½ feet apart. Silvery foliage, forms a rounded mound. Full sun. Zones 4-10, not heat-tolerant.

ARUNCUS AETHUSIFOLIUS (KOREAN GOATSBEARD) 9-15 inches tall, space 1-2 feet apart. Dark green compound leaves, plumes of creamy white flowers. Blooms in summer. Partial shade. Zones 4-7.

ARUNCUS DIOICUS (GOATSBEARD) 4-7 feet tall, space 3 feet apart. Tall plumes of white flowers, abundant compound leaves. Full sun to partial shade. Blooms in summer. Zones 3-7.

ASARUM EUROPAEUM (EUROPEAN WILD GINGER) 5-8 inches tall, space 8-12 inches apart. Heart-shaped evergreen foliage, small greenish-brown flowers. Partial to full shade. Blooms in spring. Zones 4-8.

ASCLEPIAS TUBEROSA (BUTTERFLY WEED) 1-2½ feet tall, space 1½ feet apart. Brilliant orange flowers in tight umbels. Full sun. Flowers in summer. Zones 3-10, not heat-tolerant.

ASTER 'PURPLE DOME' 2-4 feet tall, space 2 feet apart. Compact plant with light purple flowers. Full sun. Blooms in late summer to early fall. Zones 4-9.

ARUNCUS GOATSBEARD *Rosaceae (Rose family)*

Goatsbeards are large, easy-to-grow, low-maintenance perennials, especially useful for the back of lightly shaded beds and borders, as well as woodland gardens. *A. dioicus* [*A. sylvester*] is well suited to face down large shrubs like rhododendrons and mountain laurel. The tall, quick-growing plumes of white, fading to cream, flowers are good for cutting. Male and female flowers are borne on separate plants. Unless seed is required, the fluffier, more upright flowers of the male plants are usually preferred. If you don't buy them in flower, it is impossible to tell the difference. To reach their full potential, goatsbeards need plenty of room and rich, fertile soil high in organic matter. Moist, water-retentive soil is ideal, but usually additional water is still needed during dry spells. If the soil can be kept sufficiently moist, goatsbeards will tolerate sunny positions, but the tips of the leaves may become brown and crisped; they are seldom satisfactory in southern zones. An organic summer mulch of leaf mold or compost is recommended, and a light dressing of complete fertilizer in spring keeps the fertility level high. Plant or divide in spring or fall. Deadhead female flowers when they fade, since the seedheads become heavy and droop in an ungainly way. Pests and diseases are seldom a problem. For limited space or for rock gardens, the ferny-leaved dwarf species *A. aethusifolius* is available; this underused species can be used as a substitute for astilbes in warm climates.

ASARUM WILD GINGER *Aristolochiaceae (Birthwort family)*

Wild gingers are found throughout the north temperate regions of the world. Their creeping rhizomes, which emit a gingery fragrance when bruised, slowly give rise to dense mats of rounded to heart-shaped deciduous or evergreen foliage. The flowers, which are pollinated by slugs, are inconspicuous. For shaded gardens, the wild gingers are hard to beat, and they make fine companions for other shade-lovers, such as ferns, astilbes, and hostas. They are widely used as edging or ground-cover plants under trees and shrubs or in dark corners. The optimum degree of shade varies from species to species. A

'Purple Dome' aster with ornamental grassses.

August flowers need not be screaming shades of orange, red, or yellow. There is also blue. A great favorite of everybody who grows it is Russian sage, or Perovskia, with almost white aromatic leaves and stems and very narrow spikes of mid-blue flowers. . . . aconites or monkshoods, which are gloriously blue as summer turns to fall . . . *Aster* x *frikartii*, with soft lavender-blue petals surrounding a small gold boss, and neat though elegant pointed leaves, blooming from late July sometimes even through November.
FROM *THE ESSENTIAL EARTHMAN, HENRY MITCHELL ON GARDENING*

Opposite: Aster x *frikartii* 'Mönch'.

slightly acid, moist, but well-drained soil is to their liking, ideally enriched with leaf mold or other organic material. A similar mulch during the summer will help to keep the soil evenly moist and on the acid side. In the spring apply a light dressing of a complete fertilizer for optimum vigor. The wild gingers resent disturbance and should be lifted only to increase stock. This is readily accomplished by division of the rhizomes in spring. New plants may be set out in spring or early fall. Our native *A. canadense* is a tough, deciduous species with broadly heart-shaped, slightly glossy, light green leaves. These are a gourmet item for slugs and snails. One of the most widely grown evergreen species is *A. europaeum*, which has beautiful glossy leaves, but is not as drought-tolerant as *A. canadense*, but this does best where summers are not too hot. Some of our native evergreen species, such as *A. arifolium* [*Hexastylis arifolium*], *A. shuttleworthii* [*H. shuttleworthii*], and *A. virginicum* [*H. virginicum*] are well adapted for southern gardens; *A. candatum*, a California native, does, well there. The latter two species have beautifully mottled dark leaves. The evergreen species seem to be less attractive to slugs.

ASCLEPIAS BUTTERFLY WEED *(Milkweed family)*

The most widely grown member of this genus is *A. tuberosa*, a showy native of dryish fields and roadsides, where the plants are fully exposed to the sky. In the garden, it is wise to try to duplicate these conditions. Although a rich soil is not necessary, a well-drained one is essential, and the best results are obtained in a position with full sun. This plant does well at Phoenix's Desert Botanical Garden; another species, *A. subulata,* is a stunning performer there, producing wandlike stems and white milkweed flowers in late spring even in the poorest desert soils. Once butterfly weed is established, it is more or less carefree, although sometimes it takes a season or two before the plants flower freely. They resent disturbance due to their deep taproots, so buy container-grown stock and handle the roots carefully–they emerge late and are sometimes forgotten and therefore damaged. This plant is protected in many states, and collection from the wild is seldom successful anyway. Propagation may be difficult, with the best results from outdoor sowing of freshly collected seed in pots, in late fall or the following spring. Stem or root cuttings are sometimes successful. Planting may be done in spring or fall. Butterfly weed is a brilliant addition to the summer flower border, where it attracts butterflies in profusion. The flowers are usually brilliant orange, although the 'Gay Butterflies' strain includes reds, pinks, and yellows All make fine cut flowers, and the ornamental seedheads may be saved for dried arrangements. Deadheading often promotes an additional flush of later blooms. Aphids are sometimes a problem. Another native, *A. incarnata,* the swamp milkweed, has soft dusty pink flowers and is useful in wet areas of sunny gardens.

ASTER ASTER *Asteraceae (Daisy family)*

The *Aster* genus is large and diverse, mostly native to North America. Asters are found growing in the wild along roadsides, in open fields, in light wood-

lands, and even near the sea, in soils that range from damp to quite dry, but seldom of great fertility. Some reach only a few inches in height, while others tower above most perennials at heights of 7-8 feet. Many of the asters on the market today are the result of the hybridizers' work, particularly in Europe, where they have been very popular for years. Blooming mostly in the late summer and fall, some make valuable additions to the rock garden and cutting gardens, while others are effective as specimen or background plants in formal gardens, coastal settings, or naturalized in open meadows. Among the best, particularly for cutting, are the *A. novae-angliae,* New England aster, cultivars. These bold clump-formers tolerate much damper soil conditions than most asters and thrive in good garden soil; they usually need to be staked. Pinch frequently to keep the plants compact. Vivid hot pink 'Alma Potschke', correctly 'Andenken an Alma Potschke', begins to bloom in late summer and continues until the cold weather. A relative newcomer, 'Hella Lacy' has strong violet flowers while 'September Ruby' is deep crimson. These and late-blooming 'Harrington's Pink' are ideal for the back of the border. The New York aster, *A. novae-belgi,* and its numerous cultivars are quite similar to the New England asters but are more prone to mildew and need division more frequently. Pinch in late spring to encourage bushier, more compact growth; the taller ones will still probably need to be staked. Well-known cultivars include 'Marie Ballard', which has double, light blue flowers, and the 1½- to 2-foot-tall 'Snow Flurry'. Be sure to plant them in well-drained but slightly moist soil. Both the New York and New England asters benefit from frequent division in the spring or early fall to maintain vigor. Mildew is a recurring problem for both these groups; thin overcrowded stems of large plants in the spring, and spray with a fungicide as necessary. The *A.* x *dumosus* group of hybrid asters is represented by such popular cultivars as pure white 'Snowsprite', which grows only 12-15 inches tall. Also low-growing,

Astilbes are an important part of the shade section of The New York Botanical Garden Perennial Garden.

ASTER NOVAE-ANGLIAE 'HARRINGTON'S PINK' (NEW ENGLAND ASTER, MICHAELMAS DAISY) 2-4 feet tall, space 2 feet apart. Clear pink flowers. Full sun. Blooms in late summer to early fall, later than most asters. Zones 4-9.

ASTER X FRIKARTII 'MÖNCH' 2-3 feet tall, space 1½ feet apart. Sturdy upright stems, lavender flowers. Full sun. Blooms in late summer to fall, Zones 5-10, not heat-tolerant.

ASTER 'PROFESSOR ANTON KIPPENBERG' 2-3 feet tall, space 2 feet apart. Low-growing plant with semidouble wisteria blue flowers. Full sun. Blooms in late summer to early fall. Zones 4-9.

ASTILBE X ARENDSII 'BRIDAL VEIL' (FALSE SPIREA) 2 feet tall, space 1½-2½ feet apart. White flowers, ferny compound leaves. Full sun to partial shade. Blooms in midsummer (mid astilbe season). Zones 4-8.

A shady area becomes a varied study of hostas, ferns, and astilbes. Since different astilbe species bloom at different times, there can be flowers from late spring to late summer. The spent blooms are interesting as well.

'Professor Anton Kippenberg', usually erroneously listed as *A. novae-belgi* 'Professor Kippenberg', sports masses of semidouble wisteria blue flowers. *Aster.* 'Purple Dome', variously listed as *A. novae-angliae* 'Purple Dome' or *A.* x *dumosus,* is more resistant to mildew than the New York asters, and most are quite compact, more in scale with smaller gardens. 'Purple Dome' is sometimes attacked by chrysanthemum lacebugs. Another hybrid, Frickart's aster, *A.* x *frikartii,* is considered by many to be in the top ten of all perennials. Its very long blooming season, low maintenance (almost mildew-free), and abundant large, single, lavender flowers make it indispensable in perennial gardens and for cutting. Its habit tends to be loose and floppy, so face it down with sturdier plants, such as Sedum 'Autumn Joy' or *Veronica longifolia* 'Crater Lake Blue', for support. Plant in full sun and mulch over the winter in cold climates for best results. Divide in spring every 2-4 years to maintain vigor. *A.* x *frikartii* 'Wonder of Staffa' and 'Mönch' are very similar, and are both readily available on the market; 'Mönch' is short-lived at Brookside Gardens in Wheaton, Maryland. Deadhead all the asters to extend blooming times, for neatness, and to prevent self-seeding. Japanese beetles may need control.

ASTILBE FALSE SPIREA *Saxifragaceae (Saxifrage family)*

False spireas, or more commonly astilbes, are among the best perennials for shaded gardens, where their beautifully dissected and durable foliage remains

ASTILBE X ROSEA 'PEACH BLOSSOM' (FALSE SPIREA) 3 feet tall, space 1½-2½ feet apart. Pale pink flowers, ferny compound leaves. Full sun to partial shade. Blooms in early summer. Zones 4-8.

ASTILBE CHINENSIS VAR. TAQUETTI 'SUPERBA' (FALSE SPIREA) 3-4 feet tall, space 3 feet apart. Narrow plumes of strong magenta flowers, strong erect stems. Full sun to partial shade. Blooms in late summer. Zones 4-8.

ASTILBE CHINENSIS 'PUMILA' (FALSE SPIREA) 1 foot tall, space 1 foot apart. Spreading, low-growing plant with raspberry-colored flowers. Full sun to partial shade. Blooms in summer to late summer. Zones 4-8.

ASTILBE X ARENDSII 'FANAL' (FALSE SPIREA) 2 feet tall, space 1½-2½ feet apart. Deep red flowers, ferny compound leaves. Full sun to partial shade. Blooms in early summer. Zones 4-8.

ASTILBE X ARENDSII 'DEUTSCHLAND' (FALSE SPIREA) 2 feet tall, space 1½-2½ feet apart. White flowers, ferny compound leaves. Full sun to partial shade. Blooms in early summer. Zones 4-8.

ASTILBE THUNBERGII 'OSTRICH PLUME' (FALSE SPIREA) 2 feet tall, space 1½-2½ feet apart. Pink flowers, ferny compound leaves. Full sun to partial shade. Blooms in early to mid summer. Zones 4-8.

ASTILBE SIMPLICIFOLIA 'DUNKELLACHS' (FALSE SPIREA) 1-1½ feet tall, space 1 foot apart. Arching panicles of pink flowers. Full sun to partial shade. Blooms early to midsummer. Zones 4-8.

RODGERSIA AESCUFOLIA (SHIELDLEAF) Close relative of *Astilboides tabularis*. 3-5 feet tall, space 3 feet apart. Huge green leaves, panicles of astilbelike flowers. Tolerates full sun, partial shade is better. Blooms in summer. Zones 4-9, not heat-tolerant.

handsome throughout the season. These clump-forming plants are just as appropriate for formal flowerbeds and borders as they are in an informal woodland garden. The most dramatic effects are created when astilbes are planted in large sweeps or waves, although well-grown specimen plants also can be striking. They make fine cut flowers, and the dried seedheads are useful for winter arrangements. The key to success in growing astilbes is to provide a deep, organically rich soil that is well drained but never dries out. Neither waterlogged nor extremely dry soil will suffice, and they will not tolerate competition from tree roots. A partially shaded site is ideal. In moderate climates, they will flourish in full sun as long as the soil can be kept sufficiently moist; but windswept or hot, humid conditions are not acceptable. They rarely succeed in southern California as perennials, although the nurseries do stock them; they are best grown as annuals. These greedy feeders benefit from a dressing of complete fertilizer each spring, as well as an organic summer mulch to keep soil temperature low and soil fertility and moisture high. During dry spells extra water is necessary. Planting may be done in the spring or fall; summer planting of container-grown stock demands extra attention to soil moisture. Propagation is easy by dividing established plants in spring when the plants are 4-6 inches tall; fall division is an alternative. After flowering the plants may be deadheaded, although many gardeners find the spent plumes to be an attractive addition to the winter garden, particularly when encrusted with frost or snow. They can remain on the plants until growth begins the following spring. Powdery mildew and Japanese beetles may attack the foliage of astilbes, but seldom become serious problems.

Nursery catalogs contain long lists of named astilbe cultivars, but the parentage of each may be complex and sometimes obscure. *A.* x *arendsii* 'Bridal Veil' ('Brautschleier') is a white-flowered German selection that flowers midway through the astilbe season. Others in this hybrid group include 'Fanal', an early flowering red with deep red young foliage, and 'Cattleya', which has rose pink flowers. This plant is short-lived in the South. *A. chinensis* var. *taquetii* 'Superba' is one of the last of the astilbes to bloom. It holds its narrow plumes of strong magenta flowers well above the foliage. Hybrids of the *A. chinensis,* Chinese astilbe, group include 'Pumila', a drought-tolerant spreading low-grower, excellent as a ground cover, with crushed raspberry-colored flowers in late summer. From the *A. japonica* hybrid group, one of the most readily available is 'Irrlicht', which has plumes of white flowers early in the season. *A.* x *rosea* 'Peach Blossom' and *A. thunbergii* 'Ostrich Plume' ('Straussenfeder') are both pink-flowered, mid-season blooming cultivars, the latter somewhat taller. The last three are often listed under *A.* x *arendsii*. For the front of the border or rock garden, low-growing cultivars from the *A. simplicifolia* hybrids, such as 'Sprite' and 'Dunkellachs', are excellent choices.

ASTILBOIDES (RODGERSIA) SHIELDLEAF *Saxifragaceae (Saxifrage family)*
Recent name changes within this Asian genus have resulted in some nomenclatural confusion. *Astilboides tabularis* [*Rodgersia tabularis*], the shieldleaf

The astilbes . . . are probably the most important flowering plants for the shaded garden. (A bonus is their bronze or green foliage.) There are so many to choose from, especially among the *A.* x *arendsii* hybrids, that you can just go for the colors. Some, especially among reds, are nearly as ornamental when they go to seed as they were in flower, and the faded spires last for months.
FROM *THE NATURAL SHADE GARDEN,* BY KEN DRUSE

ASTRANTIA MAJOR (MASTERWORT) 2-3 feet tall, space 1-1½ feet apart. Greenish white or pinkish flowers, 1½ inches across. Full sun or partial shade. Blooms in summer. Zones 4-9, not heat-tolerant.

AURINIA SAXATILIS (BASKET-OF-GOLD) 1-2 feet tall, space 1 foot apart. Spoon-shaped leaves, masses of brilliant yellow ¼-inch flowers. Full sun. Blooms in early spring. Zones 4-10.

BAPTISIA AUSTRALIS (WILD BLUE INDIGO) 3-6 feet tall, space 3 feet apart. Blue green foliage, 1-inch blue flowers. Full sun to partial shade. Blooms in early summer. Zones 3-10, heat-tolerant.

BELAMCANDA CHINENSIS (BLACKBERRY LILY) 2-3 feet tall, space 1 foot apart. Orange-spotted flowers, shiny blackberrylike fruit. Full sun to partial shade. Blooms in summer. Zones 5-10, heat-tolerant.

rodgersia, is the only species whose name has changed, but most catalogs still list it under its old name. The other species of *Rodgersia* have remained in that genus. By any name, these are superior plants for large, bold foliage effects, either as specimens or for massing in light woodland borders or beside water. Their plumy sprays of flowers are interesting but of secondary importance. Although shieldleafs will succeed in full sun as long as the soil is consistently damp, they really thrive in cooler, partially shaded locations. Soil should be deep and well amended with plenty of organic material to retain adequate moisture. They must not dry out, demanding deep watering during times of drought to avoid browning of the handsome foliage. A spring application of fertilizer and an organic summer mulch are recommended to retain fertility and keep the soil evenly moist. Fall planting is successful only in mild-winter regions. Where winters are cold, spring planting is preferable, and winter protection with evergreen boughs or salt hay is recommended. If stock increase is desired, divide older plants as growth commences in early spring. *Rodgersia pinnata, R. aesculifolia,* and *R. sambucifolia* are also worth seeking.

ASTRANTIA MASTERWORT *Apiaceae (Carrot family)*

Only *A. major* is commonly available, but this species is gaining in popularity as a long-blooming plant for lightly shaded borders and for cutting. The flowers also dry and press well for craft items. Often listed is the cultivar 'Margery Fish', which is quite similar to the species, but is reputed to have larger flowers; 'Rubra' has rosy bracts. These combine well with *Viola cornuta*. 'Sunningdale Variegated' is an elegant but hard-to-find cultivar grown for its beautiful yellow- and cream-splashed foliage. Masterworts require a deep, fertile soil that remains moist during hot weather, but is well drained at all times. While they will grow in full sun in the North, they show off best in partially shaded places and are happiest where nights are cool. Plant in spring or early fall, but keep well watered during times of drought. To retain fertility, apply a light dressing of complete fertilizer annually. Plants are easy to raise from seed sown in spring or summer, or established plants may be divided in early spring or fall. Deadhead to avoid self-seeding and to encourage longer blooming. Few pests and diseases attack masterworts, although the handsome foliage may be attacked by slugs in damp places.

AURINIA (ALYSSUM) BASKET-OF-GOLD *Brassicaceae (Mustard family)*

Long a mainstay of rock and wall gardens in spring, *A. saxatilis* [*Alyssum saxatile*] is one of the best companions for minor bulbs like squills, grape hyacinths, and crocuses. This undemanding perennial requires no more than a lean, free-draining soil in full sun. Overly rich or well-fertilized soils are not to its liking, and the resulting soft, floppy growth is unattractive. Planting can be done in spring or fall. Do not mulch. After flowering, shear the plants hard to avoid seed production and to retain a compact shape. The base of the plants becomes woody even during the first season, but new growth will usually break after trimming. In warm zones and where it is to be used in tempo-

It is the composition of different groups of plants, at different heights, with form, foliage, and flower variations, that gives each border its unique character. Borders are three-dimensional and different planes and masses allow light and shadow to play on flower and foliage while ground-hugging plants contrast with soaring spires of stately neighbors. Each individual border plant has its own qualities . . . and groups are put together so that a balanced pictorial composition results–an artistic masterpiece as well as a convincing demonstration of horticultural skills.
FROM *BORDERS*, BY PENELOPE HOBHOUSE

Baptisia australis flowers.

rary spring displays, basket-of-gold is best treated as a biennial. Spring seeding out-of-doors will produce strong, healthy stock to set out in the fall. Double-flowered *A. s.* 'Flore-Pleno' and variegated forms, such as *A. s.* 'Dudley Neville Variegated', must be propagated from cuttings of vegetative growth in spring or early summer. Other cultivars include a compact form 'Compactum' and 'Silver Queen', which has soft yellow, rather than brilliant yellow flowers.

BAPTISIA FALSE INDIGO *Fabaceae (Pea family)*

The most popular species of this native genus is *B. australis*, the wild blue indigo. In the wild it is found in light woods and in open places where the soil is moist. In the garden, it is a fine addition to the flower border, meadows, native plant gardens, or may be planted in those sometimes difficult transitional areas between formal gardens and woodlands. While not in the top ten as a cut flower, the inflated, dark-colored pods that follow are useful for dried arrangements. Wild blue indigo performs best in full sun or just a little shade and favors deep, reasonably fertile, well-drained soil. A light application of complete fertilizer in early spring will offset poorer soils. Either spring or fall planting is satisfactory, but newly planted stock should be protected with a winter mulch for the first season. In common with many of the pea family, baptisias resent disturbance. Dig only to propagate by division when it is really necessary. This should be done early in spring before growth commences. Retain at least 3 eyes per division and shorten the roots to 3-4 inches. Seeds should be sown outside as soon as they ripen, but they will overwinter before germination occurs. Seeds indoors will require scarification or other preparatory treatment to enable water to penetrate the hard seedcoat. Maintenance is minimal; staking may be necessary in shaded places. Unless the fruits are required, the plants can be sheared into rounded or domed shapes, which adds a bulky shrublike effect to a design. Powdery mildew sometimes becomes a problem in shaded places or where air movement is restricted.

BEGONIA GRANDIS HARDY BEGONIA *Begoniaceae (Begonia family)*

Begonia grandis is the hardy member of a very large tropical genus widely grown for its colorful, attractive foliage and lovely flowers. Native to China and Japan, hardy begonia can stand temperatures down to 0°F. if its tuberous base is protected by mulch and not allowed to freeze. It's a very decorative plant, with large beautiful leaves colored red on the underside and sprays of pink flowers that open from red buds. Grow in sun or shade, with a moist humusy soil. Begonias propagate from bulbils that develop in the leaf axil and then drop to the ground. The cultivar 'Alba' has white flowers; 'Simsii' produces larger flowers than most.

BELAMCANDA BLACKBERRY LILY *Iridaceae (Iris family)*

Both species in this genus (also called leopard flowers) are native to China and Japan. *B. chinensis* is becoming popular in this country as an ornamental, for its shiny blackberrylike fruits as much as for its orange-spotted flowers; once finished, the flowers twist up tightly. *B. flabellata* 'Hello Yellow' is a wonderful smaller (10-inch) cultivar with the typical blackberrylike fruit. Both are fairly easy to grow and are unusual additions to summer and early fall flower borders. Group several plants together to get a telling display. Blackberry lily grows best in full sun positions, in well-drained, reasonably fertile soil. Apply additional water during dry periods. A light spring application of a complete fertilizer is also recommended. Planting may be done in spring or fall, but newly planted stock should be protected with a winter mulch. Propagation is most satisfactory by seed sown in spring, either out of doors or indoors at about 70-80° F. Germination will take 2-4 weeks. Some gardeners prefer to divide the rhizomes in spring or early summer. Iris borer may attack the rhizomes with devastating effect; dig and destroy as soon as damage is seen; do not compost the foliage to prevent overwintering of borers. Leaf scorch causes an unsightly browning of the irislike leaves. Do not deadhead, or the attractive black glossy fruits will not form. Self-seeding is not a problem.

BERGENIA PIGSQUEAK *Saxifragaceae (Saxifrage family)*

Bergenias are native to temperate Asia, where they colonize large areas in widely differing habitats. In the garden, these bold perennials are grown as much for their substantial leaves as for their rather coarse red, pink, or white flowers. They are particularly effective massed or as a ground cover beside streams and ponds, along paths, between shrubs, and at the front of borders. The large cabbagey leaves, so popular with flower arrangers, provide a contrasting foil for ferns, fringed bleeding hearts, and other plants with finely textured foliage. Many are more or less evergreen, and when the temperature falls their leaves often become strongly flushed with purple or maroon. The best winter color appears on plants that are grown in full sun; in windswept places, however, the effect is lost, as winter burn disfigures the leaves. Bergenias appreciate protection from the midday sun, especially in the South, so a partially shaded position is ideal. At the Chicago Botanic Garden, heavy clay soils provide enough moisture to protect from burn. The soil should be deep and well drained, fairly rich in organic matter, although they will tolerate all but the driest or most waterlogged places. Spring planting is recommended so that the plants are well established before cold weather. Fall plantings must be well mulched for their first winter; in warm climates, mulching is not needed for cold protection, but does help retain moistures. Be alert for slug damage. Propagation is best in spring, when the thick rhizomes may be divided. Replant deeply. Seeds may be started out of doors in late fall or early spring, but seed-grown plants are seldom true to type since many bergenias are hybrids. Fall planting is best for southern California; it gives the plant a chance to get established before the heat of summer. Perhaps the most widely available species is *B. cordifolia,* the heart-leaved bergenia, which is evergreen as far north as Chicago. Its leaves turn burgundy color in winter. *B. crassifolia* is also widespread and has somewhat smaller leaves. Lesser grown are the

Bergenia x 'Bressingham White', a British introduction, has clean white flowers.

hybrids, of which many are named. *B.* x 'Bressingham White' is one of the best, but the foliage does not color well in the winter.

BOLTONIA BOLTONIA *Asteraceae (Daisy family)*

Only one species of this North American genus is currently in cultivation. In the wild *B. asteroides* is found in open places in sandy or gravelly free-draining soils, as well as in wetter places. They are adapted, therefore, to a wide range of soils in cultivation and grow best in full-sun positions, although they will tolerate slight shade. Where there is sufficient soil moisture or the soil is rich, the plants will spread fairly quickly, which may or may not be an advantage. In large gardens *B. asteroides* is a good subject for the back of the border, where its hundreds of white asterlike flowers top stems up to 7 feet. The straight species combines well with other tall fall-bloomers, such as *Aster* 'Coombe Violet' and *Rudbeckia nitida* 'Herbstonne', as well as some ornamental grasses, but it may be too weedy for some tastes. Where space is a concern, the shorter cultivar 'Snowbank' is recommended, as is 'Pink Beauty', which puts on a real show for 4-6 weeks. Both make good cut flowers as long as the stems are plunged in deep water in a dark cool place for conditioning. Light staking is sometimes necessary even when grown in full sun, particularly in windy places; it is essential in the shade or in richer soil. Other maintenance is minimal. Planting may be done in early spring or fall, as can propagation by division. Regular division is needed every 2-3 years to retain vigor. Seed of the cultivars will not come true. Deadheading is advisable to avoid self-seeding, although if this is not a problem the dead stems can provide an added architectural dimension to winter gardens.

BRUNNERA SILBERIAN BUGLOSS *Boraginaceae (Borage family)*

Siberian bugloss, also known as perennial forget-me-not and heart-leaved brunnera, is a favorite, low-maintenance perennial for spring, shaded gardens. It is particularly valuable as a ground cover along stream banks, in light woodlands, and under deciduous trees, but also looks well grouped at the front of borders or along paths. *B. macrophylla* requires a rich, well-drained but moisture-retentive soil, high in organic material; it does not thrive in the clay soil of the Chicago Botanic Garden. Extra water is beneficial during periods of drought. Moisture retention and fertility are best maintained by applying a summer mulch of compost or leaf mold. In southern climates, a shaded position is essential, but where summers are gentler shade is necessary only during the hottest parts of the day. Divide or take root cuttings in early spring to increase stock; either spring or fall planting is successful. Deadhead after flowering to avoid self-seeding. This plant is often bothered by slugs and snails in California, and by foliar nematodes at Brookside Gardens in Wheaton, Maryland. Some cultivars have striking patterns on the large heart-shaped leaves; those of 'Langtrees' are edged with silvery spots, while 'Variegata' has leaves bordered with creamy white.

BEGONIA GRANDIS (HARDY BEGONIA) 1-2 feet tall, space 1-2 feet apart. Bright green leaves with colored veins, small pink flowers. Full sun to partial shade. Blooms late summer to early fall. Zones 6-9.

BERGENIA CORDIFOLIA (PIGSQUEAK) 1½-2 feet tall, space 2 feet apart. Cabbagelike leaves, small deep pink flowers. Partial shade. Blooms in spring. Zones 3-10.

BOLTONIA ASTEROIDES (BOLTONIA) 2-2½ feet tall, space 1 foot apart. Asterlike flowers on many-branched, erect stems. Full sun to partial shade. Blooms in late summer to fall. Zones 3-10, heat-tolerant.

BRUNNERA MACROPHYLLA (SIBERIAN BUGLOSS) 1 foot tall, space 2 feet apart. Clumps of dark green heart-shaped leaves, tiny blue flowers. Full sun to partial shade. Blooms in late spring to early summer. Zones 3-10, not heat-tolerant.

CAMPANULA CARPATICA 'BLUE CLIPS' (CARPATHIAN HAREBELL) 8-18 inches tall, space 1-1½ feet apart. Clumps of leafy branching stems with medium blue flowers. Full sun or partial shade. Blooms in late spring or summer. Zones 3-10.

CAMPANULA LATIFOLIA (MILKY BELLFLOWER) 3½-5 feet tall, space 2 feet apart. Erect, branching stems, light blue, dark blue, or white flowers. Full sun to partial shade. Blooms in late spring to late summer. Zones 6-10.

CAMPANULA GLOMERATA 'JOAN ELLIOTT' (CLUSTERED BELLFLOWER) 1½ feet tall, space 2 feet apart. Clumps of erect stems, funnel-shaped violet flowers. Full sun or partial shade. Flowers in spring to summer. Zones 3-10.

CENTAUREA MACROCEPHALA (ARMENIAN BASKET FLOWER, YELLOW HARDHEAD) 2-4 feet tall, space 2 feet apart. Saw-tooth leaves, bright lemon-yellow thistle-type flowers. Full sun. Blooms in summer. Zones 3-9.

CAMPANULA BELLFLOWER *Campanulaceae (Bellflower family)*

This large genus provides the gardener with many of the most valuable perennials for ornamental use. Campanulas come in many sizes, from tall erect ones like *C. lactiflora,* milky bellflower, and *C. latifolia,* great bellflower, to sprawling or mat-forming species like *C. portenschlagiana,* Dalmatian bellflower, and *C. carpatica,* Carpathian harebell. The tall species are admirable subjects for the back of the flower border, while *C. glomerata,* clustered bellflower, and *C. persicifolia,* peach-leaved bellflower, enhance the middle sections. For best effect group in threes, fives, or sevens. The low-growing bellflowers are attractive as edging plants at the front of the border, in planters, or in wall and rock gardens. While tolerant of partial shade, most species grow best in full sun, except in the hottest parts of the country, where they appreciate noonday shade. A well-drained, average soil, slightly acid to alkaline, is generally sufficient; the low-growing rock-garden types require a cool, moist but well-drained root run. Irrigate during periods of drought. A light dressing of fertilizer every other year is beneficial, but only for the larger types. Most divide readily in the spring or fall, and cuttings of young growth root easily. Seed germinates freely. The taller types require staking; the removal of spent flowers avoids self-seeding. Slugs are an ever-present danger, and rots of the crown and roots may be troublesome. Diligent plant hygiene really pays off. While most nurseries carry a fairly extensive list of bellflowers, among the most popular are *C. glomerata* 'Joan Elliott' and *C. carpatica* 'Blue Clips' and its white form 'White Clips', all of which are especially suited to limited spaces. The violet-purple flowers of *C. glomerata* 'Joan Elliott' are good for cutting and in the border combine well with the soft yellow of *Achillea* x 'Moonshine'. Long-blooming *C. carpatica* 'Blue Clips' is a suitable companion for the hybrid pinks, both in the rock garden or at the front on the border. *C. porscharskyana* has trailing stems and star-shaped blue flowers, is hardy as far north as Zone 3, and thrives in southern California as well.

Campanula glomerata 'Joan Elliott'.

CENTAUREA KNAPWEED, CORNFLOWER *Asteraceae (Daisy family)*

Only a few of the thistle-flowered knapweeds are appropriate for ornamental use, but these are easy subjects for the wild garden, the flower border, or as cut flowers. *C. macrocephala,* Armenian basket flower or yellow hardhead, and *C. montana,* perennial cornflower or mountain bluets, are both readily available from nurseries and thrive where plenty of sun is available. The soil should be reasonably fertile and moisture retentive. A light dressing of fertilizer in early spring may be necessary where soils are poor; very dry or wet soils, as well as too much shade, results in weak, spindly growth. Both planting and propagation by division may be done in either early spring or in the fall. After flowering, deadhead to prevent self-seeding and cut the plants back. A second flush of bloom sometimes will result. Several diseases attack knapweeds, especially stem rot, rust, and aster yellows. Remove affected plants and destroy them. *C. montana* tends to wander, particularly in northern climates, and can become a noxious weed; it benefits from staking. One of the best of the knap-

At Brookside Gardens in Wheaton, Maryland, leadwort is planted with miniature bulbs like *Galanthus, Iris reticulata,* and *Scilla*. It leafs out to cover the unsightly bulb foliage, then provides blue flowers in late summer and red foliage color in the fall. It is cut back in late fall to better show off the bulbs in the spring–almost year-round interest is achieved in the same spot. At Berry Botanic Garden in Portland, Oregon, leadwort is planted with other fall bloomers such as *Sedum* 'Autumn Joy'.

weeds is *C. hypoleuca* 'John Coutts' [*C. dealbata* 'John Coutts'], an easily propagated repeat-bloomer with rose-pink flowers. Regrettably this is not grown by as many nurseries as it deserves, but it is worth seeking. Several states, including Colorado and Washington, have classified species of this flower as noxious weeds; *C. macrocephela* is among the most invasive species.

CENTRANTHUS RED VALERIAN *Valerianaceae (Valerian family)*

In American gardens, these European natives (also called Jupiter's beard) are represented only by *C. ruber,* the red valerian. Its cultivars 'Alba', 'Atrococcineus', and 'Roseus' are white, deep red, and rose pink respectively. All make fine, long-blooming additions to sunny borders–they sometimes flower sporadically through the whole summer–and are also useful as cut flowers. Though quite tolerant, they do best where the soil is well drained and on the poor side, with a pH of neutral to alkaline; they also survive in arid climates. Extra water is needed only during periods of extreme drought. Soft spindly growth results from too rich a soil as well as a shaded position. Poorly drained soils may cause root rot. Plant in spring or early fall, leaving sufficient space between plants to accommodate their rather billowy habit. After flowering, deadhead to avoid self-seeding, which can become a nuisance. In southern California, they are often found in waste places and are excellent in difficult spots because they take much drought and abuse. Propagation is best by basal cuttings taken in the spring, or the plants may be divided at that time. Division every three years or so maintains vigor and avoids woody or leggy growth; cutting back hard in midsummer also discourages legginess. Vegetative rather than seed propagation is essential to retain the true cultivars. No serious pests or diseases attack red valerian.

CERATOSTIGMA LEADWORT *Plumbaginaceae (Leadwort family)*

Leadwort, *C. plumbaginoides* [*Plumbago larpentae*], sometimes called plumbago, is an excellent front-of-the-border, edging, or ground-cover plant that displays its intense purplish blue flowers toward the end of the season. It is one of the last plants to leaf out in spring. As the weather turns colder, the foliage turns a striking reddish color, extending the season of interest. The best fall color is found on plants grown in full sun, although a slightly shaded position is also acceptable. Soil must be well drained, organic, and reasonably fertile; overly rich, organic soils may result in the plants spreading too rapidly and becoming invasive. Additional water during dry times is helpful; an early spring application of diluted complete fertilizer helps maintain vigor. Spring planting is preferable, particularly in the North, where recently planted material is readily heaved out of the ground during freezing weather. A winter mulch is routinely advised in Zones 6 and colder; it is not found necessary at the Denver Botanic Garden. In the spring, build up stock by root cuttings or more easily by division. In mild winter regions leadwort is evergreen; prune hard in the spring to encourage fresh, new growth. Pests and diseases are seldom a problem.

CENTRANTHUS RUBER 'ROSEUS' (RED VALERIAN) 1½-3 feet tall, space 1-1½ feet apart. Rose pink flowers on erect stems. Full sun to partial shade. Blooms in late spring to early fall. Zones 4-10, not heat-tolerant.

CERATOSTIGMA PLUMBAGINOIDES (LEADWORT) 1 foot tall, space 1½ feet apart. Low-growing foliage with intense purplish blue flowers. Full sun or partial shade. Blooms late summer to early fall. Zones 5-10.

CHELONE LYONII (PINK TURTLEHEAD) 2-4 feet tall, space 2 feet apart. Oval, coarsely toothed leaves, clear pink flowers. Partial shade. Blooms late summer to early fall. Zones 4-10, not heat-tolerant.

DENDRANTHEMA X GRANDIFLORUM [CHRYSANTHEMUM X MORIFOLI-UM] (GARDEN CHRYSANTHEMUM) 1-6 feet tall, space 1½ feet apart. Brightly colored flowers in many colors, varying in size and shape. Full sun. Blooms late summer to fall. Zones 4-10.

CHELONE TURTLEHEAD *Scrophularicaceae (Figwort family)*

The turtleheads are so named for the shape of the flowers, which loosely resembles the open-mouthed head of a turtle. These native plants are found in the eastern and southern states along rivers, beside lakes, and in damp woodlands, where the soil remains evenly moist and is high in organic content. In the garden, while they adapt well to average border conditions, they are at their best planted beside ponds and streams. Increase the water-holding capacity of the soil with liberal amounts of organic matter and irrigate during dry times. Routinely apply an organic summer mulch. Stress caused by drought increases the susceptibility to mildew disease, which is not only unsightly but also weakens the plant. Fertilization is unnecessary if the soil has been adequately prepared. Turtleheads prefer to grow in full sun, but will tolerate lightly shaded positions. At planting time, in spring or early fall, take care not to bury the crowns of the plant more than 1 inch below the soil surface. Propagate by division at the same time or take stem cuttings from late spring to midsummer. Control of leaf spot and powdery mildew may be necessary with a fungicidal spray. Thinning the number of stems on vigorously growing plants improves air circulation and inhibits the spread of powdery mildew. *C. lyonii*, the pink turtlehead, and *C. obliqua*, rose turtlehead, are most commonly cultivated. The latter blooms well into the fall and is a lovely companion for some of our native asters. Both are good cut flowers and provide interest in winter.

CHRYSANTHEMUMS *Asteraceae (Daisy family)*

Recent revision of the genetic boundaries of the *Anthemideae* order, of which chrysanthemums are members, has required changes in the names of several common chrysanthemums, including the garden chrysanthemum and the Shasta, Nippon, and painted daisies. In this book, we have grouped these plants under chrysanthemums and listed each of their new names.

DENDRANTHENA x GRANDIFLORUM [CHRYSANTHEMUM X MORIFOLIUM] (Garden chrysanthemum) This vast and varied group of hybrids includes many flower types (divided into 13 classifications by the National Chrysanthemum Society) and colors. Most are vigorous clump-formers with sturdy, upright stems, some of which are branched or woody. Most gardeners grow garden chrysanthemums from purchased potted plants, which are sold everywhere; they brighten fall gardens when most other perennials have faded. These should always be planted before the hottest part of the summer, but after all danger of frost has passed. Pinch stems regularly to encourage compact, bushy growth until the beginning of July in short-season climates and the end of July in warmer zones; they should not be allowed to flower until late summer or early fall. Taller varieties should be staked. Although they are usually used as annuals, garden chrysanthemums overwinter well if provided with light protection in cold climates. They should be divided every 2-3 years, discarding any woody growth. They do best in rich, well-drained soil and need full sun and frequent applications of fertilizer. They are susceptible to spider mites and aphids.

Although the Greeks named the Chrysanthemum "Golden Flower," the earliest recorded reference to the flower comes from Confucius, who in *Li-Ki* (Ninth Moon) extolled "the chrysanthemum with its golden glory." These small, mostly single, usually yellow wildflowers were a far cry from the ebullient blooms that characterize current mums. In the 9th century, the Japanese embraced the mum as a garden plant, and the new forms they developed were jealously guarded and long confined to Japan. In the mid 19th century, Robert Fortune was able to carry a few plants to Britain, resulting in a major breakthrough in Western mum culture when British and French botanists further improved the Japanese cultivars. America's first experience with mums was in 1798, with the introduction of a variety called 'Dark Purple' by John Stevens of Hoboken, New Jersey, but it was not until the 1920 'Fortune' that more varieties were available. In 1932, Alex Cumming of Bristol, Connecticut crossed existing garden varieties with the Korean mum (*Dendranthem zawadskii*), creating vigorous, handsome plants that eventually became available in a wide variety of colors and forms. Practically all hardy mums have ancestries stemming back to the Korean hybrids.

Opposite: A field of garden mums at The New York Botanical Garden mixes early and late season varieties.

A border of hardy mums shows just a few of their colors.

LEUCANTHEMUM x SUPERBUM [CHRYSANTHEMUM x SUPERBUM, C. MAXIMUM] (Shasta daisy) These popular hybrid daisies are easy to grow, readily available in most nurseries, and superb as cut flowers, with a long blooming season. Many cultivars are on the market, both single and double forms. Of the singles, 'Alaska' is one of the best, although 'Majestic' has larger flowers on longer stems for cutting. Another single, 'Snowcap', is compact with bushy plants better suited to the flower border. Of the doubles, 'Aglaya' is easy to find; the first of the double-flowered cultivars, 'Esther Read', is seldom offered today. The double-flowered cultivars are best planted in light shade, although in the North the singles can tolerate exposed positions. The soil must be well drained but moist, amended with plenty of organic material; they will not tolerate wet feet in the winter, but additional water is needed during dry times. Shasta daisies are heavy feeders; fertilize routinely in spring and again during the growing season for best results. To extend the blooming period, deadhead religiously; they can often be coaxed to continue to flower into the fall. Initial planting and subsequent division may be done in either spring or early fall. The plants are not long-lived and require division every 2-3 years to maintain vigor. Seed-grown plants are variable, although some cultivars are available as seed. Aphids are sometimes troublesome.

NIPPONANTHEMUM NIPPONICUM [CHRYSANTHEMUM NIPPONICUM] (Nippon daisy, Montauk daisy) This Japanese native has become a standby of many American fall borders. To perform at its best, it should be planted in spring or early fall in ordinary well-drained garden soil, in a full-sun position. It also tolerates sandy soils well and thrives in coastal gardens. The rather succulent leaves store moisture, and additional water is seldom necessary. Nippon daisies make large, shrublike plants that frequently become leggy and woody at the base. Cut them back almost to ground level as growth commences in the spring to force low young shoots; fertilize lightly afterward. Where the growing season is long, pinch the foliage back by ½-⅓ in early June, and the subsequent shoots by 2-3 nodes in early July. Where fall comes early, the delay caused by pinching may result in the flowers being frosted before they open. Propagation is best by rooting terminal cuttings in late spring or early summer. Pests and diseases are seldom serious. The shrublike proportions of Nippon daisies are useful in mixed flower gardens, particularly for the middle to back of the border. It must be remembered that the "legs" and "ankles" of these plants are not always elegant and are improved by the camouflage of dense, lower-growing plants in front. Excellent in combination with ornamental grasses.

TANACETUM COCCINEUM [CHRYSANTHEMUM COCCINEUM] (Painted daisy, Pyrethum) This is one of the finest perennials for cutting and also assorts well with bulbs in the late-spring border. Painted daisies can be planted in early fall, but spring planting is preferable, particularly in the North. In warm regions, where they are not at their best, shade them from the full heat of

LEUCANTHEMUM X SUPERBUM 'ALASKA' (SHASTA DAISY) 1-2 feet tall, space 1 foot apart. Spoon-shaped leaves, yellow-eyed 1- to 2-inch daisy flowers. Full sun. Blooms in early summer. Zone 3-10, heat-tolerant.

NIPPONANTHEMUM NIPPONICUM (NIPPON DAISY) 1½-2½ feet tall, space 2 feet apart. Bushy, well-branched plant with Shasta-like 2½-inch daisies. Full sun. Blooms in fall. Zones 5-10, heat-tolerant.

TANACETUM COCCINEUM (PAINTED DAISY, PYRETHUM) 1-2½ feet tall, space 1½ feet apart. Full sun. Blooms late spring to early summer. Zones 4-10.

CHRYSOGONUM VIRGIANUM (GOLDENSTAR) 4-12 inches tall, space 1 foot apart. Bright green leaves, small star-shaped yellow flowers. Full sun to partial shade. Blooms spring to fall. Zones 5-10, heat-tolerant.

CHRYSOPSIS VILLOSA (GOLDEN ASTER) 1-5 feet tall, space 2 feet apart. Bushy plant with wide corymbs of bright yellow flowers. Full sun. Blooms in late summer to early fall. Zones 4-10.

CIMICIFUGA RACEMOSA (BUGBANE) 3-8 feet tall, space 2 feet apart. Wandlike racemes of white flowers on wiry stems. Full sun to partial shade. Blooms in summer. Zones 3-10, not heat-tolerant.

COREOPSIS LANCEOLATA 'EARLY SUNRISE' (TICKSEED) 1-2 feet tall, space 2-3 feet apart. Semidouble yellow flowers, finely divided foliage. Full sun. Blooms in early summer to summer. Zones 5-10, heat-tolerant.

COREOPSIS VERTICILLATA 'MOONBEAM' (TICKSEED) 2 feet tall, space 2 feet apart. Erect, bushy plant with feathery foliage and pale yellow daisy flowers. Full sun. Blooms in summer to fall. Zones 3-10, heat-tolerant.

the day, but in temperate climates they thrive in full sun. Soil should be well drained and high in organic matter to maintain moisture; additional water is needed during dry periods. Avoid the weak floppy growth promoted by overfeeding; a very light spring application of a complete fertilizer will suffice. Well-grown painted daisies need attention. Their loose habit of growth calls for light staking, and routine deadheading extends flowering. After blooming time, cut the plants back hard to encourage reblooming and stockier growth. A winter mulch is recommended in cold regions. Spring or early fall division every 2-3 years helps to maintain vigor; discard the woody inner parts of the plant. Build stock with the young divisions; seed-grown plants are seldom true to name. Several cultivars have been developed for the cut-flower industry, including 'Robinson's Pink' and Robinson's Rose', both long-stemmed 'Robinson' hybrids. As a border plant, perhaps more compact 'James Kelway' with single, crimson flowers, is better suited; 'Pink Bouquet' is a good double-flowered cultivar. Pests avoid painted daisies for it is the natural source of the insecticide Pyrethrin. Leaf spot and mildew are seldom troublesome.

CHRYSOGONUM GOLDENSTAR, GREEN-AND-GOLD *Asteraceae* *(Daisy family)*

Both common names aptly describe *Chrysogonum virginianum*, a diminutive native of light woodlands of the northeastern and southeastern states. Valuable in rock gardens or as a ground cover, its perky golden flowers, set off by bright green leaves, enliven lightly shaded areas on the edge of woodlands or wild gardens. In the South, it is evergreen, but flowering usually stops during hot weather; where summers are cooler, flowering continues sporadically throughout the season, with a second autumnal flush. Plant in spring or early fall in light dappled shade or in sun if soil moisture can be maintained. Goldenstars do not like to dry out and prefer a moist well-drained soil containing a moderate amount of organic material. An organic summer mulch is recommended; additional fertilizer is unnecessary. Protect from harsh snowless winters. Increase stock in spring or early fall by division. Named cultivars include 'Allen Bush' and 'Mark Viette'. This popular little plant is low on maintenance and long on charm.

CHRYSOPSIS GOLDEN ASTER *Asteraceae (Daisy family)*

Not a true aster, this daisylike native North American grows wild in dry, sandy soil. The yellow flowers, borne in August and September in clusters, add welcome color to the fall border. Golden asters are very easy to grow, in light soil and sun or partial shade. They are fully hardy and easy to propagate by seed or division in the spring. To promote branching and increase bloom, pinch back shoots an inch or two after growth is well established. *C. mariana,* Maryland golden aster, is a low-maintenance and showy species. It grows 1-3 feet tall, with flowerheads 1½ inches across. *C. graminifolia* has silvery foliage and ½-inch-wide flowers. *C. falcata* grows just 8 inches high.

AWARDS

When looking through catalogues or nurseries, you will often come upon perennials that have received awards. Questions arise: Why did the plant receive an award, and who bestowed it?

Perennials are given awards by plant societies (see page 217 for a list of them). Awards are voted upon by the entire membership of the society or by member judges who have met the requirements to be a judge designated by that society.

The Perennial Plant Association annually awards a "Perennial Plant of the Year," given to the plant that receives the most votes from the association membership.

According to regional director Matt Horn, to be eligible a plant must meet certain requirements, including:

1. It must be available commercially.

2. It must be vegetatively propagated.

3. It must be reasonably hardy in most areas of North America.

Some specialized societies such as the American Hemerocallis Society awards a medal (Stout Silver Medal) which is the highest award bestowed upon a daylily by members of the society that have been trained as garden judges. To be eligible, a plant must pass through a series of prerequisite awards in which it has distinguished itself in many areas of the country.

plant selector

We have not had much success with delphinium. We start them in the greenhouse and plant them out every spring. We have joined the Delphinium Society, where we can get seeds from British hybrids, which produce better plants and flowers than 'Pacific Hybrids', but so far we haven't had any better luck with hardiness.
KIM JOHNSON,
OLD WESTBURY GARDENS

Delphinium do well here. They thrive in our cool climate and alkaline soil and actually are even more successful in the northern part of the state. They usually last about 3 years if they are mulched in winter.
RICHARD ISAACSON, MINNEAPOLIS LANDSCAPE ARBORETUM

We grow delphinium as annuals, forcing them in the greenhouse and planting outside in the spring.
SUSAN NOLDE,
BROOKSIDE GARDENS

Delphinium do poorly in the South. They need nighttime temperatures of 55-65° F., and we rarely go down below 70° F. in the summer.
ROBERT BOWDEN, ATLANTA

We've had some mild success with delphinium. Usually they last only 3-4 years, but I have one seedling that's lasted 8 years and has been moved twice. I garden in rich soil, mulch, minimize watering and fertilizing, and do not cut back after flowering.
GALEN GATES, CHICAGO BOTANIC GARDEN

Delphinium are not as difficult as people believe. Mold and mildew problems can be controlled or avoided by watering early in the day so that water evaporates quickly.
DR. LINDA McMAHON, BERRY BOTANICAL GARDEN, PORTLAND, OREGON

CIMICIFUGA BUGBANE *Ranunculaceae (Buttercup family)*

Bugbanes slowly make large specimen plants, planted most effectively in open woodland gardens or grouped at the back of flower borders, where their imposing size is an asset. Plant in spring or fall in a lightly shaded position; they will tolerate fairly heavy shade, but bloom will be lighter. In sunny places they are satisfactory only if the soil is kept evenly moist, and even then their normally dark green leaves may yellow. A deep, well-drained soil amended with copious amounts of acidic organic matter is the ideal, and additional water is usually beneficial during dry summers. Routinely apply a light dressing of complete fertilizer in early spring. In the summer, a mulch of leaf mold helps to maintain an evenly moist soil. Staking is seldom required except in windy places, and few pests or diseases are serious. Bugbanes are best left undisturbed except when stock must be built up by division, in early spring or fall. Erratic germination of fresh seed sown as soon as it is ripe is an option, but flowering of young plants may not occur until the fourth year. Deadhead for neatness or allow the quite attractive fruiting spires to dry on the plants. Perhaps the most popular bugbane is the native American, summer-blooming *C. racemosa*, otherwise known as black cohosh or black snakeroot. *C. simplex,* the Kamchatka bugbane, its cultivar 'White Pearl' (which flowers just before frost at the Chicago Botanic Garden), and *C. ramosa* 'Atropurpurea', the purple-leaved bugbane, bloom later and combine beautifully with autumn-flowering Japanese anemones. *C. ramosa* 'Brunette', a stunning European cultivar, has even better purple color.

COREOPSIS TICKSEED *Asteraceae (Daisy family)*

This easy, drought-tolerant and heat-loving genus includes many fine subjects for the perennial garden, for cut flowers, or for naturalizing large rough areas. All demand full sun and will not bloom as freely even in lightly shaded places. Ordinary or even poor soil that is well drained is satisfactory, although pink *C. rosea* (which is very invasive) prefers it to be slightly moist. This species is the only one that benefits from additional water during dry periods. Although tickseed is hard to find in desert climates, they do very well when grown from seed there. If the soil is poor, a light spring application of a complete fertilizer may be given, but beware of giving too much, which will result in soft spindly growth. Many new cultivars of tickseed have appeared on the market in recent years, improvements on the species in terms of compact habit and longer blooming times. Perhaps the favorite is *C. verticillata* 'Moonbeam', which bears its pale yellow daisy flowers well into the fall. It combines particularly well with silver-leaved plants like *Salvia argentea*. Other cultivars of our native thread-leaf coreopsis include the brilliant yellow 'Zagreb', similar but smaller than the species. *C. auriculata* 'Nana' has orange to gold flowers; if deadheaded regularly, it flowers even longer than 'Moonbeam'. For the front of sunny borders, compact *C. lanceolata* 'Goldfink' is hard to beat; the species tends to flop, but is a good cut flower if staked. All may be planted in spring or fall and can become invasive under good conditions. Propagate the cultivars by division in the spring, and deadhead if possible to avoid unwanted seedlings, which will be inferior, and to prolong bloom. Rust and powdery mildew are only occasionally a problem.

DELPHINIUM LARKSPUR *Ranunculaceae (Buttercup family)*

From north temperate regions of the world, these stately plants are basically not difficult to grow, but are best treated as short-lived perennials, since they tend to die out after a few years. To get the best, results they require special attention in the garden and in no way can be considered low-maintenance plants. Delphinium grow best in deep, slightly acid to alkaline and well-drained soil that has been amended with plenty of aged, well-rotted manure or compost. They are greedy feeders and should receive an annual spring application of a complete fertilizer as well as a routine organic mulch in summer to retain moisture and fertility. A sheltered position in full sun is ideal, although delphinium appreciate light shade during the hottest times of the day. They are not at their best in hot climates, where they are often grown as annuals. Strong winds must be avoided, and even the taller sorts demand careful staking of the long flower spikes to protect them from damage. Planting, not too deeply, may be done in early spring; rooted cuttings or spring-sown seedlings may be set out in early fall. Since the plants are short-lived, it is wise to keep a supply of young plants coming along. Fresh delphinium seed germinates readily out of doors in spring or summer; cover it completely to eliminate all light. Basal cuttings of young growth can be root-

Though certainly not easy to grow, delphinium are a stunning addition to the perennial border.

Delphinium x *belladonna.*

ed in the spring, using only solid, not hollow, stems. A gourmet item for slugs and snails, delphinium are also attacked by many other pests and diseases. The worst of these are aphids, borers, and mites, botrytis, or gray mold blight, crown rot, and mildew. A regular spray program that incorporates a miticide, insecticide, and fungicide is recommended. Scrupulous attention to garden hygiene reduces the likelihood of attack. Deadhead at the base of the spent flower spike to encourage a second flush of bloom from the laterals. For those willing to undertake so much maintenance, delphinium are the most glorious and rewarding of perennials. Much breeding work has been done, resulting in several superior hybrid groups and strains. *D.* x 'King Arthur', one of the California 'Round Table' series, is a particularly good dark blue selection. *D.* x *belladonna* has many cultivars, such as 'Bellamosa', dark blue, 'Casa Blanca', pure white, and 'Clivedon Beauty', with sky blue flowers. Less showy, but with intense blue flowers on shorter stems, *D. tatsiense* deserves to be more widely available. *D. tricorne*, a shade-loving native plant, produces 18-inch-tall rich blue flowers in midspring.

DIANTHUS PINK *Caryophyllaceae (Pink family)*

Properly grown in cottage gardens since medieval times, pinks and carnations have an intoxicating fragrance that few of us can resist. Sadly, many of the newer sorts have lost their fragrance, but some heirloom ones are being rescued. To a garden designer, the persistent grassy, usually gray-green foliage of the perennial dianthus is invaluable, providing a contrast to the greens of other foliage, even in winter. The perennial pinks are excellent for the fronts of borders, in rock gardens, and especially in dry walls. As a cut flower, the fragrant ones are appealing for low arrangements and, of course, are used in potpourri. The cottage pink *D.* x *allwoodii* has retained its fragrance and is available in cultivars such as double red 'Ian', double pure white 'Aqua', and semidouble, fringed pink 'Essex Witch'. The strain 'Alpinus' has single 2-inch flowers in mixed pinks and reds which also are very fragrant. Maiden pink *D. deltoides* has abundant but small flowers with only a light fragrance. It makes large mats of grassy green foliage, which at blooming time is almost completely obscured by flowers. Low-growing cheddar pinks (*D. gratianopolitanus*) are particularly suitable for rock gardens. Except for *D. arenarius*, which prefers light shade, dianthus grow best in sunny places, where the soil drains freely; most prefer sweet or alkaline soil. Many dianthus are from alpine regions of the world and have adapted to thin, well-drained soils. Avoid too much water and high-nitrogen fertilizers, both of which promote soft, weak growth, susceptible to rot. Propagate every few years since the species are generally short-lived; heel or terminal cuttings are best and root readily taken in early summer. Plant new stock in spring or early fall; mulch with evergreen boughs, at least for the first winter to prevent heaving, sun scald, and dehydration. Regular deadheading encourages reblooming and keeps the plants neat. Slugs and snails are fond of dianthus but can be deterred by applying a collar of limestone chips round the plant, which also keeps the soil sweet.

DELPHINIUM ELATUM 'MAGIC FOUNTAIN PURE BLUE' (LARKSPUR) 3-8 feet tall, space 2-3 feet apart. Erect stems with cylindrical racemes of pale blue flowers. Full sun. Blooms spring to summer. Zones 3-10, not heat-tolerant.

DELPHINIUM ELATUM 'PACIFIC GIANTS' (LARKSPUR) 3-8 feet tall, space 2-3 feet apart. Erect stems with cylindrical racemes of flowers in a wide range of colors. Full sun. Blooms spring to summer. Zones 3-10, not heat-tolerant.

DIANTHUS GRATIANOPOLITANUS 'TINY RUBIES' (CHEDDAR PINK) 6-8 inches, space 12 inches apart. Fringed, double red flowers. Full sun. Blooms in late spring. Zones 5-10, not heat-tolerant.

DIANTHUS X ALLWOODII 'HER MAJESTY' (PINK) 1-1½ feet tall, space 1½ feet apart. Fringed, double white flowers. Full sun. Blooms in summer. Zones 4-10, not heat-tolerant.

Dicentra spectabilis.

DICENTRA BLEEDING HEART *Fumariaceae (Fumitory family)*

The bleeding hearts are among the best-loved perennials for shaded borders and rock gardens, as well as natural woodland gardens. The most showy is the common bleeding heart, *D. spectabilis*, a Japanese native, which carries its pink and white or all white (*D. s.* 'Alba') strings of valentines on elegantly arched stems. Its foliage becomes shabby and tends to die back in response to hot, dry weather, and the resulting gap in the border will need to be filled. Native Americans *D. eximia*, fringed or wild bleeding heart, and *D. formosa*, western bleeding heart, are less showy, but bloom over a much longer period and retain their attractive ferny foliage throughout the season—a definite asset in the garden. These species are extremely similar and both variable. Good selections, such as *D. e.* 'Alba', *D. f.* 'Luxuriant', and 'Adrian Bloom', should be sought. In fact, the latter two are often attributed to *D. eximia*, or may be hybrids. All the bleeding hearts grow best in light shade where the soil remains evenly moist with a high organic content. None will tolerate water-logged winter conditions or dry summer ones; water during droughts. Planting may be done in spring or fall. A winter mulch is a necessity during the first winter for recently planted stock, but is recommended routinely in cold areas. Divide as growth commences in spring except for *D. spectabilis*, which may be divided after flowering but before it dies to ground level. New divisions should have at least 3 eyes. Fresh seed germinates easily, but will not come true from the cultivars. Self-seeding often occurs unless the plants are deadheaded, frequently germinating in unlikely sunny spots. The seedlings are usually inferior. Pests and diseases are seldom a problem, although stem rot sometimes needs control.

DICTAMNUS GAS PLANT *Rutaceae (Rue family)*

This elegant member of the citrus and rue family is a tough perennial, ideal as a specimen in sunny borders or flower gardens. *D. albus (D. fraxinella, D. f. albus)* and its attractive purplish-mauve cultivar 'Purpureus' are not grown as widely as they deserve. This may be because propagation is tricky, and young plants are slow to become established, both traits that cause problems for nurserymen. The common names gas plant or burning bush refer to the fact that the plant exudes a volatile gas from the base of the flowers. The dark green leaves and fruits are deliciously lemon scented. Since gas plants resent disturbance, think carefully about where to plant and then prepare the soil thoroughly in advance. Soil should be deep and rich with plenty of well-rotted organic material to retain moisture; waterlogged soil is not acceptable. If there has been adequate preparation, additional fertilizer each spring is unnec-essary, but water must be given during severe drought. Spring planting of 2-year-old pot-grown stock is recommended. To propagate, sow fresh seed out of doors in the fall. These will not germinate until the following spring, and germination is unpredictable at best. The seedlings take 3-4 years to become

DICENTRA FORMOSA 'BACCARAL' (BLEEDING HEART) 1-2 feet tall, space 1-1½ feet apart. Mounds of finely dissected foliage, heart-shaped flowers. Partial to full shade. Blooms in spring to summer. Zones 3-10, not heat-tolerant.

DICENTRA FORMOSA 'LUXURIANT' (BLEEDING HEART) 1-2 feet tall, space 1-1½ feet apart. Blue-green foliage, carmine-red flowers. Partial to full shade. Blooms in spring to summer. Zones 3-10, not heat-tolerant.

DICENTRA SPECTABLIS (BLEEDING HEART) 2-3 feet tall, space 1½ feet apart. Looser habit than *eximia*, broad heart-shaped flowers. Partial to full sun. Blooms in spring to early summer. Zones 3-10, not heat-tolerant.

DICTAMNUS ALBUS (GAS PLANT) 2-3 feet tall, space 2½ feet apart. Showy pure white flowers in racemes on vertical stems. Full sun. Blooms in late spring to summer. Zones 2-9, not heat-tolerant.

DIGITALIS PURPUREA 'GIANT SHIRLEY' (FOXGLOVE) 2-4 feet tall, space 2½ feet apart. Hood-shaped flowers on erect stems, variety of colors. Full sun. Blooms in summer. Zones 3-9.

ECHINACEA PURPUREA 'BRIGHT STAR' (PURPLE CONEFLOWER) 2-4 feet tall, space 1½-2 feet apart. Rosy pink rays with maroon disks. Full sun. Blooms in summer. Zones 3-10, heat-tolerant.

ECHINACEA PURPUREA 'WHITE SWAN' (PURPLE CONEFLOWER) 1½-3 feet tall, space 1½-2 feet apart. Pure white rays with maroon disks. Full sun. Blooms in summer. Zones 3-10, heat-tolerant.

ECHINOPS RITRO (GLOBE THISTLE) 2-3 feet tall, space 1½ feet apart. Round, spiky flowerheads, 1½ inches in diameter. Full sun. Blooms in summer to early fall. Zones 3-10.

established. Root cuttings or division in early spring are alternate propagation methods, but are not advisable, due to additional disturbance. Deadheading is optional, since the dried star-shaped seedpods are quite attractive. No serious pests or diseases attack these truly low-maintenance perennials

DIGITALIS FOXGLOVE *Scrophulariaceae (Figwort)*

The common foxglove *Digitalis purpurea* is the most ornamental of this genus. It is one of the essential components of cottage gardens and has been grown for medicinal purposes since the Middle Ages. Elsewhere a drift of foxgloves blooming in a lightly shaded woodland garden is a memorable sight. Several hybrid strains are on the market, of which 'Giant Shirley' [Shirley Hybrids] and 'Excelsior Hybrids' are best known. The common foxglove is in reality a self-seeding biennial, but others such as the strawberry foxglove, *D.* x *merto-nensis,* and the straw or small yellow foxglove, *D. lutea,* are perennial. Foxgloves may be planted in spring or fall in well-drained, organically rich soil that never dries out. An organic mulch is advisable in the summer, and winter protection helps to prevent heaving and discourages crown rot. Although they grow well in full sun in the North, they are at their best in light shade on the edges of woodlands or among shrubs. In hotter climates shade is essential, and additional water is necessary during dry periods. Fertilize lightly in early

A gardener seeking reliable, long-lasting display will appreciate purple coneflowers. Their large, showy blossoms last for up to 2 months, and when combined with rudbeckia, as shown below, they fulfill anyone's need for bright summer colors.

The round blue flowerheads of
Echinops ritro contrast beautifully with
the flat corymbs of bright red *Achillea*
'Fire King'.

spring. The perennial sorts are propagated by division in early spring, but *D. purpurea* can be allowed to self-sow or seed can be collected and sown out of doors as it is ripe. Deadheading avoids self-seeding and may encourage a second flush of bloom, but of course it removes the ripening seed, of which there is an abundance. Japanese beetles and slugs often require control; poor air circulation encourages attacks of powdery mildew.

ECHINACEA PURPLE CONEFLOWER *Asteraceae (Daisy family)*

Our native purple coneflower, *E. purpurea,* may be at its best in informal meadow and wildflower gardens, but it also makes a valuable addition to more formal areas and to cutting gardens. A position in full sun is ideal, although light shade during the hottest part of the day is tolerated. Soil need not be rich (though gardeners at the Chicago Botanic Garden find that coneflowers do better in richer soil), but it must be well drained. Purple coneflowers tolerate dry conditions well, and there is seldom need for additional water, even during drought conditions; they are a favored plant at the Desert Botanical Garden in Phoenix. It is wise to grow these long-blooming perennials on the lean side, saving extra fertilizer and water for more greedy plants. Purple coneflowers are also a good choice to grow in urban areas, since they also tolerate pollution without ill effect. However, the butterflies and bees that are so fond of them may be scarce in polluted areas. Increase stock in spring by division, or start from seed, which can be saved in the fall. Such cultivars as 'Bright Star' and 'White Swan' must be propagated vegetatively to remain true to name. During the blooming period, rigorous deadheading not only keeps the plant attractive, but also encourages the formation of new flower buds. Powdery mildew and Japanese beetles are the worst problems, but controls applied before the situation becomes serious will usually be effective. In the coldest regions, a light winter protection is beneficial.

ECHINOPS GLOBE THISTLE *Asteraceae (Daisy family)*

The globe thistles are admired as much for their coarse, thistlelike foliage, often silvery white beneath, as for their perfectly round heads of blue flowers, so useful for cutting and dried arrangements. Although their botanical nomenclature is confused in the trade and many plants are mislabeled, look for cultivar names such as 'Veitch's Blue' and 'Taplow Blue', both usually listed under *E. ritro*. Well-drained but not overly rich soil in full sun is preferred, although a little noontime shade is tolerated. Fertilize only lightly in spring where soil is poor, and water sparingly during extended dry periods. It is easily grown in southern California. Maintenance is minimal, although tall plants may need staking. Deadheading is also advisable to maintain vigor and extend flowering and promote a second blooming, as well as to limit self-seeding. Planting is in spring or fall, at which time large clumps may be divided. Root cuttings are another method of propagation, but seed-grown plants may include a high proportion of inferior ones. As usual the cultivars must be propagated vegetatively. Few pests and diseases attack globe thistles.

Epimediums are a very useful group of plants. Most will tolerate dry shade conditions–even competition from tree roots, where few plants will survive. Their heart-shaped leaves spread beautifully.

EPIMEDIUM BARRENWORT *Berberidaceae (Barberry family)*

Barrenwort is considered to be among the very finest of shade plants, assorting well with other shade lovers, such as hostas, ferns, and astilbes. One of the favorites is *E. grandiflorum*, particularly its deep pink cultivar 'Rose Queen', which forms clumps ideal as specimen plants. White-flowered *E.* x *youngianum* 'Niveum' is also slow to spread but lends itself well as an edging or specimen plant. *E.* x *versicolor* 'Sulphureum', which has yellow flowers, spreads readily, and if planted close, 6-12 inches apart, it will form an elegant but tough ground cover. Although their flowers are fleeting, the new foliage of epimediums is often rimmed or veined with red and remains handsome throughout the season. In mild areas some are evergreen, while the leaves of others turn an attractive tan color where winters are cold. The leaves can be left on the plants until the early new growth begins in spring; tattered foliage should then be removed. Barrenworts do best in soils high in organic matter to retain soil moisture. However, most will tolerate dry shade conditions, even competition from tree roots, where few plants will survive. An annual mulch of organic material is particularly beneficial under such poor conditions, but is recommended for all plantings. Set out new plants either in spring or fall, and mature plants may be divided then as well. Seed-grown plants are variable and slow to reach a good size. Occasionally crown rot may be a problem, but otherwise barrenworts are pest- and disease-free.

EUPATORIUM BONESET *Asteraceae (Daisy family)*

Most of the bonesets are found in the wild in tropical America, but a few grow in temperate regions, and these make good garden plants for flowerbeds

VIEWPOINT

IRRIGATION SYSTEMS

We find that a drip irrigation system uses less water, and, because it doesn't soak the foliage, it helps deter diseases.
DONALD BUMA,
BOTANICA, WICHITA

We use oscillators that we move around; we would prefer soaker or drip irrigation, but have not done that yet because of cost. We do use drip irrigation in field production of mums.
KIM JOHNSON, OLD WESTBURY GARDENS, NEW YORK

Overhead irrigation works well for us; we do not have a serious water shortage here, but do need to supply water during our dry summers. We don't use overhead watering if the plant is prone to fungal disease.
RICHARD ISAACSON, MINNEAPOLIS LANDSCAPE ARBORETUM

We use both overhead and drip irrigation. Overhead irrigation is used in our wildflower beds and grasslands display area. It works very well with large, somewhat unconsolidated plantings. In the main part of the garden, we are systematically installing drip irrigation, which uses less water, waters the plants more thoroughly when and where they need it, is convenient for the large number of plants we have, and is relatively inexpensive.
MARY IRISH,
DESERT BOTANICAL GARDEN

For tall plantings, when water is limited, drip irrigation is ideal. Soakers are beneficial for hedges and foundation plantings. But I feel overhead is best for most perennial gardens because it provides the opportunity to dig and try new plants and to better arrange existing plants; this digging can damage soaker hoses.
GALEN GATES, CHICAGO BOTANIC GARDEN

and borders. Our native joe-pye weed, *E. purpureum*, and its purple-flowered cultivar 'Atropurpureum' are dramatic, bold plants for the back of large borders, but may be out of scale in a confined space. They need a constant supply of water in full sun, coupled with the cooler nights of northern gardens. Blue mist flower or hardy ageratum, *E. coelestinum*, appears much like a 3-inch version of the familiar annual ageratum. *E.* x 'Gateway' is a compact hybrid of *E. purpureum* with purple stems and flowers. Beware: this late-summer bloomer spreads freely underground in moist soils, but under dry conditions is less aggressive. Cut the stems back once or twice during the season to maintain stockier plants; it may need staking. Full sun or light shade is advisable, where it combines beautifully with *Boltonia* 'Pink Beauty', or fountain grass, *Pennisetum alopecuroides*. In dry and shaded woodland areas, *E. rugosum*, the white snakeroot, can be most effective. Since it is so aggressive, it is not recommended for the border, but the fluffy white flowers really enliven dim areas in the early fall. Try them with *Aster divaricatus*. Spring is the best time to plant new plants or divide old ones of all these species. A summer mulch to conserve soil moisture and a winter mulch to avoid heaving are both recommended. Regular spraying with a fungicide against powdery mildew and an insecticide against aphids and leaf miners are suggested for blue mist flower and white snakeroot. Both should be deadheaded routinely.

EUPHORBIA SPURGE *Euphorbiaceae (Spurge family)*

This large, diverse group of plants is native to tropical, subtropical, and temperate regions of the world. All have in common a toxic milky sap that may cause a painful skin rash. In spite of this shortcoming, many make fine garden plants that deserve to be grown more widely. Those included here demand free-draining, average to poor soil in full sun in the North or partial shade in hot climates. They are truly low-maintenance perennials, requiring division of the fleshy roots only to increase stock in spring. Terminal cuttings may be rooted in summer. Either spring or fall planting is successful. One of the best of the spurges for the flower border is *E. griffithii*. The cultivar 'Fireglow' is usually offered and is becoming more readily available. Flowering a little earlier, cushion spurge, *E. polychroma {E. epithymoides}*, displays brilliant chartreuse bracts surrounding the tiny flowers. In the fall, the rounded clump of leaves turns reddish. Best in cool climates. It tends to run away and is often found 12-24 inches away from where it was planted. The blue green, spiraled leaves of *E. myrsinites* make this a fine rock-garden plant or an edging that works with many color schemes; it is the best spurge for southern California. Try it on the edge of shade with purple-leaved *Viola labradorica*.
Note: Another species, *E. euulens,* is listed as a noxious weed in Colorado, Washington, and other states; avoid it.

FILIPENDULA MEADOWSWEET *Rosaceae (Rose family)*

Native to the eastern United States *F. rubra*, queen-of-the-prairie, is a magnificent bold plant, perhaps seen at its best when massed alongside streams or

EPIMEDIUM X RUBRUM (BARRENWORT) 6-12 inches tall, space 1-1½ feet apart. Fresh green leaves, with red veins and margins; many racemes of dainty pink flowers. Full to partial shade. Blooms in spring. Zones 4-8.

EUPATORIUM PURPUREUM (JOE-PYE WEED) 4-6 feet tall, space 2-4 feet apart. Large clumps of vigorous stems with large flat pink or purple flowers. Full sun to partial shade. Blooms in summer to early fall. Zones 3-10.

EUPHORBIA GRIFFITHII 'FIREGLOW' (SPURGE) 2-3 feet tall, space 2 feet apart. Slender erect stems; small flowers with showy orange-red bracts. Full sun to partial shade. Blooms in late spring. Zones 5-9.

EUPHORBIA POLYCHROMA (CUSHION SPURGE) 1½-2 feet tall, space 2 feet apart. Clumps of sturdy stems; small flowers with chartreuse bracts. Full sun to partial shade. Blooms in spring to late spring. Zones 3-9.

FILIPENDULA RUBRA 'VENUSTA' (QUEEN-OF-THE-PRAIRIE) 6-8 feet tall, space 4 feet apart. Very tall plant with large panicles of feathery peach-pink flowers. Full sun to partial shade. Blooms in summer. Zones 3-9.

GAILLARDIA X GRANDIFLORA 'GOBLIN' (BLANKET FLOWER) 2-3 feet tall, space 1½ feet apart. Erect plant with large dark red flowers, bordered in yellow. Full sun. Blooms early summer to fall. Zone 3-10.

GALIUM ODORATUM (SWEET WOODRUFF) 6-12 inches tall, space 1 foot apart. Sprawling ground cover of attractive whorled leaves with tiny white flowers. Partial to full shade. Blooms in late spring. Zones 3-9.

GAURA LINDHEIMERI (WHITE GAURA) 3-4 feet tall, space 1-2 feet apart. Slender erect stems with willowlike foliage and white flowers with clawed petals. Full sun. Blooms in early summer to fall. Zones 6-10, heat-tolerant.

lakes, where the soil does not dry out. Its best-known cultivar, 'Venusta', affectionately called Martha Washington's Plume, has somewhat stronger pink flowers than the species, but they are difficult to distinguish. In any case, both make fine additions to cooler gardens; hot dry conditions are not to their liking. As long as the soil is well prepared and does not dry out, *F. rubra* can also be grown as a specimen plant in the border, although it needs space. The large cotton-candy plumes of flowers are very showy, but the foliage tends to become scruffy after flowering. Deadhead the spent stems to the ground for neatness and to prevent self-seeding. Spring planting is advisable, especially in the North. These shallow-rooted plants tend to heave in cold winters; mulch with evergreen boughs or salt hay. Fertilize lightly and mulch routinely in spring to provide nutrients and maintain an evenly moist soil. Divide in spring or fall to increase stock and to assure flowering vigor. For smaller gardens or at the front of the border, white-flowered dropwort, *F. vulgaris*, is an excellent choice. Its double cultivar *F. vulgaris* 'Flore-Pleno' has slightly larger flowers and combines well with *Salvia nemorosa* 'East Friesland'. Both grow well in drier soils. The meadowsweets are sometimes attacked by mildew and red spider mites, especially in hot dry climates.

Gaura grows up to 4 feet tall and produces tall flower spikes of white tinged with rose from late June into fall. The delicate flowers provide an attractive foil to bolder plants.

GAILLARDIA BLANKET FLOWER *Asteraceae (Daisy family)*

One of the easiest and most rewarding perennials, blanket flowers bloom over a very long period and require little more than deadheading to keep them producing flowers. They are as appropriate in the wild or meadow garden as they are in cutting gardens or at the front of flowerbeds. Blanket flowers demand a well-drained soil in full sun and tolerate the hottest and driest conditions well. Most widely grown is the hybrid blanket flower *G.* x *grandiflora*, a cross between perennial *G. aristata* and annual *G. pulchella*; the two latter species are both excellent under desert conditions. Several cultivars have been named, including 'Goblin' and 'Burgundy', a taller plant bearing deep wine flowers. Unfortunately, all of the cultivars are short-lived and should be propagated every 2-3 years by rooting summer cuttings or dividing healthy plants in spring or early fall. Seed-grown plants are variable, and the cultivars will remain true to name only through asexual propagation. Plant in spring or early fall and provide a summer mulch to discourage competition from weeds. Since so much energy goes into flower production, an annual spring fertilizing is beneficial. Pests and diseases are seldom troublesome.

GALIUM SWEET WOODRUFF *Rubiaceae (Madder family)*

Although sweet woodruff, *G. odoratum*, is frequently found in herb gardens, it makes a fine ground-cover plant for shaded places or may be used as an underplanting for such shrubs as rhododendrons and mountain laurel. While light shade is desirable in northern zones, it is required where summers are hot, but too much shade will result in premature dieback. The foliage of sweet woodruff smells of new-mown hay. Traditionally sprigs were used for flavoring May wine, but now it also finds itself in potpourris and stuffed into

hiking boots to deodorize them This plant does best grown in slightly acid, moist soil with plenty of organic matter, although once established it romps through much drier and poorer soils, sometimes becoming invasive. However, it is so pretty that it is seldom considered a nuisance. A light dressing of fertilizer every few years encourages healthy growth where it is slow. Set out new plants or divide in spring or early fall, and apply a summer mulch to retain moisture in the soil. The only maintenance is cutting back the tan-colored, overwintered leaves before the onset of spring growth. It is a great ground cover for difficult places. At the Chicago Botanic Garden, foliage turns brown in early summer, but quickly refoliates if it is cut back.

GAURA LINDHEIMERI WHITE GAURA *Onagraceae (Evening primrose)*

Native to Texas through Louisiana, white gaura grows 3-4 feet tall and produces tall flower spikes of white tinged with rose from late June into fall. As they age, the whites give way to pale rose, but all color phases are present on the plant at the same time, creating a lovely effect. Gaura prefers well-drained soil and full sun and is a valuable perennial for the South because it tolerates both heat and humidity equally well. Gaura can be readily increased from seeds sown in the spring or by cuttings taken in summer.

GERANIUM HARDY GERANIUM, CRANESBILL *Geraniaceae (Geranium)*

Hardy geraniums–not to be confused with annual geraniums of the genus *Pelargonium*–are enjoying a wave of popularity among American gardeners, as more and more species, hybrids, and cultivars become available. Hardy geraniums are native in temperate regions, but are from diverse habitats. Some are suitable only for rock gardens, while those mentioned here are well adapted to less specialized areas of the garden. *G.* x 'Johnson's Blue' is a fine hybrid between *G. himalayense* and *G. pratense*, sometimes listed under the latter. In

Above and right: Small and delicate geranium flowers grow on a bushy plant that forms a neat, rounded mound.

GERANIUM X 'JOHNSON'S BLUE' (HARDY GERANIUM) 1-2 feet tall, space 2 feet apart. Sprawling habit, violet blue flowers. Full sun to partial shade. Blooms in late spring to early summer. Zones 4-10, not heat-tolerant.

GERANIUM SANGUINEUM VAR. STRIATUM (DWARF BLOODY CRANESBILL) 1 foot tall, space 1½ feet apart. Low mounds of deeply divided leaves, saucer-shaped pink flowers with darker veins. Full sun to partial shade. Blooms in late spring to summer. Zones 4-10, not heat-tolerant.

GEUM X BORISII (AVENS) 1 foot tall, space 1 foot apart. Small pale orange flowers, wedge-shaped leaves. Full sun to partial shade. Blooms in early summer. Zones 5-10, not heat-tolerant.

GYPSOPHILA PANICULATA 'PINK FAIRY' (BABY'S BREATH) 1½-4 feet tall, space 4 feet apart. Small pink flowers on tangled, multibranched stems. Full sun. Blooms in summer. Zones 3-10, not heat-tolerant.

VIEWPOINT

LATE-SEASON PERENNIALS

Among the latest flowers to bloom in our perennial beds are *Helianthus salicifolius,* and *Aster tartaricus.*
SUSAN NOLDE,
BROOKSIDE GARDENS

For late fall we plant late mums, *Chystanthemum pacificum, Salvias* (including some that are not winter-hardy), *Cimicifuga simplex, Helianthus salicifolius, Boltonia,* asters, and *Helenium.*
KIM JOHNSON AND NELSON STERNER, OLD WESTBURY GARDENS, NEW YORK

Perennials for late summer and fall include *Physostegia* 'Vivid', *Aster novae-angliae,* and *Lobelia cardinalis.* Shrubs such as *Hamamelis virginiana* and crocus bulbs also bloom at the same time.
GALEN GATES,
CHICAGO BOTANIC GARDEN
DESERT BOTANICAL GARDEN

Something is blooming here year-round. But aloes and mesembs predominate in winter, and in late fall it is is Black dalea (*Dalea frutescens*) red fairyduster (*Calliandra californica*), asters, brittlebush (*Encelia farinosa*) and the three justicias (*Justicia californica, J. spicigera,* and *J. ovata.*)
MARY IRISH, DESERT BOTANICAL GARDEN

spite of its somewhat sprawling habit, its long blooming time and sterile, clear blue flowers have made it popular as a specimen plant. For the front of any borders, *G. sanguineum* var. *striatum {G. s. lancastriense}*, dwarf bloody cranesbill, is hard to beat. After a late spring flush of bloom, it continues to produce its crimson-veined pink flowers sporadically throughout the season. In the wild garden, the native *G. maculatum* and its white cultivar 'Album' are attractive. Other worthwhile cranesbills include *G. macrorrhizum,* bigroot geranium, excellent as a drought-tolerant ground cover in sun or shade and Armenian geranium, *G. psilostemon,* whose brilliant magenta flowers, veined with black, top 2- to 4-foot floppy stems. Most hardy geraniums require a full-sun to partly shaded position in the North, but demand light shade from hot sun elsewhere. Soils must be well drained but only of average fertility. A light annual dressing of complete fertilizer will supply sufficient nutrients. Plant in spring, especially in the North, so that the plants are well established by the onset of winter; in southern California, fall plantings succeed as well. Mulch in summer to cut down on weed competition. After flowering, if the foliage of some sorts becomes straggly and shabby cut it back to encourage a new flush of leaves. Most species may be propagated by sowing fresh seed, or by division in spring. Many reseed themselves, creating an informal look. Pests and diseases are few, although rusts may attack the foliage.

GEUM AVENS *Rosaceae (Rose family)*

Geums are useful plants for the front of the border or the rock garden, since their foliage remains good-looking well after the blooms are spent, and some even have interesting fruiting heads. Among the most readily available are *G.* x *heldreichii* 'Georgenberg', more often listed under *G.* x *borisii,* which has pale orange yellow flowers followed by buff seedheads. Scarlet-flowered *G. coccineum* 'Red Wings' [*G. quellyon* 'Red Wings'] is an excellent choice for mass plantings; it is a favorite at Maryland's Brookside Gardens, where it sometimes blooms for 12 weeks if deadheaded. Avens are native in temperate and arctic regions and are at their best where the summer nights are cool but the winters are not frigid. In hot climates, they are seldom satisfactory, even in partly shaded places. Full sun to light shade is ideal, with well-drained fertile soil that does not dry out too quickly. Water avens, *G. rivale,* needs damp conditions. Both spring and fall planting are successful; light winter protection is routinely recommended but is essential for fall-planted stock. Increase by division in spring or early fall; some species and cultivars, such as yellow-flowered *G. chiloense* 'Lady Stratheden', come true from seed, which must be sown as soon as it is ripe. In spring, apply a light dressing of a complete fertilizer to maintain fertility, and give extra water during dry times to help keep the foliage healthy. Cut back after blooming for neatness and to encourage a second flush of flowers. Pests and diseases are seldom a problem; mites sometimes attack it, but cutting back ususally solves the problem.

GYPSOPHILA PANICULATA BABY'S BREATH *Caryophyllaceae (Pink)*

This native of Eurasia is treasured for its large, billowy, see-through clouds

Toward the end of summer, the bold colors of *Gaillardia* and *Helenium* fill the perennial garden at The New York Botanical Garden.

of tiny single or double white flowers. Baby's breath is a long-time favorite as a filler in fresh flower arrangements, lightening the bulkier elements. It's equally useful dried. In the garden, its airy grace masks unattractive or dying-back neighboring foliage and lightens and harmonizes bold, dense clumps. Baby's breath blooms profusely and is easy to grow in full sun and very well-drained soil. Although it tolerates a soil with average fertility and pH, it prefers slightly alkaline soil. Addition of lime at planting time is beneficial, as the common name chalk plant indicates. Baby's breath has deep roots, so it does not transplant well. Start from plants, or sow seed directly, in a permanent location, allowing 3 feet between plants to accommodate its bushiness. It's best to stake plants before or as flowering stalks grow so that when the flower mass matures, it doesn't droop to the ground. A peony ring, grow-through plant supports, or stakes pushed into the ground around the clump and tied together with string are ideal. Propagate by leaf cuttings, taken from fresh new foliage. For dried bouquets, pick flowers when fully open. Baby's breath will often rebloom in late summer if cut back after flowering. Protect with mulch after the ground freezes. 'Bristol Fairy' is a popular double white. 'Pink Fairy' grows to 18 inches, with very light pink flowers that produce a less dense flowering cloud. 'Compacta Plena' is low-growing. *G. repens* is creeping baby's breath, a 6- to 8-inch alpine native that is excellent in well-drained rock gardens; 'Rosea' is the most common cultivar, with rosy pink flower clusters.

HELENIUM SNEEZEWEED *Asteraceae (Daisy family)*

At one time, the foliage of sneezeweed was dried and ground up as an inexpensive substitute for snuff. Today, they are among the best perennials to pro-

Hellebores are often the first flowers to bloom, arriving soon after–and sometimes before–the last frost.

vide color in the late-summer and fall garden, and for cutting. It is a favored plant at many gardens because it seldom needs staking and spreads quickly. Most of those listed in nurseries are cultivars or hybrids of the native *H. autumnale*, Helen's flower. Among the best-known are 'Butterpat' and 'Bruno', which has rusty red flowers. Some newer, superior European introductions include 'Gartensonne', 'Kugelsonne', and 'Feuersiegel'. *Helenium hoopesii* blooms earlier and is valuable in wet soils. Ideally sneezeweeds should be planted in full sun; light shade is acceptable, but fewer flowers on weaker stems often result. A deep, highly organic soil that does not dry out totally is best. It is wise to fertilize sparingly in spring and supply a summer mulch of organic material annually. Stock may be planted in spring or fall, and division in the spring every 2-3 years is necessary to retain vigor. The new growth of overly vigorous plants should be thinned out in the spring to allow light and air to penetrate; later on pinch back by half to produce bushier though later-blooming plants. Tall spindly growth results from too little light or from overly rich soil. Staking is often necessary, particularly for the taller sorts, even when they are well grown. After flowering cut back and thin out, especially if there are pest or disease problems, such as aphids or powdery mildew.

HELIANTHUS SUNFLOWER *Asteraceae (Daisy family)*

Several of these tall, sun-loving natives make splendid additions to late-summer and fall borders, assorting particularly well with asters and ornamental grasses. They are also suitable for open meadow gardens and other informal areas where their showiness is impressive and their spreading vigor is an asset. The willow-leaved sunflower, *H. salicifolius,* is frequently offered, and *H.* x *multiflorus* cultivars, such as 'Loddon Gold' and the extremely invasive 'Miss Mellish', are widely grown. Well-drained soil that is somewhat lean is best; a light, spring application of fertilizer is recommended for poor soils, but too much fertilizer will produce excess foliage. Water deeply during droughts for best results. To encourage flowering divide the plants at least every 2-3 years, in spring or just after flowering time. Use extra divisions for stock build-up or root cuttings of young growth in early summer. Since sunflowers are so tall, pinch the new growth once or twice in late spring or early summer to ensure bushier plants. This will, however, delay flowering until too late in the season in some northern gardens, and they will probably still need staking. Thin out crowded plants in spring and deadhead to maintain vigor. Aphids and powdery mildew can be serious.

HELLEBORUS HELLEBORE *Ranunculaceae (Buttercup family)*

As well as their most welcome late-winter or very early spring flowers, these members of the buttercup family are rapidly gaining in popularity among discerning gardeners for their handsome, mostly evergreen foliage. Although somewhat temperamental, the best-known is the pristine Christmas rose, *H. niger*. In some places, these are grown under the protection of a cold frame to supply cut flowers for the Christmas market. The Lenten rose, *H. orientalis,* is

HELENIUM AUTUMNALE 'BUTTERPAT' (SNEEZEWEED) 4-5 feet tall, space 1½ feet apart. Red and yellow daisylike flowers on strong erect stems. Full sun. Blooms late summer to early fall. Zones 3-10, heat-tolerant.

HELIANTHUS SALICIFOLIUS (SUNFLOWER) 6-8 feet tall, space 2 feet apart. Thick, drooping stems with numerous large, yellow flowerheads. Full sun. Blooms late summer to early fall. Zones 4-10.

HELLEBORUS NIGER (CHRISTMAS ROSE) 8-12 inches tall, space 1½ feet apart. Cup-shaped, nodding flowers open pure white and turn blush pink; dark, evergreen foliage. Partial to full shade. Blooms in late winter to early spring. Zones 3-9, not heat-tolerant.

HELLEBORE ORIENTALIS (LENTEN ROSE) 2 feet tall, space 2 feet apart. Small clusters of cup-shaped, nodding pink, deep purple, pale green, or white flowers. Partial to full shade. Blooms in late winter to early spring. Zones 3-10, not heat-tolerant.

HEMEROCALLIS 'BECKY LYNN' (DAYLILY) 20 inches tall, space 24 inches apart. 6-inch rose-blend flowers with green throat on semievergreen plant. Full sun. Blooms midseason; reblooms. Zones 4-9.

HEMEROCALLIS 'CONDILLA' (DAYLILY) 20 inches tall, space 24 inches apart. Golden-orange double 4½-inch flowers on dormant plant. Full sun. Blooms midseason. Zones 3-9.

HEMEROCALLIS 'HYPERION' (DAYLILY) 40 inches tall, space 24-30 inches apart. 5-inch primrose-yellow flowers with green throat on dormant plant. Full sun. Blooms mid to late season. Zones 3-9.

HEMEROCALLIS 'JOAN SENIOR' (DAYLILY) 25 inches tall, space 24-30 inches apart. Near-white 6-inch flowers with green throat on evergreen plant. Full sun. Blooms midseason. Zones 3-9.

easier and usually blooms a little later, with flowers ranging from white, often speckled with maroon, through pink to purple. *H. foetidus* and *H. argutifolius* {*H. corsicus*} are becoming more available and are well worth trying. All bloom over an extended period and are still attractive even after the inconspicuous petals and stamens have dropped. Hellebores thrive in lightly or partly shaded places, where the soil has been thoroughly prepared with an abundance of organic material. Since the roots resent disturbance, do not skimp on the initial soil preparation. Maintain high fertility with an annual dressing of compost or well-rotted manure each fall and a light spring application of fertilizer. Frequent, deep watering is necessary in dry weather. Plant in spring or early fall. If you must divide the plants to build stock, this is best just after flowering, but otherwise do not disturb them. *H. orientalis* in particular hybridizes and self-sows quite freely; it is fun to grow on your own seedlings, but only fresh seeds will germinate readily. Black spot and crown rot are occasional problems. All parts of hellebores are poisonous to humans and animals.

HEMEROCALLIS DAYLILY *Liliaceae (Lily family)*

Daylilies are the most popular perennial in the United States. They are native to Korea, China, eastern Siberia, and Japan, but have become naturalized throughout parts of Europe and North America. Their popularity has triggered extensive breeding work in several countries but especially the United States. Today there are thousands of named cultivars on the market, some better suited to particular parts of the country than others. Daylilies are easy to grow, adaptable, and versatile, but all grow best planted where they will receive sun throughout the day. That is not to say that if your garden is lightly shaded at some time of the day you will not be able to grow daylilies, but do look for a sunny site. Many daylilies will perform fairly well where there is sun for only part of the day, but none do well in

Above: 'Theron', the first red daylily, was bred by Dr. Arlow B. Stout, a pioneer of the modern hybrid daylily who worked at The New York Botanical Garden. Some of Dr. Stout's hybrid cultivars are the result of cross-pollinating two species, while others are a series of complex cross-pollinations that required 20 or more years to achieve. The New York Botanical Garden's Arlow B. Stout Daylily Garden includes several of the species that Dr. Stout used as building blocks, most of his original hybrids, as well as a bed of Stout Medal Award Winners, chosen by American Hemerocallis Society judges.

Left: The Daylily Walk at The New York Botanical Garden features over 200 different daylilies.

DAYLILY COLORS, SIZES, SHAPES

Daylily flowers normally have six similar floral segments called tepals. Their color, shape, and size vary from one cultivar to the next.

•A self-colored daylily has all tepals the same color.

•When two separate colors are displayed it is termed a bicolor.

•If the tepals are rimmed in a different color it is considered an edged cultivar.

•Some cultivars display a zone of darker color near the base, which is called the eyezone. It can be wide, spreading out far onto the tepals, or just a narrow band of color.

•A watermark is the reverse; the tepals display a pale color zone at the base.

•The American Hemerocallis Society has classified daylilies by flower size. A miniature has flowers less than 3 inches in diameter, small-flowered cultivars have flowers from 3-4½ inches, and large-flowered cultivars have flowers over 4½ inches, in diameter. This classification does not address the stature of the plant.

•Certain hybrid daylilies appear to be double. The degree of doubling can vary, even among flowers of the same plant. Doubleness results either when the number of tepals is multiplied or when the stamen filaments mutate into tepallike structures. Double daylilies first arose as mutations of single-flowered types.

•When the tepals curl backward, the daylily is termed recurved.

•Spider daylilies are those having long narrow tepals suggesting the legs of a spider. The inner tepals of a true spider must be at least 5 times as long as wide.

deep shade. In northern climates protect the dark-colored cultivars, deep reds and violets, from intense afternoon sun, which may cause "burning" or darkening of the tepals. In the South and Southwest very light afternoon shade is advisable for all colors. Avoid sites where the plants will have to compete with shallow-rooted trees or ground covers. The ideal soil for daylilies is well-drained, slightly acid loam amended with plenty of organic material to retain moisture for the fleshy rootstocks. A summer mulch helps to cut down on weed competition and slows evaporation at the soil surface. Supply plenty of water during dry times to maintain healthy foliage and encourage flowering; daylilies, though tolerant of drought, will not perform at their best in dry soil. A single dressing of slow-release fertilizer applied in late spring or several applications of liquid fertilizer throughout the season are recommended. Set out new plants, no deeper than 1-1 ½ inches below the soil surface, from containers or bare root at any time during the growing season. In cold climates avoid planting too late into the fall. They must be well rooted prior to the onset of cold weather; a porous mulch applied after the ground has frozen discourages heaving. After several years of vigorous growth, mature plants will have fewer and fewer flowers. This indicates the need for division of the whole clump to rejuvenate it, sometimes a daunting task that requires a strong back and bold approach. Lift the entire clump and divide off strong healthy pieces to replant in enriched soil. Increase stock by division or remove proliferations, which sometimes form at the base of leaf scars on the flower scape. Seed germinates readily, but due to the hybrid background of daylilies, the resulting seedlings are seldom exact duplicates of the parents. Deadhead daily, except where seed is required. Spent flowers are not only unsightly, but seed formation drains strength from the plants; it is important to deadhead below the ovary to prevent seed formation. Several pests and diseases attack daylilies. One of the most widespread and severe is soft rot or crown rot, a bacterial disease present in the soil or brought in on newly purchased material. All parts of the plant are affected, resulting in a slushy mess. Remove all infected plants and treat with mild chlorine bleach before replanting elsewhere, if they are worth saving. The surrounding soil should be removed or sterilized. If a cold period follows warm spring weather, spring sickness may appear. This causes distorted and stunted growth that sometimes remains for weeks until the plant finally grows out of it. Some cultivars are more susceptible than others. Be alert for signs of aphids, thrips, and spider mites, which are the most serious pests of daylilies. Slugs often attack young emerging leaf growth, and earwigs cause unsightly holes in open flowers and buds.

No sunny garden should be without daylilies. They are often massed, and by selecting early, mid-season, and late cultivars the flowering season may last three months or more, at least in the North. In warmer climates reblooming is more common. Rebloomers are less available for the North; 'Stella de Oro', 'Happy Returns', and 'Jason Salter' are reliable. It is helpful

Opposite: A range of daylily colors, shapes, and sizes.

DIPLOID AND TETRAPLOID DAYLILIES

The ploidy of an organism refers to the number of chromosomes contained within the organism. The combination and arrangement of the chromosomes, or genetic material, will determine both the expressed and unexpressed characteristics of the organism.

With daylilies, the typical number of chromosomes is 22, which represents two sets of eleven. This is known as the *diploid* condition; the prefix *di* means "two." All of the daylily species are diploid except *H. fulva,* which is triploid, having three sets of chromosomes.

Tetraploid daylilies were first contrived by the alteration of typical diploid daylilies using the chemical colchicine. The resulting plants had twice the typical number of chromosomes; the prefix *tetra* means "four," indicating four sets of eleven chromosomes. Since the late 1950s when this process was first developed, the tetraploid daylily has progressed rapidly. New tetraploid hybrids show many superior characteristics, such as increased adaptability, excellent foliage, and flowers with greater substance and more vivid coloration.

to visit local display gardens, nurseries, or botanical gardens to see the best daylilies for your area. In steep or erosion-prone parts of the garden, the tough soil-binding rootstocks of daylilies effectively hold the soil and can be planted close as a low-maintenance ground cover. In the perennial garden, the mounding linear leaves of daylilies are an attractive foil for other perennials and shrubs. Look for cultivars with a high number of proportionally spaced flower buds to lengthen flowering time, as well as repeat bloomers. Though only "beautiful for a day," the color range of the modern hybrids is staggering, and some are even fragrant.

HEUCHERA CORAL BELLS, ALUM ROOT *Saxifragaceae (Saxifrage family)*

These are old standbys for the front of perennial borders, and the recent selections of our native coral bells are better than ever. Most result from breeding work using *H. sanguinea, H. americana,* and *H. micrantha.* In catalogs, the cultivars are usually listed as *H.* x *brizoides*; widespread are pink 'Chatterbox', 'June Bride', which has white flowers, and 'Mt. St. Helens', a good red. The popular, maroon-leaved cultivar 'Palace Purple' is a superb foliage plant. Try it with *Achillea* x 'Moonshine' or with variegated (*Liriope muscari* 'Variegata') or silver-foliaged plants (*Stachys byzantina* 'Silver Carpet'). Select with care since the color intensity varies from plant to plant; it may become washed out under intense sun. Any of these are excellent in rock gardens, as edging plants, for the front of the border, or as ground-cover plants, where their semievergreen to evergreen foliage remains handsome throughout the year. They are also useful cut flowers over a long season. A sunny or lightly shaded spot, particularly in hot climates, is suitable for coral bells. At Phoenix's Desert Botanical Garden, heucheras are the stars in deep shade, blooming nearly all summer long; they are valued as shade plants at the Huntington Botanical Garden in southern California, as well. They prefer a well-drained soil enriched with organic matter to retain moisture in summer. Fertilize lightly each spring and water regularly during hot weather. Spring planting is recommended, except in mild climates, since the roots are shallow and subject to frost heaving; apply a winter mulch after the ground is frozen. Divide in spring to build stock or when the plants become woody to restore vigor. Deadhead to prolong blooming time. Pests and diseases are few.

HIBISCUS MOSCHATUS ROSE MALLOW *Malvaceae (Mallow family)*

When seeking perennials that have large flowers, the rose mallow is an obvious choice, with flowers reaching a diameter of up to 12 inches per individual bloom, though more commonly 6-8 inches. Among the best cultivars are 'Southern Belle', with 10-inch pink, red, or white flowers on a 4- to 6-foot-tall plant, and 'Disco Belle', which produces smaller flowers on a shorter plant. 'Lord Baltimore', a sterile cultivar with 10-inch red flowers, does not produce unwanted seedlings, a problem with some other cultivars. Rose mallows are usually grown in full sun; they can tolerate partial, but not full, shade. They

HEMEROCALLIS 'JOLYENE NICHOLE' (DAYLILY) 14 inches tall, space 24 inches apart. Rose-colored 6-inch flowers with green throat on evergreen plant. Full sun. Blooms midseason; reblooms. Zones 3-9.

HEMEROCALLIS 'KINDLY LIGHT' (DAYLILY) 28-30 inches tall, space 24-30 inches apart. Yellow flowers with narrow segments (spider form) and green throat on dormant plant. Full sun. Blooms mid to late season. Zones 3-9.

HEMEROCALLIS 'MARY TODD' (DAYLILY) 26 inches tall, space 24-30 inches apart. Gold buff 6- to 7-inch tetraploid on semi-evergreen plant. Full sun. Blooms midseason. Zones 3-9.

HEMEROCALLIS 'STELLA DE ORO' (DAYLILY) 12-18 inches tall, space 18-24 inches apart. Golden yellow 2- to 3-inch flowers with green throat on dormant plant. Full sun. Blooms early season; reblooms. Zones 3-8.

CLASSIFICATIONS OF HOSTAS

- Small hostas are up to 8 inches in height. They are best suited to shaded rock gardens or between the roots of trees where the soil is poor and shallow. 'Sea Sprite' and 'Chartreuse Wiggles' are examples.
- Edging types are 8-12 inches tall. These are especially useful for edging shaded beds or borders, woodland paths and walkways. Here their rapid growth and vigor inhibits weeds and eliminates the tedious task of edging. 'Ginkgo Craig' is a good cultivar.
- Ground covers range from 12-15 inches tall. These, such as 'Shade Fanfare' and 'Gold Standard', can be planted singly or massed at close spacing.
- Background types may reach 24 inches. They are usually planted as feature plants or a centerpiece around which the rest of the shade garden is designed. Good examples are 'Sum and Substance' and *H. sieboldiana* 'Elegans'.
- The largest hostas are called specimens. These are 2-4 feet tall, usually slow growing and excellent as accent plants. *H. tokudama* 'Aureo-Nebulosa' and 'Wide Brim' fall into this category.

prefer soils that are evenly moist and contain a good deal of organic material, but will grow well and naturalize in wet areas. They will not tolerate extreme dryness and should be kept watered in times of drought. They respond well to an annual light application of a complete fertilizer. Rose mallows should be planted in spring or fall from seeds, seedlings, or transplants. Prune old stems to the ground in early winter; deadheading helps control invasive tendendcies.

HOSTA PLANTAIN LILY, FUNKIA *Liliaceae (Lily family)*

For shaded gardens, hostas are the most popular perennials in American gardens today. Most species are native to Japan, but a few come from China and Korea. As well as the species, there are thousands of cultivars on the market, the results of extensive breeding and selection programs. There must be few nurseries and garden centers in the country that do not carry at least three or four cultivars of hosta. The specialist mail-order nurseries may carry fifty or more, particularly the most recent and expensive introductions. Hostas are notoriously unstable and frequently display different juvenile and mature leaf form, especially those that have been propagated by tissue culture. If a new variation can be stabilized, it may be registered with the American Hosta Society and marketed under its own name. Hostas are typically grown for their foliage, although their scapes of lavender, purple, or white flowers are not unattractive; some, particularly those with *H. plantaginea* in their parentage, make sweetly fragrant cut flowers and can be dried. The wide diversity of foliage is prized by flower arrangers. In habit hostas range from neat compact mounds under 8 inches tall, well suited for rock gardens and as edgings, to wide lush plants up to 48 inches in height, ideal for use as background plants or specimens. The leaves display a mind-boggling array of shapes, textures, and colors. You can choose cultivars with rounded, heart-shaped, lance-shaped, or oval leaves, with shiny, waxy, or puckered surfaces, and with wavy or smooth edges. Some are as small as a thumbnail, others as large as a basketball. The foliage varies in color; blues, greens, or variegated, in combinations of blue with yellow, white, or green, or green with yellow or white.

Hostas are easy to grow, but most are at their best in partial shade. Some cultivars adapt better to sunnier places than others, while others will take deeper shade. Only where the summer sun is not intense will the shade lovers be successful in an open place. Hostas are tolerant of a wide range of soils, excepting beach sand and those that are waterlogged. The ideal is a well-drained loam, amended with plenty of organic material. They must not dry out and need extra water in times of drought; a well-prepared soil eliminates the need for water on a regular basis. Watering early in the day is recommended, since slugs and snails are serious pests of damp environments. Fertilize sparingly so as not to encourage soft rank growth, which is subject to pests and diseases. Propagate established plants by division and plant young ones either in spring before the leaves are fully expanded or in fall. Slugs, snails, and deer are the worst pests of hostas.

HEUCHERA X BRIZOIDES 'FREEDOM BELLS' (CORAL BELLS) 1-2 feet tall, space 1-1½ feet apart. Wiry stems with many tiny bright red flowers. Full sun or partial shade. Blooms spring to summer. Zones 3-10.

HEUCHERA MICRANTHA VAR. DIVERSIFOLIA 'PALACE PURPLE' (ALUM ROOT) 1-2 feet tall, space 1-1½ feet apart. Large, wrinkled, maplelike leaves with spectacular bronze red color, tiny white flowers. Full sun to partial shade. Blooms late spring to early summer. Zones 4-10.

HIBISCUS MOSCHEUTOS 'SOUTHERN BELLE' 4-6 feet tall, space 3 feet apart. Huge red, pink, or white flowers on tall bushy plants. Full sun. Blooms midsummer to fall. Zones 4-9, heat-tolerant.

HOSTA SIEBOLDIANA 'ELEGANS' (PLANTAIN LILY) 18-24 inches tall, space 24-36 inches across. Background hosta; large bluish leaves; white flowers with light fragrance. Shade to 1/4 sun. Blooms mid to late summer. Zones 4-8.

HOSTA 'GINGKO CRAIG' (PLANTAIN LILY) 6-10 inches tall, space 12 inches apart. Edging hosta; green lance-shaped leaves with bright white margin. Shade to ¾ sun. Blooms midsummer. Zones 4-8.

HOSTA 'JANET' (PLANTAIN LILY) 16 inches tall, space 20-24 inches apart. Ground-cover hosta with variegated leaves, pale lavender flowers. Shade to ¾ sun. Blooms late summer. Zones 4-8.

HOSTA TOKUDAMA FLAVO-CIRCINALIS (PLANTAIN LILY) 12-18 inches tall, space 18 inches apart. Specimen hosta; bluish-green leaves with yellow edges. Shade to 1/4 sun. Blooms mid to late summer. Zones 4-8.

HOSTA SIEBOLDIANA 'MIRA' (PLANTAIN LILY) 24-40 inches tall, space 24-36 inches apart. Background hosta; large greenish-blue leaves, white flowers with lavender tint. Shade to 1/4 sun. Blooms in spring. Zones 4-8.

The usual remedies for slugs may be applied, but general hygiene goes a long way to eliminating their hiding and breeding places. Deer repellents are useful on a hit-or-miss basis. Expensive electric fences may be the only solution, but new repellents are being developed that are more effective.

IBERIS CANDYTUFT *Cruciferae (Mustard family)*

Candytuft, actually a subshrub rather than an herbaceous perennial, is a very popular plant, used at the front of the border, and for rock gardens and walls. The most popular species is *I. sempervirens*, perennial candytuft or edging candytuft, which produces dark green foliage and clusters of pure white flowers. Although it flowers best in full sun, candytuft will bloom as long as it gets a few hours of sunlight each day; it does require well-drained soil; the addition of lime is helpful. A hard shearing after flowering promotes compact growth. In cold climates, a winter mulch is needed to protect stems. Propagate by layering or cuttings taken in early summer, or sow seeds outdoors in spring.

INULA INULA *Asteraceae (Daisy family)*

Only one or two species of this yellow daisy genus are worthy of a place in the garden. Swordleaf inula, *I. ensifolia*, is probably the best, especially where space is a consideration. Its small stature, ease of culture, and long-blooming, cheerful flowers earn it a place at the front of sunny borders as well as in the cutting garden. Elecampane, *I. helenium*, is rather coarse and may reach 6-7

Hostas form an integral part of most shade gardens, providing striking foliage as well as flowers.

HOSTA TOKUDAMA 'AUREO-NEBULOSA' (PLANTAIN LILY) 18-20 inches tall, space 24 inches apart. Specimen hosta; puckered green-blue foliage suffused with yellow in center; white flowers. Shade to 3/4 sun. Blooms early summer. Zones 4-8.

IBERIS SEMPERVIRENS (CANDYTUFT) 1 foot tall, space 3 feet apart. Spreading subshrub with dark green leaves and pure white flowers that turn light pink. Blooms in spring to early summer. Full sun to partial shade. Zones 3-10, heat-tolerant.

INULA ENSIFOLIA (SWORDLEAF INULA) 1-2 feet tall, space 1 foot apart. Stiff unbranched stems with solitary bright yellow flowers. Full sun to partial shade. Blooms in summer. Zones 3-9.

IRIS 'BEVERLY SILLS' (TALL BEARDED IRIS) 35 inches tall; space 8-15 inches apart. Lacy pink standards and falls. Full sun. Blooms early to mid season. Zones 3-10.

feet. It has been grown in herb gardens for many years, but can be useful at the back of informal plantings, as can *I. magnifica,* which is a little showier. Inulas demand little outside well-drained, but moist soil in a full-sun position. Wet or overly fertile soils are to be avoided. Both spring and early fall are acceptable times for planting and propagation by division. Seeds germinate readily in the spring. Stake the large species and deadhead to extend flowering. Powdery mildew may be a problem, especially in dry seasons.

IRIS BEARDED HYBRIDS (X GERMANICA) BEARDED IRIS

Iridaceae (Iris family)

Undoubtedly the blooms of bearded iris are among the showiest of all perennials. Such is their popularity that few gardeners or nongardeners would fail to recognize them. Today's hybrids display an incredible range of colors, shapes, and forms, with more named cultivars arriving annually. They vary greatly in height. The short or dwarf beardeds grow to 16 inches, are the earliest to bloom, and are ideal in sunny rock gardens. The intermediates may reach 27 inches and seldom need staking in the border; they generally bloom slightly later. Last to bloom and the most popular are the tall bearded irises; some cultivars may reach 3 feet or taller. These often require staking, as the large spectacular flowers tend to be top heavy. The well-known orris root, *I.* x *germanica* 'Florentina', and *I. pallida* 'Variegata', so useful as a foliage plant, belong in this group. The talls are at their best grown in a formal setting with other irises. Both the intermediates and talls make attractive, though short-lived cut flowers. The culture of the different groups is similar. All do best in a full-sun position where the soil drains freely. The rhizomes and fleshy roots of bearded iris are subject to rot, particularly in winter, where drainage is poor. These greedy feeders require good fertile soil and benefit from an annual application of complete fertilizer. A dressing of lime is advisable in acid soils. New plants may be set out from containers from local garden centers in spring, but the special-

IRIS TERMS

Irises are spectacular flowers with three of everything: upper petals (standards), lower sepals (falls), pollen-carrying anthers, and pollen-receiving stigmas. Terms used to describe iris coloration include:

• Amoena (pleasing): white or tinted standards with colored falls.

• Bicolor (two-color): light or medium standards and deeper contrasting falls.

• Blend: combination of two or more colors (one always being yellow).

• Plicata (pleated): stitched or stippled margin color on white background.

• Self: an iris of uniform color.

• Variegata: yellow or near yellow standards with deeper falls, which may be either varied or solid tones of brown or purple.

Left: The iris beds at The New York Botanical Garden.

ist nurseries seldom ship until one or two months after flowering time. Beware of planting too late in the season; the young plants need sufficient time to root well into their new surroundings before the onset of cold weather. As they become overcrowded, every 3-4 years, older plants require division, preferably after blooming. At this time it is critical to check for the evil-smelling, soft rhizome rot associated with iris borer, and only to replant solid healthy plants. If borer damage is suspected, destroy any infected material and remove contaminated soil around the clump. In hot climates most gardeners plant the rhizomes covered with an inch or two of soil. Traditionally in colder climates the horizontal rhizomes are planted to about half their depth, so that the surface could be ripened by the sun. To facilitate this, the leaves of the intermediates and tall bearded irises were cut back to 8-12 inches into a fan shape, a month or two after flowering time. Today most gardeners across the country plant the rhizomes just below the soil surface, after reducing the foliage to 6-8 inches. Be alert for aphids and thrips, which mar the flowers and spread virus diseases; control with insecticides.

The beauty of the iris can be enjoyed in a mass planting or in a single flower.

IRIS CRISTATA DWARF CRESTED IRIS *Iridaceae (Iris family)*

This eastern North American native is one of the fragrant beauties of spring shade gardens, where if it is happy it will form large matlike colonies. As well as the species, charming cultivars such as the white 'Alba', light blue 'Shenandoah Sky', and deep blue 'Summer Storm' are on the market. While at their best in shaded or partially shaded gardens, at least during the heat of the day, these woodlanders will tolerate full sun as long as the soil can be kept evenly moist. Plant in spring or fall in loose, humus-rich soil or leaf mold, which is well drained but moisture retentive. Fertilization and additional water are seldom necessary given good soil. Unfortunately these same soil conditions are most attractive to slugs, which disfigure the leaves and flowers. Established plants divide readily in the early fall, at which time fresh seed may be collected and sown. However, germination is a slow and irregular process. In cold areas fall plantings should be protected from winter heaving by a mulch of evergreen boughs or salt hay. Dwarf crested iris combine most attractively with *Chrysogonum virginianum*, *Aquilegia canadensis*, and *Helleborus*.

IRIS ENSATA (IRIS KAEMPFERI) JAPANESE IRIS *Iridaceae (Iris family)*

The Japanese irises grown in American gardens today are a far cry from the unimpressive native species found in Siberia and northern China as well as Japan. The modern beauties are the result of extensive work by Japanese hybridizers over several centuries, so that now double and peony-form cultivars as well as the more familiar single-flowered forms are available. All the modern cultivars have large flowers ranging in color from white through pinks, lavenders, purples, and violets as well as reddish gold; many are conspicuously striped, streaked, or veined. For example, 'Moonlight Wave' and 'Henry's White' are both good whites, 'Pink Lady' is pale pink, and 'Kumo-

VIEWPOINT
DIVIDING IRISES

We divide irises every 2-3 years,
when their centers begin to die out.
DONALD BUMA,
BOTANICA, WICHITA

It is important to divide and sterilize
irises every 4-5 years; all the dead tissue must be cut away.
ROBERT BOWDEN, ATLANTA

We divide irises when the rhizomes
become crowded, when flowering
declines, when we find pest problems, or rotting rhizomes; it is usually
done every 3-5 years. We often
replace with new rhizomes to upgrade
our collection.
KIM JOHNSON, OLD WESTBURY
GARDENS, NEW YORK

We divide irises every 3-4 years,
when the clumps are quite large.
GALEN GATES, CHICAGO
BOTANIC GARDEN

no-Obi' ('Band of Clouds') has lilac-striped flowers. Select from the catalogs according to your own color preference; some catalogs and nurseries also indicate if a particular cultivar is early or later blooming. Japanese iris prefer to grow in full sun, but will tolerate shade for part of the day. They should be planted in fall or early spring in acid soil, rich in organic matter, which remains damp to wet during the growing season. An organic mulch helps to retain moisture. These greedy feeders not only require a high level of moisture during the growing season, but also should be fertilized routinely in early spring. Where winters are cold, keep the plants drier during the winter months and protect from heaving with a mulch of evergreen boughs or salt hay. Every 3-4 years, just after blooming or in the early fall, lift and divide the plants to retain vigor and to increase stock. Iris thrips sometimes attack the flowers; deadhead regularly. Although Japanese iris grow well in shallow standing water, they also adapt to moist border conditions and are excellent cut flowers.

IRIS PSEUDACORUS YELLOW FLAG *Iridaceae (Iris family)*

The European yellow flag iris has become naturalized so widely in northeastern North America that it is often considered a native. Thriving in wet places, or at least where the soil is constantly moist, they also tolerate well-prepared border soil readily. In the landscape, their upright sword-shaped foliage helps visually to break up the flat edges of a pond or stream bank, where they are most effective massed with other moisture-loving plants, such as *Lobelia cardinalis* (cardinal flower), and *Primula japonica* (Japanese primrose). Several cultivars are on the market, and these are best planted in the border, grouped or as specimen plants. In spite of its name, 'Alba' has pale cream flowers; 'Bastardii' is primrose yellow. The double-flowered 'Flora Plena' is offered only occasionally. As a foliage plant the yellow and cream striped-leaved 'Variegata' is outstanding. The latter needs a little shade to avoid leaf burn, the rest are happy in full sun; flowering is less prolific even in partial shade. Keep the soil moist at all times, particularly during dry spells; yellow flag iris may even be planted into shallow water. Both spring and early fall plantings are successful. Established plants divide readily throughout the growing season; it takes 2-3 years for seed-grown plants to reach flowering size. At Old Westbury Gardens, on New York's Long Island, this flower is cut back to keep the plant neat and to control its invasive tendencies. Iris borer may attack the rhizomes; remove and destroy any infected plants, sanitizing thoroughly before replanting with clean stock.

IRIS SIBIRICA SIBERIAN IRIS *Iridaceae (Iris family)*

Originally from central Europe and Russia, Siberian irises are among the most reliable perennials for American gardens, blooming just after the bearded iris and before the Japanese iris. In the garden they are suitable as specimen plants, in mixed borders, and on awkward banks prone to erosion, their tough roots serving admirably to hold the soil. They are attractive, though short-

IRIS 'BRIDE'S HALO' (TALL BEARDED IRIS) 36 inches tall, space 8-15 inches apart. Yellow-gold margins on pure white flowers. Full sun. Blooms early to mid season. Zones 3-10.

IRIS 'MYSTIQUE' (TALL BEARDED IRIS) 36 inches tall, space 8-15 inches apart. Light blue upright standards, deep purple falls. Full sun. Blooms midseason. Zones 3-10.

IRIS 'WABASH' (TALL BEARDED IRIS) 35 inches tall, space 8-15 inches apart. White standards, purple falls slightly edged in white. Full sun. Blooms midseason. Zones 3-10.

IRIS 'VICTORIA FALLS' (TALL BEARDED IRIS) 36 inches tall, space 8-15 inches apart. Purple upright standards and falls. Full sun. Blooms midseason. Zones 3-10.

IRIS CRISTATA 'ALBA' (DWARF CRESTED IRIS) 6-10 inches tall, space 1 foot apart. Yellow-crested white flowers, sword-shaped leaves arranged in fans. Full sun to partial shade. Zones 6-9.

IRIS ENSATA (JAPANESE IRIS) 2-3 feet tall, spaced 11/2 feet apart. Sword-shaped foliage, flat purple, blue, or white flowers. Full sun to partial shade. Blooms in summer. Zones 5-10.

IRIS PALLIDA 'VARIEGATA' 3-4 feet tall, space 2 feet apart. Lavender blue flowers, distinctive striped foliage. Full sun. Blooms in late spring. Zones 3-10

IRIS PSEUDACORUS (YELLOW FLAG) 2-5 feet tall, space 11/2 feet apart. Sword-shaped leaves, pale to deep yellow flowers. Partial shade. Blooms in early summer. Zones 4-9.

lived, cut flowers; for best results cut when the buds show color. Siberians, as well as the other irises, have fascinated the hybridizers, resulting in a large selection of cultivars, mostly blues, violets, and whites of varying heights and with differing blooming times. One of the most popular is deep violet 'Caesar's Brother'; 'Flight of Butterflies' is dark blue with conspicuous veining. Among the whites slightly ruffled 'White Swirl', lightly marked with yellow in the throat, is excellent. Bicolors include yellow and white 'Star Cluster' and light blue and dark blue 'Canford'. To ensure free blooming, plant Siberian iris in full sun or in no more than half shade; in hot climates, shade at midday. Fall planting is best where winters are mild, but spring is a better time in cold areas. Be sure to mulch the first winter after planting. A neutral to acid, well-drained soil, high in moisture-retaining organic material is ideal; where the soil dries out rapidly, supply extra water to keep it evenly moist. Fertilize lightly each spring and after flowering for best results. In time older clumps become overcrowded or die out in the center, indicating the need for division. This can be done as growth commences in spring or cut the foliage and divide in fall, replanting the young, healthy outer parts of the plant. Iris thrips may need control. Deadhead to prevent self-seeding.

Kirengeshoma's bell-shaped flowers grow on a large, bold plant.

KIRENGESHOMA PALMATA YELLOW WAXBELL *Saxifragaceae* *(Saxifrage family)*

Kirengeshoma is an unusual choice for late-summer color in the shade garden, providing a wonderful texture contrast to azaleas and hemlock. This native of Japan and Korea is a large, bold plant with maplelike leaves and clusters of yellow, bell-shaped, pendulous flowers with thick, waxy petals. After flowering, interesting horned seed pods appear. This is a low-maintenance plant that requires no staking or deadheading, best for Zones 5-9. Grow in light to moderate shade and moist, well-drained acid soil. Space plants 3 feet apart, and cut to the ground after frost. *K. p. koreana* is quite similar.

KNIPHOFIA TORCH LILY *Liliaceae (Lily family)*

Most of the torch lilies on the market today are hybrids or cultivars of species, particularly of *K. uvaria*, found in tropical and southern Africa and Madagascar. Gradually, knowledgeable American gardeners are becoming more comfortable with using these bold and often imposing plants. The vertical accents provided by their stiff swordlike leaves are no less important to a garden designer than the spikes of often hot-colored flowers. Flowering time varies from late spring to late summer and even fall. In a collection of torch lilies, the season might open in early summer with 'Earliest of All', with soft coral flowers, followed by 'Springtime', which has spikes of coral and yellow flowers on 3- to 4-foot stems. Pale yellow 'Ice Queen' and hot orange-red 'Wayside Flame' are both late bloomers, up to 4 feet in height, but 'Little Maid', creamy white, seldom tops 2 feet. There is something for everyone. They assort well with shrubs and many finer-foliaged perennials, providing

French lavender (*Lavandula dentata*), also known as fringed or Spanish lavender, is more tender than English lavender and must be grown as an annual or pot plant north of Zone 9.

architectural accents in beds and borders. Plant in full sun except in very hot regions, where they appreciate light shade during the hottest times of the day. Deep, well-drained soil, enriched with plenty of organic material is important; torch lilies will not survive wet winter conditions, whatever the zone (though gardeners at Portland's Berry Botanical Garden report that they do well in the wet winters of the Pacific Northwest, they do not survive winter at Chicago Botanic Garden). Fertilize in spring and water frequently during dry weather. In the North, planting and division of older plants is best in spring; either spring or fall is satisfactory where winters are milder. Protect the crowns from winter damage by tying the leaves over the crown or mulching with dry leaves or evergreen boughs. While slow at first, once established torch lilies require very little maintenance.

LAMIUM DEAD NETTLE *Lamiaceae (Mint family)*

These low-growing, more or less evergreen members of the mint family have a bad reputation for taking over. However, their invasive tendencies are an asset when used as a ground cover, and for that purpose they are invaluable. The spotted dead nettle, *Lamium maculatum*, and its cultivars are most widely used and are not quite as aggressive as *L. album*. The pink-flowered cultivar 'Beacon Silver' and its white-flowered counterpart 'White Nancy' are high in the popularity polls; their emerald-edged silver leaves enliven many a shaded garden. 'Chequers' is not as showy, but the bright green, silver-flashed leaves are a particular joy in winter when the growing tips become purplish, accentuating the green and silver. The foliage combines well with *Liriope muscari* 'Variegata' in the winter garden. Dead nettles are ideal in lightly shaded beds, borders, or woodlands, but are too aggressive for all but the largest rock gardens. Avoid too much shade, which gives rise to spindly, untidy growth. Plant in well-drained soil that remains evenly moist, although they will often tolerate dry shade. Plant in spring or fall and keep pinched for neat, bushy growth. Fertilize lightly only in alternate years. To propagate take cuttings in early summer, or divide in spring or early fall. Stay alert for slug damage. Closely related *Lamiastrum galeobdolon*, yellow archangel, is often overlooked except as a ground-cover plant. The best cultivar is 'Herman's Pride' , which has striking silver markings on the leaves and yellow flowers. It tolerates more shade than *Lamium*.

LAVANDULA ANGUSTIFOLIA SSP. ANGUSTIFOLIA ENGLISH
LAVENDER *Lamiaceae (Mint family)*

Lavender has been grown for centuries for its wonderfully fragrant flowers and foliage coupled with its attractive appearance in the garden. This bushy, branching, semievergreen shrub produces showy flowers and silvery gray-green foliage that remains attractive through the winter. Lavender flowers and leaves are widely used in sachets and potpourris, and cut flowers are a fine visual and aromatic addition to fresh or dried arrangements. Grow lavender in full sun, in a light, sandy, well-drained and alkaline soil. It is tolerant of poor,

IRIS SIBIRICA 'CAESAR'S BROTHER' (SIBERIAN IRIS) 2-4 feet tall, space 3 feet apart. Erect clump-former, blue or violet flowers. Full sun to partial shade. Blooms in late spring to early summer. Zones 4-10.

KIRENGESHOMA PALMATA (YELLOW WAXBELL) 3-4 feet tall, space 2-3 feet apart. Erect purple stems, pale yellow flowers. Partial shade. Blooms late summer to early fall. Zones 5-9.

KNIPHOFIA UVARIA (TORCH LILY) 3-4 feet tall, space 3 feet apart. Gray-green, sword-shaped foliage, 8- to 10-inch pokers of red, yellow, and orange flowers. Full sun. Blooms spring to fall. Zones 6-10.

LAMIUM MACULATUM 'BEACON SILVER' (SPOTTED DEAD NETTLE) 1-1½ feet tall, space 1 foot apart. Silver leaves edged in green, small rosy pink flowers. Partial to full shade. Blooms in spring to late summer. Zones 3-10.

Many perennials can be dried for use in permanent arrangements by hanging them upside down in a dry place for several weeks. Lavender, delphinium, and yarrow make excellent dried flowers.

dry soil. Many cultivars do not breed true to type from seed, so purchase small plants or start from divisions (in spring) or stem cuttings (from spring to late summer). Clip plants back during the first year to keep them from flowering and to encourage lateral branching. Spacing depends on variety and the eventual size you wish the plant to attain; you may plant as close as 12 inches for miniature hedges or up to 4-6 feet apart for spreading. Lavender is also fine for winter pot culture, in the greenhouse or on a sunny windowsill. Water pots infrequently, and maintain nighttime temperatures of 40-50° F., and daytime temperatures 5-10° warmer.

Lavender plants develop a woody base with age and eventually become quite straggly. You can avoid having to replace older plants by pruning in the spring or after flowering to maintain a compact shape. Lavender benefits from a mulch of 1 inch of coarse sand. For maximum fragrance, harvest the flowering stems in early blossom. Hang in small bunches to dry, or spread out on a screen. Pick leaves anytime. Provide plants with winter protection, such as pine boughs, after the ground freezes.

Among generally available cultivars, 'Alba' has white flowers and 'Jean Davis' offers pink blooms. 'Munstead' is a popular dwarf with deep lavender flowers. 'Twickle Purple' is very fragrant, with soft lavender flowers and broader, more silvery leaves. 'Hidcote' grows to 12 inches, with deep purple flowers. 'Provence' bears wonderfully fragrant violet flowers on 2-foot stems and becomes an impressive 3-foot shrub with soft gray-green foliage. French lavender (*L. dentata*) is more tender, and needs to grown as an annual or an indoor pot plant north of Zone 9. Lavandin (*L.* x *intermedia*) has large gray leaves twice the size of English lavender, topped by thick dark purple flower spikes; it is also hardier than other lavenders, and its flower buds are bigger and better for harvesting.

LIATRIS BLAZING STAR, GAYFEATHER *Asteraceae (Daisy family)*

It comes as a surprise that these natives belong to the daisy family. Both the lack of petallike ray florets and the arrangement of the flowers in a spike belie their familial affiliation. Although at home in formal beds and borders, they are especially well suited to growing in meadow or wild gardens (where they attract butterflies) and are often included in "instant meadow" garden mixtures. As a cut flower they are superb, with strong stems and spikes that curiously open from the top down. Plant the tuberous roots in a sunny position for best vigor, in rich, well-drained soil. Amend with organic material prior to planting, to retain summer moisture. It is seldom necessary to water even during dry spells, but wet feet in winter are not tolerated (except for *L. spicata*). Plant in spring or early fall and do not disturb except to build stock. Propagate in spring by cutting through the roots, retaining at least 2 or more eyes per division. *L. spicata* 'Kobold' is most frequently offered. It has lost much of the loose charm of other gayfeathers and is rather compact, with spikes of dark purple flowers reminiscent of Indian clubs. The tall gayfeather, *L. aspera*, is a less formal plant, but it may need to be staked. Look for the cultivars 'White Spires' and purple 'September Glory' to grace late-summer and fall gardens. Deadhead after blooming time to prevent self-seeding and an untidy appearance. Generally low-maintenance; they become weak when overfertilized. They are occasionally bothered by root-knot nematodes.

LIGULARIA LIGULARIA *Asteraceae (Daisy family)*

Ligularias are grown both for their large masses of handsome leaves as well as for their imposing flowers. They are well suited as specimen plants for the middle to back of the border, but may be at their best in large stands beside ponds, lakes, or streams, where the soil remains moist. Under these conditions, they thrive in full sun, but where soil tends to dry out or in windy places, they benefit from some shade during the heat of the day. They do not perform well in southern California because of slugs, snails, and hot, dry summer days. The large leaves are most unattractive "flying at half-mast" at midday! Ligularias are greedy feeders and should be fertilized each spring in addition to receiving heavy dressings of well-rotted manure or compost each spring or fall. Initial soil preparation for spring or early fall planting should include copious amounts of organic material. Propagation is by division in spring or fall. *Ligularia* 'The Rocket', variously listed under *L. stenocephala* or *L. przewalskii*, is widely available and is grown for its flowers, rather than its foliage, as is *L. dentata*. 'The Rocket' is an attractive companion for soft yellow daylilies, such as 'Hyperion'. Bigleaf ligularia or golden groundsel, *L. dentata {L. clivorum}*, has particularly interesting kidney-shaped, coarsely toothed leaves, which in the cultivar 'Desdemona' are deep purple, especially on the

Spiky *Ligularia* contrasts well with feathery *Inula*; although their colors are similar their shapes and textures are strikingly different.

At The New York Botanical Garden, *Liriope* is used to edge peony beds. *Liriope* also works well with bulbs, which can grow through it.

undersides. The rather shaggy, orange daisy flowers may be enjoyed by some, but others are content to remove them before they bloom. The foliage of 'Desdemona' assorts well with many of the large-leaved hostas. Be alert for slug damage throughout the season.

LIMONIUM LATIFOLIUM SEA LAVENDER *Plumbaginaceae (Plumbago)*

Often incorrectly called statice, sea lavender–like baby's breath–produces an airy cloud of tiny flowers, usually in shades of lavender to pink. The 180 species of *Limonium* are found growing in salt marshes around the world. The flowers hold their color for a long time, so they are excellent for both fresh and dried arrangements. The light airiness of the plant lightens up dense areas of the border very effectively, and the late-summer bloom perks up the garden. Grow in full sun in somewhat sandy soil; overly fertile or heavy soil will produce weak stems that require staking. Sea lavender will thrive in a seaside garden, as it is resistant to salt spray. Start from seed sown in early spring or late fall; plants require 3-4 years to reach flowering size. Space established plants 18-24 inches apart; they can be increased by division in very early spring. For variation in color, try a combination of 'Blue Cloud', 'Violetta', and 'Collier's Pink'.

LIRIOPE LILYTURF *Liliaceae (Lily family)*

Native to Japan, China, and Vietnam, these lily relatives have become indispensable in American gardens for their tough versatility and ease of culture. They are valued as impenetrable ground covers massed in sun or shade, as well as for edgings at the front of beds and borders, foundation plantings, and along woodland paths. Under urban conditions, their tolerance of pollution and heat is unbeatable. Big blue lilyturf, *L. muscari*, is the species grown most widely, and many cultivars are on the market. 'Majestic' is popular, as is 'Big Blue', taller than some at 15 inches. 'Variegata' has yellow margins to its strappy leaves and is especially effective during northern winters when there is little interest. Try it with *Ajuga* 'Catlin's Giant'. In full sun 'Silvery Sunproof' is a good variegated cultivar. Hardier *L. spicata*, creeping lilyturf, is a better choice where temperatures dip below -10° F., in spite of its invasive tendencies. While lilyturf tolerates full sun, most are at their best where they are shaded during the heat of the day. Almost any type of soil is satisfactory as long as the drainage is adequate; even during droughts additional water is unnecessary. None of these cultivars are hardy in Chicago; they are grown extensively at Phoenix's Desert Botanical Garden under steady irrigation and usually in some shade. Plant in spring or fall. As growth commences in spring, cut back the overwintered foliage and fertilize lightly. Build stock by dividing the plants anytime from spring till fall. *L. spicata* may self-sow. Be alert at all times for slug and snail damage. In warm regions, closely related mondo grass, *Ophiopogon*, is widely used as a mass ground cover, but it is hardy only to Zone 7. However, *O. planiscapus* 'Arabicus', with its almost-black

LAVANDULA ANGUSTIFOLIA SSP. ANGUSTIFOLIA (ENGLISH LAVEN-DER) 2-3 feet tall, space 2-6 feet apart (12 inches apart for hedge). Arching spikes of purple flowers. Full sun. Blooms in summer. Zones 5-8.

LIATRIS SPICATA 'KOBOLD' (SPIKE GAYFEATHER) 1½-3 feet tall, space 1½ feet apart. Bright purple wands on erect stems. Full sun. Blooms in summer to fall. Zones 3-10, heat-tolerant.

LIGULARIA STENOCEPHALA 'THE ROCKET' (LIGULARIA) 3-4 feet tall, space 2-3 feet apart. Large cutleaf foliage and spikes of yellow flowers. Full sun to partial shade. Blooms summer to late summer. Zones 4-10, not heat-tolerant.

LIMONIUM LATIFOLIUM (SEA LAVENDER) Rounded mass of leathery evergreen foliage, tiny white flowers. Full sun. Blooms in mid to late summer. Zones 3-10.

LIRIOPE MUSCARI 'VARIEGATA' (LILYTURF) 1-2 feet tall, space 1½ feet apart. Green and cream striped foliage, spikes of small lavender flowers. Blooms in fall. Full sun to full shade. Zones 5-10, heat-tolerant.

LOBELIA CARDINALIS (CARDINAL FLOWER) 3-4 feet tall, space 1 foot apart. Racemes of brilliant red flowers on tall stems. Full sun to full shade. Blooms in late summer. Zones 2-9, not heat-tolerant.

LUPINUS RUSSELL HYBRIDS (RUSSELL HYBRIDS LUPINE) 3-4 feet tall, space 1½-2 feet apart. Abundant compound leaves, long, dense racemes in a great variety of colors. Full sun to partial shade. Blooms in late spring to early summer. Zones 4-9

LYCHNIS CHALCEDONICA (MALTESE CROSS) 3-5 feet tall, space 1 foot apart. Upright stems, deep red flowers with deeply notched petals. Full sun. Blooms in summer. Zones 3-10, not heat-tolerant.

leaves, is a little hardier and makes a striking foliage accent plant to Zone 6.

LOBELIA LOBELIA *Lobeliaceae (Lobelia family)*

Many gardeners are familiar with the annual lobelias, but the perennial sorts are less well known. Cardinal flower, *L. cardinalis*, and great blue lobelia, *L. siphilitica,* are both natives and deserve a place in the ornamental garden. They are particularly effective massed alongside streams, beside ponds, and in other informal places where moisture is plentiful. They are also attractive in lightly shaded borders and thrive if the soil is properly prepared. Enrich them with plenty of organic matter prior to planting to help retain summer moisture. A summer mulch is also advisable, but be sure to keep it away from the crowns; lobelias do not tolerate drying out, but will rot if they are smothered in winter. They do well in shade at the Desert Botanical Garden in Phoenix if planted near water. Either spring or fall planting is successful; light winter protection of evergreen boughs or salt hay is essential for new plantings. Lobelias are not long-lived but usually self-sow. Keep young plants coming on as replacements. Fresh seed is best sown out of doors in fall to germinate after a cold period; divide established plants in spring.

LUPINUS LUPINE *Fabaceae (Pea family)*

Hybrid lupines are used in flower borders—particularly in cooler climates—to add height and vertical interest to the flower garden. The most widely available group is the Russell Hybrids, developed in England in the 1930s and valued for their wide range of colors, which includes yellow, orange, purple, and pink. Gallery hybrids, which also come in a wide range of colors, are more compact in size. *Lupinis hartwegii,* a Mexican native*,* and *Lupinus subcarnosus* (Texas bluebonnet) are annuals. Lupines need well-drained, acidic soil and full sun, but dislike heat and high humidity. Amend neutral or alkaline soil to acidify it before planting lupines. Container-grown seedlings are available at nurseries in the North. Although the seed of some species is difficult to germinate, most hybrids are grown readily from seed. Plant in spring in the North; in the South, lupines can be treated as annuals with seedlings planted in November for spring bloom.

LYCHNIS CAMPION *Caryophyllaceae (Pink family)*

As a strong accent in sunny summer gardens, *Lychnis chalcedonica*, Maltese cross or scarlet lightning, is hard to beat. Its brilliant vermillion flowers, borne on strong stems, stand out well and bloom over several weeks if deadheaded routinely. The white-flowered form 'Alba' has chalky white flowers and is often hard to find in nurseries, but is worth seeking. There is also a pink cultivar, 'Rosea', and it double-flowered cultivar, 'Plena'. Well-drained average soils are satisfactory; a light annual dressing of a complete fertilizer is recommended, but extra water is required only during times of drought. This short-lived perennial should be divided in spring or fall every 3-4 years to maintain vigor, but if some flowers are allowed to set seed, these will frequently self-

Lobelia siphilitica, **great blue lobelia.**

Some invasive plants, like *rudbeckias, lysiymachias,* and *lythrum* are good for quick color. Some, like variegated gout weed, should only be used in a controlled situation–in a container or in an area surrounded by walkways or bricks. Attention to deadheading is a must so that the plant won't reseed itself.
KIM JOHNSON AND NELSON STERNER, OLD WESTBURY GARDENS, NEW YORK

My own philosophy on aggressive weeds is that when they are used in the middle of a totally urban area and kept under some control, they might work. But those with property on the edge of a natural area or park needs to take great care not to plant aggressive, weedy plants. *Pennisetum setaceum,* a very nice-looking ornamental grass, is a pernicious weed, very successful at seeding itself; we no longer recommend or sell it.
MARY IRISH, DESERT BOTANICAL GARDEN

I think every plant has its place! There are some plants in this book–*Cenaurea montana, Lysimachia clethroides, L. nummalaria, Macleaya microcarpa, Matteuccia struthiopteris, Monarda,* and *Phlaris*–that are aggressive and need to be handled appropriately, in heavier soil, steep slopes, shorelines, etc. Be sure to create a barrier at planting time.
GALEN GATES, CHICAGO BOTANIC GARDEN

Readers should be aware that *Lythrum* has been banned in Minnesota; even cultivars that are advertised as sterile and noninvasive have been found to reseed.
RICHARD ISAACSON, MINNEAPOLIS LANDSCAPE ARBORETUM

Surely there are substitutes for the most invasive plants. . .
KATHY MUSIAL, HUNTINGTON BOTANICAL GARDEN

sow. Initial planting may be done in spring or early fall. Rose campion, *Lychnis coronaria,* is also widely grown, as much for its silvery gray, woolly leaves as for its screaming cerise flowers. Happily there is a white-flowered cultivar, 'Alba'. Rose campion is also short-lived but self-sows freely and should be propagated from seed. Its tolerance of hot, dry, and rather poor soils makes it especially valuable in some gardens.

LYSIMACHIA LOOSESTRIFE *Primulaceae (Primula family)*
Although several species of this genus are used as ornamentals, they have earned a reputation as thugs, to be avoided in garden settings. The gooseneck loosestrife, *L. clethroides,* is a case in point, in spite of its ease of culture and elegant flowers, so good for cutting. These plants adapt well to full sun or partial shade, where the soil is organically rich and slightly moist or even wet. Where there is shade, drier soils suffice; in dry weather they benefit from regular watering. Plants may be set out in spring or fall and should be widely spaced since they make large plants. Propagate by spring or fall division or sow seeds; they seed themselves freely unless deadheaded. Once gooseneck loosestrife becomes esablished, it is hard to eradicate and romps freely. Hard to find *L. ephemerum* is a much more refined plant, which forms elegant stands of gray green foliage and is not invasive. In dry soil in partial shade, yellow loosestrife or circle flower, *L. punctata,* is not hard to control, but where soils are damp it, too, becomes a pest. It is at its best in informal plantings alongside water. *L. nummularia,* creeping Jenny or moneywort, makes a fine ground cover, in which case its invasiveness is an asset. However, beware of allowing it to invade a lawn. The yellow-leaved cultivar 'Aurea' brightens shady spots.

LYTHRUM LOOSESTRIFE *Lythraceae (Loosestrife family)*
Their common name notwithstanding, *Lythrum* are unrelated to *Lysimachia,* but share the bad reputation for invasiveness. Huge areas of North American wetlands have been colonized by the European purple loosestrife and its relative the wand loosestrife, *L. virgatum,* to the point where several states have banned their sale. This is unfortunate since they provide needed pizzazz to late summer borders that may be looking a little tired. The cultivated forms are less invasive, but it is prudent to deadhead routinely; although they are self-sterile, they breed promiscuously with either of the species. Breeding has produced several excellent cultivars, including 'Morden's Pink', 'Robert', which has good fall foliage color, and 'Firecandle'. Plant in spring or early fall in full sun or light shade, where the soil is rich and remains moist. Water in hot weather. Divide established plants in spring or early fall or take cuttings during the summer. Japanese beetles are the most serious pest of loosestrifes.

MACLEAYA (BOCCONIA) PLUME POPPY *Papaveraceae (Poppy family)*
These bold, beautiful plants from China and Japan adapt readily to gardens elsewhere. Both *M. cordata,* common plume poppy, and similar *M. microcarpa,* small-fruited plume poppy, are spectacular as specimen plants as well as being

LYSIMACHIA CLETHROIDES (GOOSENECK LOOSESTRIFE) 2-3 feet tall, space 3 feet apart. Upright plant with tiny star-shaped flowers on curved racemes. Full sun to partial shade. Blooms in mid to late summer. Zones 3-10, not heat-tolerant.

LYTHRUM SALICARIA 'MORDEN'S PINK' (LOOSESTRIFE) 3-5 feet tall, space 2 feet apart. Very vigorous erect stems with willowlike leaves and spikes of hot pink flowers. Full sun to partial shade. Blooms in summer to fall. Zones 3-10, not heat-tolerant.

MACLEAYA CORDATA (COMMON PLUME POPPY) 8 feet tall, space 2-3 feet apart. Strong vertical stems with very large lobed leaves and many tiny white flowers. Full sun to partial shade. Blooms in summer. Zones 4-10, not heat-tolerant.

MONARDA DIDYMA 'CROFTWAY PINK' (WILD BERGAMOT, BEEBALM) 2½-3 feet tall, space 1½ feet apart. Large clumps with dark green opposite leaves and rose pink flowers with leafy bracts. Full sun to partial shade. Blooms in summer. Zones 4-10, not heat-tolerant.

Loosestrife provide needed pizzazz to late-summer borders that may be looking a little tired; unfortunately, the plant's invasive tendencies have caused it to be banned in some areas and avoided in others.

effective background plants for larger borders. Allow plenty of space and site where their aggressive habit will not present future problems. Only in the hottest climates is a lightly shaded site preferred; otherwise plant in full sun, in spring or fall. Deep, organically rich soils that drain freely are ideal, although leaner, drier soils serve to inhibit their roving. To encourage rapid colonizing, fertilize lightly in spring; in some gardens, the plants need no encouragement and are aggressive to the point of invasiveness. Root pruning of the young suckers in spring also serves to slow their spread; the offshoots may be used to build stock. Combine with maiden grass *Miscanthus sinensis* 'Gracillimus', or face down with *Rudbeckia nitida* 'Herbstonne' for autumnal effect. Beware: this plant emits an orange sap that can stain skin and clothes.

MONARDA WILD BERGAMOT, BEEBALM *Lamiaceae (Mint family)*
As popular with butterflies, bees, and hummingbirds as with gardeners in the ornamental garden, the wild bergamots attract the added dimension of wildlife to outdoor spaces. They are ideal in wild gardens and meadows and make fragrant, long-blooming additions to summer borders. In the wild, these native North Americans are found growing in full sun or partial shade, often in transitional areas where meadows meet the woodlands and the soil is lean, but usually moisture retentive. In the garden the wild bergamots tolerate a wide range of soils as long as there is sufficient water-holding organic matter to keep it evenly moist. Mulch in summer and water deeply during

NEPETA X FAASSENII 'DROPMORE' (CATMINT) 1-2 feet tall, space 1½ feet apart. Gray-green leaves, profuse small lavender flowers. Full sun. Blooms early to late summer. Zones 3-10, not heat-tolerant.

OENOTHERA MISSOURIENSIS (MISSOURI PRIMROSE) 9-18 inches tall, space 2 feet apart. Prostrate dark green foliage, large yellow flowers. Full sun. Blooms in summer. Zones 4-10, heat-tolerant

PAEONIA 'BEV' (PEONY) 34 inches tall, space 36-48 inches apart. Double; pink 6½-inch flowers, lightly scented. Full sun. Early to midseason. Zones 2-10.

PAEONIA 'BLAZE' (PEONY) 32 inches tall, space 36-48 inches apart. Single; 2-3 rows of bright red rounded petals. Full sun. Early season. Zones 2-10.

PEONY CATEGORIES

The American Peony Society recognizes 4 different forms of peony flower:

1. Singles have 5 or more petals surrounding a central boss of fertile pollen-bearing anthers.

2. Doubles have 5 or more guard petals surrounding a mass of anthers and carpels modified to appear as a mass of petals. There is no trace of typical stamens in the double form.

3. Semidoubles have 5 or more guard petals surrounding a center intermixed with petal-like carpels and distinct pollen-bearing stamens.

4. Japanese types have flowers with 5 or more guard petals and a center consisting of a larger mass of staminodes (modified stamens with aborted non-pollen-bearing anthers). Anemone types are classified with the Japanese types by the American Peony Society.

times of drought to avoid stress and leaf drop. Stress leaves the plants more vulnerable to attacks of powdery mildew, an unsightly and common problem remedied by routine sprays of fungicide. Avoid overfertilizing; the resulting excessive, soft growth is readily attacked by mildew and usually requires staking. Thin the new growth in early spring to increase air movement. It is prudent to plant beebalm well away from other mildew-prone plants, such as lilacs, garden phlox, and black-eyed Susan. Numerous cultivars and hybrids of beebalm are available. Soft rose-colored 'Croftway Pink' is popular; 'Mahogany' has strong dark red to maroon flowers. One of the best whites is 'Snow White', while 'Violet Queen' (a hybrid of *M. fistulosa*) and 'Blue Stocking' are good purplish blues. All spread freely and should be divided in spring or fall every 2-4 years to keep them in check and maintain flowering vigor. Cuttings of young spring growth root readily. Deadhead regularly to extend flowering.

NEPETA CATMINT *Lamiaceae (Mint family)*

Its gray-green aromatic foliage alone earns *Nepeta* a place in many of the best gardens, especially where the design calls for a subtle foil for brilliant floral effects. Traditionally a standby of herb gardens, catmint is also useful in borders, as a billowy edging to paths and walkways, or as an airy underplanting for roses. The Persian nepeta, *N. mussinii*, is the most readily available sort, but this may not be the most desirable, since it self-seeds abundantly. A better choice is the sterile hybrid Faassens catmint *N. x faassenii*. These two are frequently confused in the trade, but should not be difficult to distinguish after flowering. The cultivar 'Six Hills Giant' is much larger, growing up to about 3 feet in height with long spikes of deep lavender blue flowers. For covering larger spaces, this is by far the best, although not many nurseries carry it. All grow best in full sun in well-drained soil that is on the lean side; it becomes floppy even in soils that are only moderately fertile. Where there is a little shade, be certain that the soil drains freely. Planting is successful in spring or fall. To build stock, divide in spring or early fall or take cuttings of new growth in late spring or early summer. After the first flush of bloom, it is advisable to cut the plants back by about half their height for neatness and to encourage a second flush of bloom in the fall. Pests and diseases are seldom a problem.

OENOTHERA EVENING PRIMROSE, SUNDROPS *Onagraceae (Evening Primrose family)*

These natives of the Western Hemisphere are popularly known as sundrops if the flowers open during the day, and evening primroses if they open in the evening, although this is not always the case. While most species are best suited to informal meadows and naturalized areas, the Missouri primrose or Ozark sundrop, *O. missouriensis*, is excellent for the front of sunny borders and in the rock garden. Its flowers usually open during the afternoon, but each persists for several days. Routine deadheading prolongs the blooming period.

PAEONIA 'DOREEN' (PEONY) 32 inches tall, space 36-48 inches apart. Japanese; fuschia-pink petals with yellow fringed center. Full sun. Midseason. Zones 2-10.

PAEONIA 'KRINKLED WHITE' (PEONY) 32 inches tall, space 36-48 inches apart. Single; white flowers with crinkled petals. Full sun. Early season. Zones 2-10.

PAEONIA 'SOFT SALMON SAUCER' (PEONY) 32 inches tall, space 36-48 inches apart. Single; pink petals that fade to white. Full sun. Early season. Zone 2-10.

PAPAVER ORIENTALE (ORIENTAL POPPY) 2-4 feet tall, space 2-3 feet apart. Large flowers with crepelike petals in a wide range of colors. Full sun. Blooms in late spring to early summer. Zones 3-9, not heat-tolerant.

The showy double flowers of peony 'Bev' contrast with its dark green foliage, which lasts through the season.

Unlike some of its cousins, it is not aggressive and may safely be planted in spring or fall in deep fertile soil, rich in organic matter. Water deeply during dry spells. To build stock divide established plants in spring or after flowering, or cuttings may be rooted in midsummer; seed germinates readily in the spring or fall. Ozark sundrops prefer the cooler summers of northern gardens. The showy evening primrose, *O. speciosa*, is true to its name. It displays profuse amounts of pink or white flowers during the day and is very vigorous. Plant in moderate to poor soil in full sun to encourage compact growth and discourage the roving of its running roots. *O. tetragona*, sundrops or four-angled sundrops, is commonly available, particularly its cultivar 'Fireworks'. It blooms in late spring with bright red buds that open to yellow. This short-lived perennial adapts well to meadow gardens, where it assorts well with Queen Anne's lace and chicory.

PAEONIA LACTIFLORA PEONY *Ranunculaceae (Buttercup family)*
Peonies are among the all-time favorite perennials. They are hardy and bloom freely in most parts of the country and above all are easy to grow. They are excellent as single specimen plants or may be grouped in mixed

or perennial borders, with shrubs or massed in all-peony beds. Those with strong stems are valued as cut flowers, and all make handsome foliage plants when out of bloom; some even display fall color. The herbaceous peonies on the market today are the result of extensive breeding programs involving more than just *P. lactiflora* in the parentage. Thousands of named cultivars are listed. The range of cultivars is staggering, with varying flower shapes and forms as well as colors from white through pinks to deep red, wine, and maroon. Blooming times vary; many specialist catalogs list early, midseason cultivars, since hot weather encourages weak stems. Peonies need full sun, but appreciate a little shade during the hottest part of the day, especially in warm climates. Lack of sun promotes sparse flowering. A frequent query is: "The old plants in my mother's garden no longer bloom well. Is it due to old age?" It is more often found that neighboring trees have grown large, blocking out sufficient light. All peonies require good drainage. Amend sandy soils with generous amounts of organic matter to improve moisture retention; heavy soils should be lightened with coarse sand or gravel, and amended with well-rotted manure, compost, or leaf mold. Peonies are deep-rooted, greedy feeders; ideally prepare the soil to a depth of 2-3 feet. Water regularly and deeply during dry weather and dress lightly with a low-nitrogen, complete fertilizer each spring for best results. Fall planting is recommended (or before new growth starts in the South), since the young shoots emerge very early in the spring. Bare-rooted plants should be set no deeper than 1-2 inches below the soil surface; deeper planting inhibits flowering. Container-grown stock may be planted at any time, but the soil level must always remain the same. If they have been planted too deeply in the container, expose the crown with a jet of water prior to planting. Peonies make large plants requiring plenty of space; avoid crowding. With enough room, peonies will bloom with minimal attention for 20 years or more, until eventually the flowers become fewer and smaller. Lift and divide these plants in the fall, carefully cutting the clump into flowering size divisions, each with at least 3 strong roots and 3-5 buds or "eyes." Smaller divisions will reach blooming size in 1-2 seasons. Discard the old decayed center. The roots are very brittle, but become more easily managed if allowed to dry out in the sun for a few hours before cutting. Protect new divisions after planting for the first winter. The large, heavy flowers of peonies almost always need extra support. Most effective is the peony hoop, a circle of heavy wire attached to metal stakes. Place this over each plant as growth commences in the spring and raise it as the plant grows to about ½ its final height. Some gardeners support each stem individually, but this involves a great deal of work if there are more than 1-2 plants. To obtain the largest blooms, remove the side buds, leaving only the terminal bud to open. This results in a shorter period of bloom and may be desirable only for special cut flowers or for exhibition. Botrytis blight is a common problem, but is easily controlled with fungicides; cut down all infected foliage in the fall and destroy it. **Never** compost infected

This may be the place to say that lists of the "best" varieties are inherently absurd, since if you dislike deep red with yellow centers, you clearly should not grow reds with yellow centers, no matter what list they appear on. Likewise, if you think the white with yellows are too elegant and want something flashier, like pinks and yellows, you should grow the pinks.
FROM *THE ESSENTIAL EARTHMAN, HENRY MITCHELL ON GARDENING*

plant remains. Root rot may be caused by poor drainage; but blast may result from low temperatures, drying out in spring, or lack of potassium. Ants are often abundant on the flower buds, feeding on the sticky "honey-dew" of aphids; a sharp spray of water usually dislodges them, but the aphids must be controlled.

PAPAVER POPPY *Papaveraceae (Poppy family)*

While the genus *Papaver* includes about 50 species of both annuals and perennials, native to Europe and Asia, the Oriental poppy is the perennial most often cultivated. *P. orientale* is a familiar and striking garden sight, with its large, flamboyantly orange-red flowers, each borne on a single stalk. Its vivid flower petals are usually blotched purplish-black at the base, and the flowers bear many black stamens. Flower buds nod, but stand erect when they are about to bloom. To use cut flowers in bouquets, sear the stem ends with a flame immediately after cutting. Oriental poppies require full sun, protection from wind, and very well-drained neutral-pH soil; standing water in the winter will cause the fleshy roots to rot. Plant root cuttings taken in late summer as soon as foliage begins to die down or purchased roots in early spring in the North, late summer or fall in the South, spacing 15-18 inches apart, for flowering 2 years later. Place 6-inch root cuttings horizontally 2 inches deep in the soil, and roots 3-4 inches deep; starting in a sandy propagation bed or frame increases success rates. Plants will not appreciate being transplanted. Oriental poppies bloom in May and June; their hairy foliage then disappears by July, leaving a gap in the border that needs filling—annuals and perennials like baby's breath are good for this. A summer mulch will keep the soil cool and moist, which Oriental poppies prefer, and will also mark the empty spot where the plant remains. A spring sidedressing of compost or all-purpose plant food is beneficial. Foliage will reappear in the autumn and persist through the winter. Many varieties of Oriental poppy are now available, in both single and double form, in a host of colors beyond the traditional flaming red, including white.

PENSTEMON BEARD-TONGUE *Scrophulariaceae (Figwort family)*

All but one species of penstemon are native to North America. Their habitats range from dry deserts and prairies to cool alpine regions and moist wood-lands. Regrettably most seem to be very specific about their cultural require-ments in the garden and are not easy to tame. *Penstemon digitalis* 'Husker's Red' is a happy exception. This recent selection from the University of Nebraska is one of the easiest to grow. It performs well in damp to normal soils that drain freely in the winter. In the hottest areas, shade lightly from the heat of the day, but elsewhere site in full sun. It makes an excellent cut flower as well as earning its place in the border. The common beard-tongue, *P. barbatus*, is also readily available, especially the cultivars 'Rose Elf', which has rosy

pink flowers, and the deep red 'Prairie Fire'. All the named cultivars must be propagated vegetatively by spring division or by terminal cuttings taken in early to late summer. Penstemons are short-lived at best, so be sure to have young plants in the wings. Protect with evergreen boughs or hay during the winter, but avoid an organic mulch in summer as it may encourage crown rot. Aphids may need control.

Perovskia atriplicifolia greets visitors at Cornell Plantations in Ithaca, New York. This plant also makes a fine addition to the perennial border.

PEROVSKIA ATRIPLICIFOLIA RUSSIAN SAGE *Lamiaceae (Mint family)*

Despite its common name, Russian sage isn't a sage and isn't exactly Russian. It's a native of Pakistan, the Crimea, and Afghanistan, an association that somehow led to its "Russian" name. This subshrub grows up to 4 feet tall and wide, and in August and September it produces a cloud of beautiful purple-blue flowers that float above fragrant and sticky silver green leaves. Russian

Phlox paniculata 'Bright Eyes' (garden phlox) is a member of the Phlox family, which contains many ornamental plants with widely varied growth habits and blooming times.

sage is very easy to grow. Purchase bushy plants and set out in spring or early summer, or take cuttings (which root easily in peaty soil or vermiculite) in midsummer. Set 2 feet apart at the back of the border, in full or partial sun and average, well-drained soil. Do not crowd or plant in heavy soil. Russian sage is quite hardy and does not need frost protection. Leave it tall in autumn—its gray stems are attractive in winter—then cut back to about 8 inches in spring when plants start leafing out all along the stems. Fertilize at this time too. It will lean toward the light and tend to flop over as it matures; staking the plants when young will remedy this problem.

PERSICARIA (POLYGONUM) SMARTWEED, KNOTWEED
Polygonaceae (Buckwheat family)
This worldwide genus has recently undergone some taxonomic revision, but the ornamentals used in American gardens undoubtedly will retain their old names for some time in the trade. Some, such as Mexican bamboo or Japanese knotweed, are rampant invasive sorts that have given the genus a bad name. However, several species have their place in the garden, particularly in light shade where the soil remains constantly moist. *Persicaria bistorta* [*Polygonum bistorta*], snakeweed, is a good clump-former for the front of the border. Its cultivar 'Superbum' is superior to the species, with larger pokers of pale pink flowers, good as cut flowers. The Himalayan fleece flower, *P. affinis* [*Polygonum affine*], is mat-forming and well-suited to open rock gardens, or makes a good ground cover. The persistent leaves turn bronze and copper in the fall. 'Darjeeling Red' is a good cultivar. None of these smartweeds must be allowed to dry out, although they are not for the bog garden. Apply an organic mulch for the summer, and water during times of drought. Planting may be done in spring or fall, at which times established plants may be divided. Pests and diseases are seldom serious.

PHLOX MACULATA WILD SWEET WILLIAM *Polemoniaceae (Phlox family)*
This eastern North American native is the earliest summer-flowering phlox to bloom. Its heads of fragrant white, pink, or purple flowers were frequently found growing in remote cottage gardens and may be considered old-fashioned. Today they are just as appropriate for summer borders, for cutting, and for fragrance gardens. Often confused with the later-blooming *P. paniculata,* wild sweet William has darker green leaves that are much more resistant to mildew. One of the best-known cultivars is the pure white 'Miss Lingard', affectionately known as the wedding phlox. Undoubtedly, it has graced many a wedding bouquet. 'Miss Lingard' is sometimes listed under *P. caroliniana* and may be a hybrid. More recent cultivars include 'Omega' with white, lilac-eyed flowers, 'Alpha' with pink flowers with a darker eye, and dark pink 'Rosalinde'. All perform best in full sun or very light shade, where the soil is evenly moist and amended with plenty of organic material. Plant in early spring or fall, although the latter is usually recommended. Fertilize lightly each spring and supply water during dry weather. As growth begins in spring,

PENSTEMON DIGITALIS 'HUSKER'S RED' (BEARD-TONGUE) 2-4 feet tall, space 2-3 feet apart. Tall erect dark red stems, with pure white flowers. Full sun. Blooms late spring to early summer. Zones 3-9.

PEROVSKIA ATRIPLICIFOLIA (RUSSIAN SAGE) 3-5 feet tall, space 1½-2 feet apart. Graceful subshrub with silvery branches filled with small, whorled lavender flowers. Full sun. Blooms late spring to early summer. Zones 5-10, not heat-tolerant.

PERSICARIA BISTORTA 'SUPERBUM' (SNAKEWEED) 2-3 feet tall, space 2 feet apart. Erect branch stems with pokers of pale pink or lavender flowers. Full sun to partial shade. Blooms in early summer. Zones 3-9.

PHLOX MACULATA 'MISS LINGARD' (WILD SWEET WILLIAM) 2-4 feet tall, space 2 feet apart. 6-inch panicles of pure white flowers. Full sun to partial shade. Blooms in early summer. Zones 3-9.

PHLOX PANICULATA 'BRIGHT EYES' (GARDEN PHLOX) 2-4 feet tall, space 2 feet apart. Clump-forming plant bears pale pink flowers with dark red eyes. Full sun. Blooms in summer to early fall. Zones 3-9, not heat-tolerant.

PHLOX STOLONIFERA 'PINK CUSHION' (CREEPING PHLOX) 6-12 inches tall, space 1 foot apart. Low-growing creeping plant bears 1- to 1½-inch bright pink flowers. Partial to full shade. Blooms in late spring. Zones 3-9.

PHLOX X 'CHATTAHOUCHEE' (CHATTAHOOCHEE PHLOX) 12 inches high, space 12 inches apart. Lavender petals with reddish-purple eyes above dark green leaves. Full sun to shade. Blooms mid to late spring. Zones 5-9.

PHYSOSTEGIA VIRGINIANA 'PINK BOUQUET' (FALSE DRAGONHEAD) 3 feet tall, space 1½ feet apart. Erect stems bear close-set tubular pink flowers. Full sun to partial shade. Blooms in late summer to fall. Zones 3-10, heat-tolerant.

thin the shoots to facilitate good air circulation and prevent overcrowding, which encourages mildew and other diseases. At about 12 inches high, pinch out the tops of the stems to force sturdier, bushier growth; well-grown plants seldom require staking. Routine deadheading extends flowering time and encourages a second flush of bloom. Propagation is generally by division. Powdery mildew is a severely disfiguring disease even on the more resistant types; routine spraying with a fungicide is recommended. Some experts suggest a summer mulch of gravel that can be removed, rather than an organic mulch, which retains the spores to reinfect the following season. Leaf spot may also be a problem.

PHLOX PANICULATA GARDEN PHLOX *Polemoniaceae (Phlox family)*
Garden phlox are one of the mainstays of sunny perennial gardens, perhaps serving as a reminder of our childhood and grandmother's cottage garden. The species is native to the eastern United States and is seldom cultivated, being largely replaced by the host of first-rate selections and cultivars available. All colors except true blue and yellow are found, with plants ranging in size from under 1 foot to 3-4 feet in height. Some, such as 'Bright Eyes', which has bright pink flowers accented with a rich rose eye, are more resistant to powdery mildew than others; select these in regions where mildew abounds. Other reliable cultivars include 'Pinafore Pink', which is similar to 'Bright Eyes', but is only 6-10 inches tall. 'Othello' is a long-blooming deep red cultivar, while 'The King' has large trusses of deep purple flowers. There are several good whites, but 'Mt. Fuji' ['Mt. Fujiyama'] is considered among the best. Garden or summer phlox are demanding, but well-grown plants are spectacular in bloom. Plant in full sun in spring or fall. Prepare the soil deeply with generous amounts of organic material to retain moisture while improving drainage; wet feet will not be tolerated in winter. Fertilize routinely each spring. Water thoroughly to keep the soil evenly moist during hot weather and apply a summer mulch. This may be organic, but some experts now recommend a gravel mulch, which avoids the retention of–and reinfection by–spores of powdery mildew; remove the gravel mulch during fall cleanup. Thin the young spring growth to increase air movement; this operation also results in larger flower trusses on stronger stems. Pinch the taller cultivars in late spring for shorter, bushier plants, which will not require staking. Deadhead to prevent self-seeding. Divide garden phlox every 2-3 years in spring or fall to maintain vigor; use extra, strong healthy pieces to build stock. On a commercial scale propagation is by root cuttings. Although garden phlox are high-maintenance perennials, they more than repay the extra work with a magnificent and long-blooming display of color.

PHLOX STOLONIFERA CREEPING PHLOX *Polemoniaceae (Phlox family)*
In the wild, creeping phlox are found in damp woodlands in the high regions of the Appalachians and southeastern states. In the garden, they are useful planted as a dense ground cover in shaded or partially shaded places, and even

Phlox subulata (moss pink) is a tough, sun-loving, low-growing plant that grows well in rock gardens and in walls.

in sun in cool climates. They spread quite rapidly, but not aggressively, from creeping stems that root at the nodes, creating a thick mat of attractive semi-evergreen foliage when not in bloom. The cultivars are showier and have larger flowers than the species. 'Blue Ridge' has lavender blue flowers, its counterpart 'Pink Ridge' is a clear pink; 'Bruce's White' is pure white with a prominent yellow eye. Well-drained, fertile soil kept slightly and evenly moist with the addition of plenty of organic matter is ideal for creeping phlox. Additional fertilizer is unnecessary if the soil has been prepared well. Either spring or fall planting is successful. The creeping stems root at the nodes, and to propagate, several young plants may be cut from a single stem; terminal cuttings may also be rooted in late spring or summer. Occasionally powdery mildew attacks creeping phlox, but they are otherwise pest- and disease-free.

PHLOX SUBULATA MOSS PINK *Polemoniaceae (Phlox family)*

In contrast to some other low-growing phlox, moss pinks are sun lovers, thriving where the soil is only of average fertility but is very well drained. They will not tolerate wet feet and will not need additional water even during times of drought. These tough, eastern North Americans are excellent in sunny rock gardens, as wall plants and edgings or as ground covers if the drainage is good. Their perky flowers are a welcome sight in spring when they bloom abundantly and combine well with Siberian squills and other miniature bulbs. The stiff, almost prickly leaves are semievergreen and seldom "brown out" during hot weather. The species has mostly been replaced by superior cultivars, such as white-flowered 'White Delight' and 'Blue Hills', which has light blue flowers with a darker eye. One of the most attractive pink cultivars is 'Emerald Pink'; 'Scarlet Flame' is a rosy pink with a darker eye. Both early spring or fall plantings are successful. After flowering, cut back lightly to encourage healthy, compact growth. Red spider mites are sometimes a nuisance during hot dry weather. The prostrate stems often root themselves at the nodes, and these can be removed to propagate; early summer cuttings may also be rooted. In exposed places, a winter mulch of evergreen boughs or salt hay is recommended for protection from intense cold, glaring sun, and winter winds.

PHLOX X 'CHATTAHOOCHEE' CHATTAHOOCHEE PHLOX
Polemoniaceae (Phlox family)

This hybrid between *P. divaricata* var. *laphamii* and *P. pilosa*, the downy phlox, was first discovered in Georgia. It is an excellent plant for lightly shaded borders, woodlands, and shaded rock gardens, where it spreads slowly and assorts well with violets and sweet woodruff. It is showier than the pale blue or lavender-flowered woodland phlox, *P. divaricata*, or its fine pure white cultivar 'Fuller's White', which are used in similar places in the garden. All these woodland phlox require well-drained but highly organic soils to do their best. The Chattahoochee phlox is somewhat more tolerant of sun than the woodland phlox, but still prefers a dappled site. Plant in spring or fall and mulch routinely each spring with leaf mold or well-rotted compost. Fertilizer is seldom necessary when the soil is well prepared. After flowering, shear the plants lightly to shape and to promote vigorous new growth. To build stock, divide in spring or early fall or take cuttings of young growth. It is important to plant in areas with good air circulation to try to cut down on powdery mildew. If mildew does become a problem, spray with a fungicide.

PHYSOSTEGIA FALSE DRAGONHEAD *Lamiaceae (Mint family)*

The only species cultivated widely is *P. virginiana,* commonly known as obedient plant. This native North American member of the mint family has earned a reputation as being somewhat of a thug in the flower border. This may be true in some places, but used with discretion, obedient plant can be invaluable, providing late color over a long period. It also makes a fine cut flower and more than earns its place in the flowerbed or border. Plant in spring or fall in full sun or light shade, where the soil is only of average fertility and on the dry side. Rich soils coupled with plenty of moisture will result in weak stems and aggressive spreading, not necessarily an asset where space is limited. Divide frequently to keep within bounds. Propagate with young divisions

The time of fullest inflorescence of the nineteenth century front yard was when phlox and tiger lilies bloomed; but the pinkish-orange colors of the latter (the oddest reds of any flower tints) blended most vilely and rampantly with the crimson-purple of the phlox . . . the front yard fairly ached. Nevertheless, an adaptation of that front-yard bloom can be most effective in a garden border, when white phlox only is planted, and the tiger lily or cultivated stalks of our wild nodding lily rise above the white trusses of bloom . . . to other members of the phlox family the old front yard owed much; the moss pink sometimes crowded out both grass and its companion periwinkle; it is still found in our gardens, in either pink or white, it is one of the satisfactions of spring.
FROM *OLD TIME GARDENS*, ALICE MORSE EARLE (1901)

PLATYCODON GRANDIFLORUS (BALLOON FLOWER) 1½-2½ feet tall, space 1 foot apart. Erect toothed stems, oval gray-green leaves and balloon-shaped purplish-blue flowers. Full sun to partial shade. Blooms in mid to late summer. Zones 3-10.

POLYGONATUM ODORATUM VAR. THUNBERGII 'VARIEGATUM' (GIANT SOLOMON'S SEAL) 1-3 feet tall, space 1 foot apart. Tall arching, leafy stems, white-edged leaves, clusters of small white flowers. Full sun to partial shade. Blooms in late spring. Zones 4-9, not heat-tolerant.

PRIMULA JAPONICA (JAPANESE PRIMROSE) 1-2½ feet tall, space 1 foot apart. Many whorls of small flowers, in a large range of colors, held high above foliage. Partial shade. Blooms in late spring. Zones 5-9.

PULMONARIA SACCHARATA 'MRS. MOON' (BETHLEHEM SAGE) 1-1½ feet tall, space 2 feet apart. Variegated green and silver foliage, small pink flowers turning to blue. Partial to full shade. Blooms in spring. Zones 3-9.

or summer cuttings. Several cultivars are available, including 'Summer Snow', which has pure white flowers and is reputed to be less invasive than the species. 'Vivid' is somewhat later-blooming than the others and produces its 2-foot spikes of bright rose pink flowers well into the fall. The most commonly offered is 'Pink Bouquet', which often needs staking. All can be cut back by about half their height in early summer to encourage bushy growth and avoid floppiness. Perhaps the most beautiful is 'Variegata', grown for its striking white-edged leaves. Its spikes of clear pink flowers seem to be overkill! Be alert for slugs where the soil is damp.

PLATYCODON GRANDIFLORUS BALLOON FLOWER *Campanulaceae*
(Bellflower family)

The common name of this Asian native refers to the flower buds, which are shaped like hot-air balloons. Long-lived and easy to grow, this perennial is tolerant of a wide range of sites and conditions. The compact form *P. g.* var. *mariesii* is offered by most nurseries and lends itself to flowerbeds, borders,

Above: The typical balloon shape of the balloon flower is clearly seen in this white cultivar. *Below:* Balloon flowers add a touch of blue to a border of daylilies.

and even rock gardens. Taller cultivars, such as 'Shell Pink' and the 'Fuji' series from Japan, also have their place and make excellent cut flowers; sear the base of the stem to prevent "bleeding." Plant balloon flowers in well-drained soil in full sun in the North, but shade lightly in hot climates. Each spring apply a dressing of fertilizer to maintain fertility; water during dry weather. The deep, fragile roots resent disturbance, but careful division is possible after growth begins in late spring. Pot-grown plants are preferred, since root disturbance is minimal; either spring or fall planting is appropriate. Spring-sown seed germinates readily in pots. To prolong blooming routinely remove spent flowers. Pests and diseases are seldom a problem.

POLYGONATUM SOLOMON'S SEAL *Liliaceae (Lily family)*

Solomon's seal is truly one of the most beautiful low-maintenance perennials for shade. The graceful arching stems provide the perfect foil for other shade lovers, such as ferns, hostas, and astilbes. Our native small Solomon's seal, *P. biflorum,* may be at its best naturalized in woodland gardens, perhaps combined with variegated hostas or low ferns. For more formal parts of the garden, the fragrant *P. odoratum* var. *thunbergii,* and particularly its variegated cultivar 'Variegatum', is useful. Its leaves retain their irregular creamy white edging throughout the season, stunning with an "echo" planting of yellow-variegated hostas. In the fall, most Solomon's seal foliage turns an attractive straw yellow. The soil should be woodsy and well drained, under dappled or light shade. Maintain soil moisture with an organic summer mulch and fertilize lightly in spring. To build stock, cut through the thick rhizomes with a sharp knife to divide them, ideally in spring. If delayed until fall, the new plants may not have sufficient time to become established before cold weather. Slugs sometimes chew the succulent young growth, which is unattractive as the leaves unfurl.

PRIMULA PRIMROSE *Primulaceae (Primrose family)*

Only a few species of this large genus are widely grown, so many of them being too fussy for all but the specialists. Mostly native to temperate regions of the Northern Hemisphere, primroses do best where summers are relatively cool. The polyantha primrose *P.* x *polyantha* is most widely cultivated. Countless millions are raised annually and sold as early spring pot plants. As soon as the ground warms up, these can be planted outside and will usually continue to bloom for several seasons. The 'Pacific Giant' strain is widespread; it has flowers of yellow, blue, red, pink, and white, mostly with yellow throats. Polyantha primroses prefer a richly organic soil that remains moist. If the soil conditions are met, they will do well even in full sun, but also thrive in dappled shade. They make ideal companions for ferns, lungworts, barrenworts, and other shade-lovers. Also fairly easy are the Japanese primroses, *P. japonica.* In time, if allowed to self-seed naturally, these will form large colonies in rich, moist to wet soil where they are partly shaded. Good cultivars include 'Miller's Crimson' and 'Postford's White', but their offspring will not remain

Opposite: A stunning combination for the shade garden: green and white Solomon's seal and hostas.

I shall never forget the morning on which a basketful of this charming plant was first brought to my door. Its flowers, of a rich magenta color, were arranged in tiers, one above another, on a spike nearly two feet in height. It was beyond all question the most beautiful species of the genus to which it belongs, and will, I doubt not, take its place as the "Queen of the Primroses."
ROBERT FORTUNE, PLANT HUNTER, WRITING ABOUT *PRIMULA JAPONICA.*

true unless the plants are isolated. Since they hybridize freely, a range of whites, pinks, reds, and crimsons results. If the roots can be kept moist, Japanese primroses will thrive in sunny places, too, and adapt well to border conditions. They are especially attractive in bog gardens, or alongside streams or ponds; best where the water is not stagnant. Others to try include cowslips *P. veris* and oxlips *P. elatior*, with pastel yellow flowers, and the pink to mauve flowered Japanese star primrose *P. sieboldii,* which is summer deciduous. Both spring and fall are good planting times. Divide established plants after flowering or sow fresh seed as soon as it is ripe. Young seedlings are best overwintered in a cold frame, prior to spring planting. Primroses are subject to winter-heaving in cold climates; protect with evergreen boughs. Slugs can be devastating in damp shady places; in sunnier spots be alert for aphid and red spider mite infestations.

PULMONARIA LUNGWORT *Boraginaceae (Borage family)*
The shade-loving lungworts are valued in the garden for their very early flowers, usually pink turning to blue, which are followed by handsome foliage, often mottled with silver. The most readily available is *P. saccharata,* Bethlehem sage, and several of its fine cultivars are on the market. 'Mrs. Moon' is an old favorite with showy, silver-spotted leaves that may reach a foot in length when well grown. 'Sissinghurst White' has recently become popular; its white flowers are beautifully set off by the speckled leaves. This combines dramatically with the maroon young foliage of some red-flowered astilbes. Others, such as 'Janet Fisk', have patches of silver marking larger leaves. All are excellent choices for the front of shaded borders or as an underplanting for rhododendrons and shrubs, in combination with bulbs and other perennials. Lungworts are at their best in filtered light shade, where the soil remains evenly moist and is high in organic material. Even in northern regions, full sun is not to their liking. Keep the soil cool and moist throughout the season with an organic mulch. An early spring application of fertilizer and regular watering through extended dry spells is recommended. Plant in early spring or early fall, at which times established plants may be divided. Slugs are fond of the succulent new growth; powdery mildew may attack plants stressed during dry weather.

RUDBECKIA CONEFLOWER, BLACK-EYED SUSAN *Asteraceae (Daisy)*
In common with so many of our North American daisies, coneflowers are sun lovers and are at their best when grown in open positions with full sun. They are easy to grow and bloom over a long period, providing strong color accents in flowerbeds, borders, and meadow gardens. They require soil only of average fertility, too rich a soil resulting in soft, floppy growth. A light spring dressing of fertilizer is valuable, however, where the soil is poor. Good drainage is essential, but watering during dry weather is advised. Both spring and fall plantings are successful; propagate from established plants by division in either season. The species will flower the first season from spring-sown

seed. Blooming time is extended considerably by regular removal of spent flowers. Probably the best-known of the coneflowers is *R. fulgida* var. *sullivantii* 'Goldsturm'–acres of it have been planted in combination with *Sedum* x 'Autumn Joy' and ornamental grasses in our nation's capital. This compact, uniform plant must be propagated vegetatively to retain its desirable characteristics, although some catalogs offer an inferior 'Goldsturm Strain'. For the back of the border, shining coneflower, *R. nitida*, is a good candidate. Its cultivars 'Herbstonne', which is perhaps the showiest, and 'Goldquelle', a double form and probably a hybrid, are readily available. Where the soil tends toward dampness, the cutleaf coneflower, *R. laciniata*, is useful. Mildews and leaf spots result in unsightly foliage and sometimes premature leaf drop; aphids can also be a nuisance.

SALVIA SAGE *Lamiaceae (Mint family)*

In the wild, this large genus grows in tropical and temperate regions throughout the world. As a group, the sages represent a wide range of good garden plants with varied uses. Annuals, such as scarlet sage, *S. splendens,* and mealy-cup sage, *S. farinacea*, are important for their constant flowering during the summer, while the common sage, *S. officinalis*, has long been used in herb gardens and kitchens. Some of the tender sorts like pineapple sage, *S. rutilans*, and Mexican sage, *S. leucantha*, are perennials of warm regions but make fine

Salvia leucantha, Mexican sage, is perennial in warm climates and can be used as an annual in northern gardens.

RUDBECKIA FULGIDA VAR. SULLIVANTII 'GOLDSTURM' (ORANGE CONE-FLOWER) 1½-2 feet tall, space 1½ feet apart. 3- to 4-inch ray flowers with bright orange petals and dark centers. Full sun. Blooms in summer to fall. Zones 3-10, heat-tolerant.

RUDBECKIA NITIDA 'HERBSTONNE' (CONEFLOWER) 5-6 feet tall, space 2 feet apart. 3- to 4-inch flowerheads, yellow rays with green centers. Full sun. Blooms late summer to fall. Zones 7-10, heat-tolerant.

SALVIA NEMEROSA 'OSTFRIESLAND' (SAGE) 1½-3 feet tall, space 1½-2½ feet apart. Spikes of purple flowers, gray-green foliage. Full sun. Blooms late spring to summer. Zones 5-10.

SCABIOSA CAUCASICA (PINCUSHION FLOWER) 1½-2½ feet tall, space 1-2 feet apart. Flat blue flowerheads, held on long peduncles. Full sun. Blooms mid to late summer. Zones 3-10, not heat-tolerant.

additions to northern summer gardens when treated as annuals. The hardier hybrid sage *S. nemorosa {S.* x *superba}* is a long-blooming perennial and has become a mainstay of countless sunny borders where the nights are relatively cool and soils remain moist. In hot climates hybrid sage is not at its best. Cultivars such as 'Ostfriesland' ['East Friesland'] and a darker species *S.* x *Superba* 'Mainacht' ['May Night'] are listed in most catalogs. All provide striking companions for other perennials, such as *Achillea* x 'Moonshine'. Spring planting is preferred, in a full-sun position where the soil is fertile and well drained, but moisture retentive. Wet feet during winter are not tolerated. Hybrid sages benefit from a winter mulch of evergreen boughs to prevent heaving, especially for the first winter. Except during severe drought, watering is probably unnecessary. Routine deadheading prolongs flowering; stake as necessary. Propagate by division in spring, or early fall where winters are mild; summer stem cuttings root readily. White fly is sometimes a problem.

Rudbeckia fulgida var. *sullivantii* 'Goldsturm'.

SCABIOSA SCABIOUS, PINCUSHION FLOWER *Dipsacaceae (Teasel)*

Only a few species of this teasel relative are grown as ornamentals. Of particular note is *S. caucasica*, loved as a cut flower for generations, as well as a good border plant where it is at its best grouped in threes or fives. Several superior cultivars are on the market today. 'Fama', an improvement of the old-fashioned 'Clive Greaves', is one of the best, with large clear sky-blue flowers on strong stems; 'Miss Willmott' and 'Bressingham White' are both good whites. Recently the more compact dove scabious *S. columbaria* cultivar 'Butterfly Blue' has become popular, due to its extremely long blooming time. However scabious are not easy; they do not care for the high heat and humidity of many North American summers and must have extra protection from intensely cold winters. They are superb in cool coastal areas, where they should be planted in full sun; elsewhere partial shade is best. Plant in spring in neutral to alkaline, richly organic and well-drained soil, which remains cool in summer. The soil must not be allowed to dry out during the growing season, or become waterlogged in winter. Fertilize sparingly with a complete fertilizer every few years. Only divide (in spring) established plants to build stock, since subsequent growth is slow. Seed may be started in spring or early summer out of doors for blooming the following season. Timely deadheading encourages flowering. Though susceptible to several fungal diseases, these seldom become serious if the plants are growing well.

SEDUM STONECROP *Crassulaceae (Orpine family)*

Relatively few species of this very large genus are cultivated in American gardens. Some of the smaller sorts, such as *S. nevii,* belong in the rock garden or in troughs or strawberry jars, where they can be enjoyed close up. Others, including *S. spurium,* the two-row stonecrop, and particularly its cultivar 'Dragon's Blood', and *S. acre,* the gold moss stonecrop, are well suited for use as ground covers. The popular taller sorts are excellent for the front to midsection of the border and have been used effectively both as specimen plants and

SEDUM X 'AUTUMN JOY' (STONECROP) 1½-2 feet tall, space 1½ feet apart. Rosettes of gray-green foliage, domes of pink flowers that turn copper. Full sun to partial shade. Blooms in late summer to early fall. Zones 4-10.

SEDUM 'RUBY GLOW' (STONECROP) 8-10 inches tall, space 1 foot apart. Small dark red leaves, flat head of dark red flowers. Full sun to partial shade. Blooms in late summer. Zones 4-10.

SEDUM SPECTABILE (SHOWY STONECROP) 1½-2 feet tall, space 1½-2 feet apart. Flat heads of white to pink flowers. Full sun to partial shade. Blooms in late summer to early fall. Zones 4-10.

SEMPERVIVUM TECTORUM (HENS-AND-CHICKS) 1-1½ feet tall, space 1-1½ feet apart. Rosettes of oval leaves with dark tips, small purplish or pinkish flowers. Full sun. Blooms in summer. Zones 5-10.

massed for long-range viewing. The best-known must be *S.* x 'Autumn Joy', variously listed by nurseries as *S. spectabile* 'Autumn Joy' or *S. purpureum* 'Autumn Joy'. It is, in fact, a hybrid between the former and *S. telephium*. Its large clusters of green buds, reminiscent of broccoli, open pink and then turn bronze to copper color. If allowed to remain on the plants into the winter, they are quite a decorative brown well into the winter. Full sun and soil that is on the poor side are preferable; too much shade or a rich soil results in unsightly flopping of the top-heavy heads. If this occurs, remember to pinch the plants to about a foot tall in mid to late June next year; this results in more, but smaller, flower clusters that will not flop. 'Autumn Joy' is popularly grown in concert with ornamental grasses and can be observed almost by the acre in our nation's capital. Showy stonecrop, *S. spectabile*, has paler pink flowers, but is otherwise similar. Its cultivar 'Brilliant' has stronger pink flowers, while those of 'Star Dust' are almost white. Another hybrid sedum well worth growing is *S.* x 'Vera Jameson'. Its deep rosy pink flowers are borne on arching or sometimes prostrate stems in midsummer, but the maroon to bronzy foliage is attractive throughout the season. Try it against the contrasting silver herbage of *artemisias* or *achilleas*.

The succulent stonecrops may be planted in spring or fall and prefer to be in full sun for most of the day, except in the hottest parts of the country, where a little noonday shade is beneficial. Very well-drained, open soil somewhat low in fertility is recommended, since weak lanky growth results from too "good" a soil, and root rot is encouraged by wet feet. Do not fertilize. Additional water is seldom necessary, as the fleshy leaves store water naturally. In hot zones, occasional watering may be advisable. Few pests and diseases attack the stonecrops, but aphids sometimes cripple the young growth of the taller types.

Left: Sedum x 'Autumn Joy' with asters and *artemisia* in The New York Botanical Garden's fall border.

SIDALCEA MALVIFLORA 'ELSIE HEUGH' (PRAIRIE MALLOW, MINIATURE HOLLYHOCK) 2-4 feet tall, space 1-1½ feet apart. Racemes of shell pink flowers with fringed petals. Full sun to partial shade. Blooms in summer. Zones 5-10.

SOLIDAGO 'PETER PAN' (GOLDENROD) 2-feet tall, space 2-3 feet apart. Many bright yellow flowers on tall erect stems. Full sun. Blooms in summer. Zones 3-10.

STACHYS BYZANTINA 'SILVER CARPET' (LAMB'S-EARS) 1-1½ feet tall, space 1 foot apart. Silvery foliage, sprawling habit; this cultivar does not produce flowers. Full sun to partial shade. Zones 4-10, not heat-tolerant.

STOKESIA LAEVIS 'BLUE DANUBE' (STOKES' ASTER) 1-2 feet tall, space 1-1½ feet apart. Large blue flowerheads with small inner florets and fringed outer petals. Full sun. Blooms in summer to fall. Zones 5-10, heat-tolerant.

SEMPERVIVUM HENS-AND-CHICKS, HOUSELEEK *Crassulaceae* (Orpine family)

The different species of hens-and-chicks are very variable and also hybridize freely, resulting in countless named forms and hybrids and nightmarish nomenclature. However, most sold in nurseries appear to be cultivars of the European *S. tectorum*, the common houseleek. *S. t.* var. *calcareum*, which has red tips to its green leaves, is widely grown. Another common type is *S. arachnoideum*, characterized by the fine webs of threadlike hairs that connect the leaf tips, hence its common name, cobweb houseleek. All demand full sun and a very well-drained soil, which should be of poor to average fertility. If it contains some organic material, watering may not be necessary during dry times, but the plants must not be allowed to dehydrate. Crown rot is a problem that arises in poorly drained soil. Spring planting is advisable, and young offsets can be removed at that time to build stock. Seed is easy to germinate, but plants are very slow to flower; interesting forms may reward the hobbyist. Hens-and-chicks are long-lived, tough, and easy, well suited to sunny rock gardens and dry walls. In small spaces, they adapt well to troughs, strawberry jars, and other containers. This is a good plant to introduce children to the joys of growing.

Above: Hens-and-chicks in an appropriate container.

SIDALCEA PRAIRIE MALLOW, CHECKERBLOOM *Malvaceae* (Mallow)

Only one species of this Californian genus is widely cultivated for ornamental purposes, *S. malviflora {S. malvaeflora}*; it is considered to be among the best low-maintenance perennials. Closely related to the hollyhocks of grandmother's garden, these lower-growing plants have the same appealing old-fashioned charm so appropriate in cottage gardens, but they are equally suitable in the midsections of sunny or partially shaded flowerbeds; they also make fine cut flowers. The species itself is seldom grown, but several superior cultivars, including shell pink 'Elsie Heugh', are widely grown. The somewhat taller, salmon pink 'William Smith' and deep rose 'Brilliant' may be harder to find. The seed-propagated strain of 'Stark's Hybrids' ('Stark's Variety') results from crossing *S. malviflora* with *S. candida*. Their colors range from pale pinks through dark rose and purple. White checkerbloom, *S. candida*, is occasionally offered, particularly its cultivar 'Bianca', which displays its white flowers accented with blue anthers in early summer. Plant prairie mallows in spring or fall in deep, fertile soil, high in organic matter. The soil must be well drained but remain evenly moist during hot weather; apply an organic summer mulch and water deeply during droughts. If allowed to dry out, the foliage becomes crisped, and flowering suffers. A light spring dressing of complete fertilizer is recommended. At their best where nights are cool, prairie mallows must be shaded from intense midday sun, particularly in southern climates. In spring propagate named cultivars by division or sow seed of the species and hybrid strains, to plant out in fall. After flowering, cut the stems back by half to encourage strong basal growth and a second flush of bloom. Protect from Japanese beetles; prairie mallows are not affected by rust, which disfigures hollyhocks.

SYMPHYTUM X UPLANDICUM 'VARIEGATUM' (RUSSIAN COMFREY) 3-5 feet tall, space 3 feet apart. Grayish green leaves, banded in cream, lilac flowers. Full sun. Blooms in summer. Zones 3-9.

THALICTRUM AQUILEGIFOLIUM (COLUMBINE MEADOW RUE) 2-3 feet tall, space 1 foot apart. Ferny foliage, corymbs of purple, pink, or white flowers. Full sun to partial shade. Blooms late spring to early summer. Zones 5-10, not heat-tolerant.

THALICTRUM ROCHEBRUNIANUM (LAVENDER MIST MEADOW RUE) 4-6 feet tall, space 1½-2 feet apart. Tall wiry stems with panicles of light purple flowers. Full sun to partial shade. Blooms summer to early fall. Zones 5-10, not heat-tolerant.

TIARELLA CORDIFOLIA (FOAMFLOWER) 1-1½ feet tall, space 2 feet apart. Clusters of heart-shaped leaves, airy racemes of white, pink, or red flowers. Partial shade. Blooms late spring to early summer. Zones 3-9.

SOLIDAGO GOLDENROD *Asteraceae (Daisy family)*

These splendid American natives have long suffered from an unjustified bad reputation. Their pollen does not cause hay fever; indeed, it is much too heavy and waxy to be borne on the wind. Witness the popularity of these flowers with bees and other insects, which visit the open flowers, adding interest to roadsides, meadows, and gardens throughout the late summer and fall. Some species do tend to be weedy and invasive, and these are best confined to meadow or native plant gardens, but many of the modern hybrid cultivars, which are so much appreciated in European gardens, are well worth growing. They provide bright color at a time when there is sometimes a lull in flowering and combine especially well with fall-blooming asters. The taller ones are good as cut flowers. One of the best is 'Peter Pan' ['Goldstrahl'], which is offered widely; more recent introductions include low-growing *S. sphacelata* 'Golden Fleece' from Mt. Cuba Center, suitable as a ground-cover plant, and clump-forming *S. rugosa* 'Fireworks' from North Carolina Botanical Garden, which blooms in late summer on 3- to 4-foot stems. This shows its best form in fairly good soil that remains moist. Most goldenrods perform best in full sun but will tolerate some shade, particularly *S. speciosa*, the noble goldenrod. They are not fussy as to soil, but it must be well drained. Beware of planting the aggressive species in rich soil; they will readily take over! The seaside goldenrod, *S. sempervirens*, is adapted to saline conditions and is useful in controlling erosion. Plant in spring or fall. Routine maintenance is limited to a light spring application of a general fertilizer only if the soil is poor, and deadheading after blooming. Additional water is seldom necessary except during extended droughts. Propagate the hybrids and cultivars by division in spring or early fall. Mildew is a widespread problem that should be controlled.

Silver-gray *Stachys* creates an excellent edging for a perennial bed; from a distance, it resembles a river running along the flowerbed.

STACHYS BETONY *Lamiaceae (Mint family)*

Only a few species of this rather large genus are grown as ornamentals, although wood betony, *S. officinalis*, has been cultivated in herb gardens since Roman times. Big betony, *S. macrantha {S. grandiflora}*, earns its place in the late-spring flower garden, particularly in cooler parts of the country. Its upright spikes with whorls of pink, purple, or white flowers are offset by the dark green, rough foliage. Perhaps the most popular betony for the flower garden is *S. byzantina {S. lanata}*, affectionately known as lamb's-ears. This forms dense mats of white woolly leaves, ideal as edgings or ground-cover plants in sunny, well-drained beds or borders. Since the flower spikes are rather unappealing and are even considered by some to detract from the overall appearance, these are often removed, but they can be cut and dried; the cultivar 'Sheila MacQueen' produces silver, flowerless spikes good for this purpose. Alternatively select the nonflowering cultivar 'Silver Carpet', a superior plant in its own right. Plant in spring or early fall in full sun, especially in the North, but some shade is recommended in hot climates. A lean, free-draining, sandy soil is preferred; excess fertility and water promote soft, disease-prone

TRICYRTIS HIRTA (TOAD-LILY) 1-3 feet tall, space 1½ feet apart. Erect stems with clasping leaves and 1-inch-long speckled flowers. Partial to full shade. Blooms early to late fall. Zones 5-9.

TROLLIUS EUROPAEUS (GLOBEFLOWER) 2 feet tall, space 1-2 feet apart. 1- to 2-inch-wide yellow globe-shaped flowers 1-2 on a stem; foliage is palmately divided and toothed. Full sun to partial shade. Blooms late spring to early summer. Zones 3-10.

VERBASCUM CHAIXII 'ALBUM' (MULLEIN) 3 feet tall, space 1½ feet apart. Vertical stems bear narrow spires of pale yellow flowers with dark red stamens. Full sun. Blooms late spring to summer. Zones 5-10.

VERONICA LONGIFOLIA 'SUNNY BORDER BLUE' (SPEEDWELL) 2-4 feet tall, space 1 foot apart. Spires of dark violet flowers on compact plants. Full sun to partial shade. Blooms early to late summer. Zones 4-10, not heat-tolerant.

growth. In hot, humid climates and where drainage is poor, lamb's ears often "melt" or rot out by midsummer, leaving unsightly gaps. Even well-grown, established plants die out in the center after a few years; divide regularly in spring. Replant the strong outer parts of the plant, discarding the centers. Deadhead to prevent self-seeding.

STOKESIA LAEVIS STOKES' ASTER *Asteraceae (Daisy family)*

This sun-loving, evergreen native from the southeastern United States is easy to grow and hardy as far north as southern New England. An excellent plant for the front of the border as well as for cutting, it requires little more than a sunny position with very well-drained, even dryish soil. In spring a light application of complete fertilizer is recommended, but additional water is seldom necessary except during extended dry spells. In cold areas it is important to plant in spring, but in milder climates either spring or early fall planting is successful. Northern plantings benefit from the protection of an evergreen or salt hay winter mulch. Stoke's asters may be started from seed, but propagate the cultivars vegetatively, either by division or from root cuttings in spring. The most popular cultivar is 'Blue Danube', but several other good cultivars are also available. A fairly recent American introduction is 'Klaus Jelitto', named for the famous German seedsman, which has larger flowers than 'Blue Danube'. 'Alba' and 'Silver Moon' are white-flowered; the latter is somewhat more floriferous. No serious pests or diseases attack Stoke's asters, which can be considered truly low-maintenance perennials.

SYMPHYTUM COMFREY *Boraginaceae (Borage family)*

The coarse, common comfrey, *S. officinalis*, has been grown for its medicinal properties in herb gardens for centuries and still has its place there. For ornamental purposes, the hybrid Russian comfrey *S.* x *uplandicum* is much showier, particularly in its scarce variegated form 'Variegatum'; the coarsely hairy but striking foliage serves to earn its place throughout the season. Try it against *Berberis thunbergii* var. *atropurpurea* 'Crimson Pygmy' or other red-leaved shrubs. The lower-growing, large-flowered comfrey, *S. grandiflorum*, serves well as a dense ground-cover plant in shade, even where the soil is dry, although growth is stronger where soil moisture is available. The species has yellow flowers, but 'Hidcote Blue' and 'Hidcote Pink' are attractive cultivars; the cream and yellow foliage of 'Variegatum' lights up shaded places all season long. Russian comfrey may be planted in spring or fall and performs best in sun to light shade. The soil should contain a fair amount of organic material to maintain even moisture, and a light dressing of fertilizer every 2-3 years will probably be sufficient. Deadhead after flowering, particularly the variegated-leaved cultivars; self-sown seedlings will seldom be true to the parents. Vegetative propagation by root cuttings or division in spring or fall is recommended. After blooming, cut back hard to force a second flush; the leafy growth adds bulk to the compost pile.

Common comfrey, *Symphytum officinalis*, has been grown for its medicinal properties in herb gardens for centuries and still has its place there.

Yucca filamentosa.

THALICTRUM MEADOW RUE *Ranunculaceae (Buttercup family)*

Several of the meadow rues are fine, low-maintenance perennials for shaded flower gardens. They are valued for their stately bearing and the airy feeling of their fluffy apetalous flowers. Their delicate fernlike foliage contrasts well with bold-leaved plants like hostas and ligularias. The columbine meadow rue, *T. aquilegifolium,* is perhaps the most widely grown and is a good companion for Siberian irises. It is the most heat-tolerant species. *T. rochebrunianum,* the lavender mist meadow rue, is valuable in the late-summer garden and is usually considered to be superior to *T. delavayi* and *T. dipterocarpum,* both of which are widely offered. In wet areas the native tall meadow rue, *T. polygamum,* and purple meadow rue, *T. dasycarpum,* are useful. All do best in light shade, particularly at midday. They tolerate a wide range of soils, but perform best in well-drained, slightly moist soil amended with plenty of organic matter. Fertilize lightly each spring and water deeply in dry weather. An organic summer mulch maintains even soil moisture and also represses competing weeds. Planting is successful in spring or early fall. Sow seeds of the species in spring or build stock by division of established clumps early in the season. The tall species may need staking, especially if overfertilized. Powdery mildew is sometimes a nuisance.

TIARELLA FOAMFLOWER, FALSE MITERWORT *Saxifragaceae*

These mostly native woodlanders are excellent choices for shaded gardens or borders, where even when not in bloom their handsome foliage contrasts as pleasingly with delicate ferns as with bold-leaved hostas. Plant in spring or early fall in a partially or fully shaded position, where the soil remains moist with generous amounts of organic material. Foamflowers do not tolerate dry soil and must be watered during the dry months. Additional fertilizer is seldom necessary. The stoloniferous Allegheny foamflower, *T. cordifolia,* is widely offered in the trade and is the best choice for a woodland ground cover; where a clump-forming plant is required, a better choice is closely related Wherry's foamflower, *T. wherryi,* which does not spread by stolons. Its pinkish flowers open in late spring. A routine summer mulch of organic material helps to retain soil moisture; mulch newly planted stock with evergreen boughs or salt hay in winter. To build stock, divide established plants in spring or early fall, or sow seed of the species in spring.

TRICYRTIS TOAD-LILY *Liliaceae (Lily family)*

This Asian genus has become popular in American gardens in the last few years both for its ease of culture and for its curiously unusual flowers, which bloom over several weeks in the fall. Toad-lilies perform best in filtered light shade, but will tolerate the full sun of northern climates and adapt well to shaded rock gardens, borders, or woodland gardens. Their often arching habit contrasts as well with upright ferns as with rounded clumps of hostas and *ligularias.* Plant in spring or fall in highly organic, rich, well-drained soil that does not dry out. A summer mulch of leaf mold or compost helps to retain

VERONICA LATIFOLIA 'CRATER LAKE BLUE' (HUNGARIAN SPEEDWELL)
1½ -3 feet tall, space 1 foot apart. Bright blue flowers on erect stems. Full sun to partial shade. Blooms late spring to summer. Zones 3-10, not heat-tolerant.

VERONICASTRUM VIRGINICUM (BOWMAN'S ROOT) 4-6 feet tall, space 1½ feet apart. Branched vertical stems with horizontal whorls of leaves and racemes of tiny pale blue or white flowers. Full sun or partial shade. Blooms late summer to fall. Zones 3-10, not heat-tolerant.

VIOLA PEDATA (BIRD'S FOOT VIOLET) 2-6 inches tall, space 10-12 inches apart. Deeply palmately dissected foliage with flat, pansylike flowers. Upper petals violet, lower petals lilac blue. Full sun to partial shade. Blooms mid to late spring. Zones 4-9.

YUCCA FILAMENTOSA (ADAM'S NEEDLE) 4-6 feet tall, space 2-3 feet apart. Spiny gray-green leaves, white bell-shaped flowers. Full sun. Blooms mid to late summer. Zones 4-10, heat-tolerant.

VIEWPOINT
FAVORITE PLANT COMBINATIONS

I like to plant *Helictotrichon semper-virens* with *Sedum* 'Autumn Joy'. Another successful combination is *Ophiopogon planiscapus* 'Arabicus' with *Imperata cylindrica* 'Red Baron'–this looks particularly nice when backlit by the sun.
SUSAN NOLDE,
BROOKSIDE GARDENS

We like to combine agaves and wild-flowers, particularly penstemon, lupines, and bladderpod; globe mal-low, brittlebrush, rocks, and hedge-hod cacti; and vines–especially sum-mer-blooming ones–in a cactus gar-den.
MARY IRISH, DESERT BOTANICAL GARDEN

Clematis 'Montana Rubens' looks wonderful when grown through shrubs or perennials. Daffodils can be interplanted with daylilies very suc-cessfully. We also like Siberian bugloss with forget-me-nots.
NELSON STERNER, OLD WESTBURY GARDENS

Some excellent combinations: *Alchemilla* at the base of a *Tsuga* (hemlock) hedge; spring bulbs under *Achillea*; Fall crocus (*Colchicum*) with *Ajuga* 'Burgundy Glow' (the pink foliage is beautiful with pink chalice-shaped flowers of the *Colchicum*); *Digitalis lutea* with *Hosta montana* 'Aureo-marginata'; and *Sedum* 'Vera Jameson' with *Dianthus superbus*.
GALEN GATES,
CHICAGO BOTANIC GARDEN

Cerotastigma plumbaginoides is very attractive with a companion planting of *Achillea* 'Moonbeam' or *Coreopsis verticillata* 'Moonbeam'.
DONALD BUMA,
BOTANICA, WICHITA

moisture. Water deeply during periods of drought. Routine fertilizing is sel-dom necessary, unless fertility drops. Be alert for slug damage. Established plants may be divided in spring or early fall; fresh seed germinates readily. Most commonly grown is the hairy toad-lily, *T. hirta*, and sometimes its unusual white cultivar 'Alba' is available. *T. h.* 'Miyazaki' is similar to the species, but its pale flowers are spotted with lilac. It may be a hybrid with *T. formosana {T. stolonifera},* which bears clusters of flowers at the ends of its stems. In time this species forms large showy clumps.

TROLLIUS GLOBEFLOWER *Ranunculaceae (Buttercup family)*

Globeflowers are natives of the Northern Hemisphere and generally do best in cool climates. They are excellent plants for moist or even wet areas and are particularly effective massed alongside streams, ponds, or lakes, as well as being useful in damp rock gardens and at the front of lightly shaded borders. The European or common globeflower, *T. europaeus*, is widely available, partic-ularly its more floriferous cultivar 'Superbus'. Try planting it with *Iris pseuda-corus* 'Variegata' for an unusual combination. Many other cultivars, including yellow orange 'Goldquelle', lemon yellow 'Earliest of All', and deep orange 'Orange Princess' are listed under *T.* x *cultorum*, a catch-all for hybrids between the European and Asian species. Our native *T. laxus*, spreading globeflower, is less showy, but is well suited to native woodland gardens. All require deeply organic soil that remains moist; water deeply during dry times. Partial or dappled shade is ideal, although full-sun positions are satisfactory if the soil can be kept damp. Each spring fertilize lightly to maintain fertility, and apply an organic summer mulch to retain moisture. Either spring or early fall plant-ing is successful. Build stock of cultivars by dividing established plants in late summer or early fall; sow seed of the species in a shaded spot as soon as it is ripe in mid to late summer. Pests and diseases are seldom a problem.

VERBASCUM MULLEIN *Scrophulariaceae (Figwort family)*

Most of the stately mulleins are biennials or short-lived perennials, and many are regarded merely as roadside weeds. However, this large genus has several garden-worthy members that are gaining in popularity and availability among the American gardening public. One of the best is *V. chaixii*, which displays its tall spikes of purplish-red centered yellow flowers throughout the season. The white-flowered variety 'Album' is an integral part of the White Garden at Sissinghurst in England. Both should be allowed to self-seed for subsequent years. The purple mullein, *V. phoeniceum*, produces tall spikes of purple, pink, or white flowers. It is one of the parents of *V.* x *hybridum*, which includes pink, salmon, or bronzy flowered 'Cotswold Hybrids'. All thrive in full sun or very little shade and are tolerant of a wide range of soils as long as they are not waterlogged. Poor drainage encourages root rot. They are gener-ally drought-resistant and seldom need additional water, even during periods of drought. Plant in spring or early fall from seeds sown out of doors the pre-vious May or June. Seed-grown plants may result in some unexpected and exciting surprises, since mulleins hybridize promiscuously. The cultivars must be raised from root cuttings, which are taken in late spring. Even without the strong vertical accents that these plants provide in the flower garden, several are worth growing for their often striking foliage.

VERONICA SPEEDWELL *Scrophulariaceae (Figwort family)*

This large genus, native to the North temperate zone, supplies the discerning gardener with a wide range of superior garden plants. They are easy to grow in full sun or partial shade, in well-drained, average soil, and need little more than an occasional watering when droughts become serious. Plant in spring or fall but do not pamper. The species germinate easily if somewhat slowly from seed; the cultivars can be divided in spring or fall or may be increased from cuttings taken during the summer. Leaf spot sometimes attacks the foliage, making it unsightly and weakening the plants. Much hybridizing has occurred among the speedwells, resulting in some with questionable parentage. One of the best is 'Sunny Border Blue', usually listed under *V. longifolia.* It is more compact than the species and is very long-blooming, making it eminently suitable for the front to mid section of flowerbeds and borders. Other selections of the long-leaved speedwell include dark blue 'Foerster's Blue' and royal blue *V. subsessilis.* The best cultivar of the Hungarian speedwell, *V. latifolia {V. teucrium, V. austriaca},* is 'Crater Lake Blue'. Its loose, brilliant gentian blue flowers enhance many a rock garden. *V. spicata,* the spiked speedwell, is involved in many of the good selections, which vary considerably in height. 'Red Fox' has rosy red flowers on 10- to 15-inch stems, while the stems of 'Blue Peter' may reach 2 feet. 'Heidekind' displays 6- to 8-inch spikes of rose pink flowers above dense mats of foliage. 'Icicle' has spikes of glistening white flowers on 1½- to 2-foot stems, excellent for cutting. A more recent introduction is 'Goodness Grows', introduced by the nursery of that name. Its spikes of purple blue flowers begin to bloom in late spring and hardly stop until frost. *V. incana,* the woolly speedwell, is worth growing just for its silvery gray leaves; its nonflowering cultivar 'Silver Slippers' is a superb foliage plant for the front of sunny borders or rock gardens. This attribute has been passed along to the pink-flowered cultivars 'Barcarolle' and 'Minuet', which are listed under *V. spicata.*

VERONICASTRUM BOWMAN'S ROOT *Scrophulariaceae (Figwort family)*

This elegant plant, native to northeastern woodlands, is particularly suitable for the late-summer garden. *V. virginicum,* also known as Culver's root and blackroot, has strong, vertical stems that grow 4-7 feet tall but rarely need staking. It sometimes takes 4 years to reach its full height. Because of this height, the plant is ideal at the back of the border; because it is a native plant, it is well-suited for use in native or wildflower gardens.It is particularly effective when planted near water. The most widely used cultivar is 'Album', which has dark green foliage that provides a striking background for the sharply white flowers. *Veronicastrum* is easy to grow in full sun or partial shade.

VIOLA VIOLET *Violaceae (Violet family)*

Most violets are found in the wild in cool regions of the world, often growing
in partly shaded hedgerows or light woodlands. In the garden many adapt
well to massed woodland plantings, where the soil is highly organic but well
drained. Other species are ideal as rock-garden and front-of-the-border plants,
in both sun and shade. One of the best-loved of the American species is the
bird's foot violet, *V. pedata,* so-named for its divided leaves, shaped like the
foot of a bird. This species is unusual among violets as it inhabits dry and
infertile soil in its natural range. Plants of the bird's foot violet are becoming
increasingly scarce in the wild and seldom transplant readily. They should
never be dug from the wild and must be cultivated only from seed-grown
nursery-propagated stock, or sow your own seed out of doors in spring or fall.
These are excellent as rock-garden plants, preferring a full-sun to partly shaded position where the soil is very well drained and somewhat poor. *V. odorata,*
the sweet violet, has long been grown as a romantic and fragrant cut flower.
Several cultivars are available, among them dark violet-blue 'Royal Robe' and
'White Czar'. All may be planted in spring or fall in a cool, partially shaded
position with rich, slightly moist soil that will not dry out. Several fungal diseases attack violets, but slugs are probably the most serious problem.

YUCCA ADAM'S NEEDLE *Agavaceae (Agave family)*

Most yuccas are found in the wild in the deserts and semideserts of the south-
western United States. In the garden they are valuable for the bold architectural interest they contribute year round. Being salt-tolerant, they are especially useful in seaside gardens, where the plant palette is somewhat limited.
Yuccas are particularly handsome when used as specimen plants or in borders,
but group plantings are also effective, and they are frequently used as a barrier
or hedge. Overcrowding results in one-sided, rather unattractive plants. The
common name Adam's needle properly refers to one of the most popular
species *Y. filamentosa.* This very long-lived plant has been found in gardens
long after the houses have been demolished, testimony to their longevity and
truly low-maintenance demands. Striking variegated cultivars include
'Golden Sword', whose bluish-green leaves are edged in yellow, and 'Bright
Edge', with green foliage edged with cream. Soapwell, *Y. glauca,* Spanish dag-
ger, *Y. gloriosa,* and other species may also be found regionally. All require full
sun to flower well, although they may grow well enough in some shade. Plant
in spring or fall in soil that is well-drained and on the lean side; poor drainage
causes rot, and excess fertilizer results in soft, lanky growth. Pests and diseases
are seldom serious. The easiest way to increase stock is by removing the offsets
during the growing season or starting from seed. Otherwise plants may be
divided or stem, rhizome, or root cuttings can be taken.

FERNS

Most ferns are nonflowering perennials that reproduce by spore rather than by seed. A large percentage of ferns are tropical and grow in rain forests, but many others are native to temperate regions of the world, some even to deserts or alpine areas. In the garden they are valued for their leaves (called fronds), which are usually very finely dissected or divided and which range in color from greenish or bluish green to a yellowish green; some are even variegated. Because many ferns have lacy, delicate-looking fronds, we tend to feel that they are fragile and hard to grow. In fact, most are just the opposite and tolerate a wide range of cultural conditions, and even some abuse.

In temperate gardens, ferns generally require plenty of filtered light, such as is found under oaks and other deep-rooted deciduous trees. The permanent deep shade that is produced by evergreens, such as pines and hemlocks, is usually too dense to give good results, but the weak, full sun of the morning or late afternoon is also acceptable. Only a few ferns, such as the aggressive, hay-scented fern, *Dennstaedtia punctilobula*, can tolerate full-sun conditions. Although most ferns require shade, gardeners often make the mistake of trying to grow them in such deep shade that they cannot thrive and at best barely stay alive.

Most ferns do best in soil that is rich in organic material and well drained, yet can hold enough moisture without becoming soggy. Some, such as royal fern, *Osmunda regalis,* tolerate wet conditions, even standing water. Loose soil, free from compaction, enables the shallow fern roots to spread easily. An organic mulch in summer helps to keep the roots cool and moist. Water deeply during dry periods; this may be necessary daily in the hottest sections of the country, but though less frequent, is just as important in cooler zones. A summer mulch helps to control weeds, which compete for water and nutrients, thereby freeing the gardener for other tasks. When necessary, hand-weeding is recommended, since cultivation tends to disturb the shallow, spreading roots.

All species of ferns can be grown from spores, which can be tricky but very rewarding. Many are more easily propagated by division in spring or early fall, in the same way as countless other perennials. The different forms and cultivars of ferns must always be propagated vegetatively, since plants grown from spores (or seeds for flowering perennials) may not come true to form and often exhibit a wide range of variability.

Ferns require little maintenance when given good growing conditions. Remove the old, dead, or collapsed fronds by cutting them off as close to the crown as possible before new growth unfurls in the spring. This opens up space and light, enabling the new fronds to grow unrestricted. Slugs and snails are the only real problems.

Ferns have an important role to play in any shaded garden. The cool effect they convey with their graceful, textured, and soft appearance is constant, as opposed to the colorful but short-lived flowers of other shade plants. They combine especially well with hostas, in all their multitude of leaf sizes and colors, but are also effective with the bold leaves of plants like hardy begonias, ligularias, Japanese anemones, and hellebores. The low-growing foliage of epimediums, brunneras, bergenias, and pulmonarias, for example, is elegantly accented by taller-growing ferns. Beyond cultural conditions, your imagination is the only limit to where ferns can enhance your garden. Use them along paths, as an underplanting for shrubs, to hide the dying foliage of spring bulbs, in quiet sitting areas, and in woodland beds and borders. Experienced gardeners understand that while many a garden looks good in flower, those that are planned with the interplay of foliage shapes, colors, and textures in mind remain interesting and good-looking throughout the season.

ADIANTUM MAIDENHAIR FERN *Adiantaceae (Maidenhair family)*

Most maidenhair ferns are found in wet tropical forests, but perhaps the most widely cultivated is a temperate species, *A. pedatum*, the northern maidenhair fern, native to the northeastern United States. This deciduous clump-former prefers a lightly shaded place, although it will tolerate deeper shade. Plant in spring or fall in loose, richly organic soil that is well drained and evenly moist, but not soggy. A range from slightly acid to slightly alkaline is preferred. Apply an annual spring dressing of organic or slow-release fertilizer to maintain fertility, and an organic mulch to keep the roots cool in summer. In dry weather, water to keep the soil evenly and consistently moist. Protect new plantings and those in exposed positions with salt hay or evergreen boughs in winter. Increase stock by division in spring or early fall, or start from spores. Slugs and snails must be controlled. This choice fern is slow to establish, but is very cold-hardy, at its best in colder rather than hotter climates. It is an excellent companion for the bold leaves of the larger hostas in shaded and woodland gardens. Other hardy species include *A. aleuticum* from the northwest and the dwarf *A. a.* var. *subpumilum*, useful for shaded rock gardens. The Himalayan maidenhair fern, *A. venustum,* forms 1-foot clumps of very delicate evergreen fronds.

ATHYRIUM LADY FERN *Aspleniaceae (Spleenwort family)*

Most of the lady ferns are found in temperate parts of the world, and a few are well suited to growing in lightly shaded woodland gardens. The most widespread is *A. filix-femina*, the European lady fern. The typical species forms a soft, loose, vase-shaped clump of thin-textured, deciduous fronds; its numerous cultivars and varieties include 'Axminster', which is more dwarf with finely cut foliage, and the red-stemmed lady fern 'Vernoniae cristatum', with frilly deep green fronds on mahogany-red stems. The North American counterpart of *A. filix-femina* is now *A. angustum*. The Japanese painted fern *A. niponicum* 'Pictum' [*A. goeringianum* 'Pictum', *A. iseanum*] is perhaps the showiest of the ferns and is well known to gardeners. This deciduous fern is also very variable, and it is wise to see the plant in leaf before buying to ensure good color variegation. All these are best planted in spring or early fall in light shade, where the soil is loose and richly organic, well drained but moisture retentive. They

ADIANTUM PEDATUM (NORTHERN MAIDENHAIR FERN) 2 feet tall, 2 feet wide, space 1½-2 feet apart. Clump-forming deciduous blackish stalk, light green leaf segments. Light shade to deeper shade. Zones 3-8.

ATHYRIUM NIPONICUM 'PICTUM' (JAPANESE PAINTED FERN) 1½-2 feet tall, 1½-2 feet wide, space 1½-2 feet apart. Mound-forming deciduous plant, with handsome, strongly-variegated fronds.

DENNSTAEDTIA PUNCTIOLBULA (HAY-SCENTED FERN) 2-3 feet tall, spreading 2 feet or more. Deciduous plant with soft, hairy green fronds; aggressive. Light shade to sun. Zones 3-8.

DRYOPTERIS ERYTHROSORA (JAPANESE RED SHIELD FERN) 1-3 feet tall, 1-3 feet wide, space 1-2 feet apart. Evergreen plant; young fronds are reddish, turning shiny green in summer, then reddish in fall and winter. Light shade to deeper shade. Zones 5-9.

should not be allowed to dry out and require deep watering to remain moist during hot weather. In spring, dress with a light application of organic or slow-release fertilizer as needed. Mulch lightly for the summer and protect from drying winter winds with salt hay or evergreen boughs. Particular forms should be propagated vegetatively, by division in spring; spore-grown stock is extremely variable, but can result in some very interesting plants. Protect from slug damage, which makes the leaves unsightly.

DENNSTAEDTIA HAY-SCENTED FERN *Dennstaedtiaceae (Hay-scented fern family)*

The only hardy species of hay-scented fern is *D. punctilobula*, found in large areas of partially shaded woods or open meadow areas of the eastern United States. In the garden it tolerates a wide range of positions and will often grow surprisingly well in full sun, although light shade is preferable. Ideally the soil should be loose and well drained, but hay-scented fern is tolerant of a wide range of soil types, except those that are compacted. This aggressive spreader should be confined to naturalized woodlands or the edge of meadows, where beautiful, large colonies will form; it is not a good choice for small areas. Plant in spring or fall, and apply an organic summer mulch. Clumps of the rhizomatous root mass may be severed in spring or fall to build stock. Hay-scented fern is difficult to eradicate from cultivated areas, so careful thought is advised before planting.

DRYOPTERIS SHIELD FERN *Aspleniaceae (Spleenwort family)*

The shield ferns (also known as wood ferns) are native to temperate regions worldwide and are commonly cultivated as garden plants in light or even deeper shade. Many of them are evergreen, an asset in the garden, and some display fine fall color. They are extremely variable, several having numerous named forms, and also hybridize with each other promiscuously. The autumn fern or Japanese red shield fern, *D. erythrosora*, is one of the best for landscape use. Its evergreen fronds emerge a coppery red and mature to shiny green, turning to bronze-red again at the onset of cold weather. Our northeastern native, the marginal shield fern, *D. marginalis*, is also evergreen with leathery, bluish-green fronds. This versatile clump-former thrives in soils that are drier than most ferns tolerate. Also clump-forming, the male fern, *D. filix-mas,* and its many forms, such as 'Undulata robusta', are deciduous in cold areas, semi-evergreen elsewhere. All can be planted in spring or fall in well-drained but evenly moist, highly organic soil. Water deeply during dry periods, and fertilize lightly with a slow-release or organic fertilizer in early spring. An organic mulch for the summer helps to keep the soil cool and moist. Where winters are cold, protect new and exposed plants with salt hay or evergreen boughs. Be alert for slugs.

MATTEUCCIA OSTRICH FERN *Aspleniaceae (Spleenwort family)*

Our native ostrich fern, *M. struthiopteris* [*M. pensylvanica*], is found in the wild in damp or even moist woodlands over a large area of the northern United States. In the garden its vase-shaped, stately habit is striking, particularly underplanted with low-growing plants such as forget-me-nots (*Myosotis*). Ostrich fern produces two different types of fronds: the conspicuously leafy, sterile ones, and the shorter, spore-bearing fertile ones, which become woody and persist through the winter, when they provide interest in the garden and are useful for dried arrangements. Furthermore the young fronds (fiddleheads) are edible and are considered a gourmet's delight. Although a lightly shaded position is preferable, full sun is tolerated if the soil remains damp. Richly organic soil that is well drained is ideal, but ostrich ferns will grow even in swampy places. Regular watering is advised during the hottest times of the year. An organic mulch is beneficial for the summer, and a winter mulch of salt hay or evergreen boughs, especially for the first winter, helps to prevent heaving. Both spring and fall planting are successful. Maintenance is limited to division of overcrowded stands in spring or early fall and removal of dead, overwintered fronds before new growth begins in the spring. There are no serious pests or diseases.

OSMUNDA FLOWERING FERN *Osmundaceae (Flowering fern family)*

Several of the temperate osmundas make good garden subjects, where they give height and grace and provide a foil for bolder-leaved plants throughout the season. They prefer fertile soils that are rich in moisture-holding organic matter but that are well drained; apply an organic summer mulch and keep the soil moist with regular watering during dry weather. These deciduous ferns may be planted in either spring or fall. To build stock, divide established plants in early spring or grow from spores. There are no serious pests. The most widely cultivated of the flowering ferns is *O. cinnamomea*, cinnamon fern, perhaps because it is the easiest. A lightly shaded moist to wet place is preferable, but if the soil remains evenly moist they will tolerate full sun. Clumps of cinnamon fern produce two types of fronds: the sterile leafy ones and the fuzzy, cinnamon-colored ones that bear the spores. The latter wither by midsummer, after the spores have been shed. The royal fern, *O. regalis,* is native to wet, acid soils in light shade, but also will tolerate soils with higher pH and full sun provided there is enough moisture available. The young fiddleheads are copper-colored when they emerge in the spring and gradually turn bright green as they mature. The spores are borne on the tips of the fronds rather than separately. Interrupted fern, *O. claytoniana,* performs best in light to full shade (but tolerates more open conditions), in slightly acidic, moist but not wet soil. Its fertile parts are borne in the middle of the sterile fronds, interrupting the leaflets with cinnamon-colored spore clusters.

POLYSTICHUM *Aspleniaceae (Spleenwort family)*

Most members of this genus are from temperate parts of the world and have leathery, evergreen foliage. Several are under cultivation, of which the most common and easiest is the Christmas fern, *P. acrostichoides*. It is native to east-

Cinnamon fern in early spring.

MATTEUCCIA STRUTHIOPTERIS (OSTRICH FERN) Up to 5 feet tall, 2-3 feet wide; space 1½-3 feet apart. Deciduous plant with upright vase-shaped sterile fronds and 1 foot tall fertile fronds that persist through winter. Light shade to full sun. Zones 2-8.

OSMUNDA CINNAMOMEA (CINNAMON FERN) 4 feet tall, 2 feet wide; space 1½-2 feet apart. Deciduous sterile fronds forming clumps; cinnamon-colored fertile fronds wither by mid-summer. Light shade to sun. Zones 1-10.

OSMUNDA REGALIS (ROYAL FERN) 4 feet tall, 4-6 feet wide, space 1½-2 feet apart. Large, deciduous, clump-forming plant with shrublike appearance; spores borne at tip of fronds. Light shade to sun. Zones 1-10.

POLYSTICHUM ACROSTICHOIDES (CHRISTMAS FERN) 2 feet tall, 2 feet wide; space 1½-2 feet apart. Evergreen leathery deep green fronds. Light shade to deeper shade. Zones 2-10.

GRASSES

Ornamental grasses are becoming increasingly more popular. Part of the reason for this is that they are being promoted by many garden designers as part of the "New American Garden" style of natural-looking landscaping. But their popularity is also a result of their great value. In addition to their beauty, they add height, color, and drama to the perennial border; many flower in late summer and into fall, with flowers persisting into the winter. They present texture in mass plantings or as backdrops or accents to the garden; they are usually easy to care for, though some species are invasive. Many make excellent cut flowers, fresh or dried.

ern North America and can be found in rocky, shaded woodlands as well as semiopen places. In the garden it is an excellent choice for the shade garden or border, where it combines well with early spring flowering bulbs, serving to hide their fading foliage. Plant in spring or fall in loose, slightly acid and well-drained soil, where the organic content is high. Christmas fern will not tolerate wet feet. Provide a winter mulch of evergreen boughs for newly set plants. If it has become shabby, the evergreen foliage may be removed before the new growth has developed, but it may be left on without harm until later. Propagation is by spores or by division in early spring. There are no pests or diseases. Other species of *Polystichum* include the holly ferns. A few of these are readily available on the market, such as Braun's holly fern, *P. braunii,* tassel fern, or *P. polyblepharum,* and the European soft shield fern, *P. setiferum,* and its numerous named variants, such as 'Congestum cristatum' and 'Herrenhausen'.

GRASSES

CALAMAGROSTIS REED GRASS *Poaceae (Grass family)*

The genus Calamagrostis includes some of the showiest of all the ornamental flowering grasses. Feather reed grass, *Calamagrostis* x *acutiflora* 'Karl Foerster' [*C. acutiflora* 'Stricta'] is a clumping grass with upright flower spikes 2- to 3-feet above its medium green foliage that appear in the late spring to early summer and ripen to a golden tan in late summer. The flower spikes will persist well into winter and are excellent when used in conjunction with fall fruiting shrubs such as winterberry (*Ilex verticillata*) or red chokeberry (*Aronia arbutifolia*). In warm climates, high temperatures can reduce the number of flower spikes. But in areas where they thrive, feather reed grasses are excellent for mass plantings or as specimen or accent plants for the mixed border. They prefer well-drained, slightly moist soil, but will tolerate heavier and wetter soils. Grow in full sun, for even light shade will reduce the amount and quality of flower spikes, or eliminate them altogether. The late-summer- or fall-blooming reed grass, *C. brachytricha* [*C. arundincea* var. *bracytricha*] flower spikes resemble bottlebrushes in shape and turn wheat-colored in fall; they do not persist through winter as the reed feather grasses do. The fall-blooming reed grass will grow and flower well in shade and can be used in the shade border or woodland garden. It need to be kept on the moist side and should be watered regularly during periods of drought. The reed grasses are rarely bothered by pests and diseases.

CAREX SEDGE *Cyperaceae (Sedge family)*

Relatively few of the sedges are appropriate for landscape use, but as they become better known, they gain in popularity. In appearance similar to many of the ornamental grasses, they are generally more tolerant of shade, and some are better suited to wet areas. Widely available *Carex morrowii,* the Japanese sedge, is a mound-forming plant with flat, thick evergreen leaves. The foliage of the silver variegated Japanese sedge *C. m.* 'Variegata' is narrowly edged with silver. Another variegated form, *C. m.* 'Aureo-variegata' [*C. hachijoensis* 'Evergold'], has a bright golden stripe down the center of its leaves. All are excellent planted closely and massed as a ground cover. The latter form is showy enough to make a fine specimen plant in rock gardens, particularly in coastal regions where it enjoys full sun; in hot climates, noonday shade is recommended. For best results keep the soil evenly moist, and divide every few years to retain vigor. Bowles golden sedge, *C. elata* 'Bowles Golden', is a showy plant with bright yellow foliage narrowly edged with green. It forms a wide, dense clump of leaves and is stunning massed on the banks of ponds, lakes, and streams where the foliage is reflected in the water. It also combines beautifully with blue-leaved hostas to enliven shaded spots. Avoid deep shade, which encourages weak spindly growth; at the Chicago Botanic Garden it tolerates sun when established. Spring is recommended for planting, mostly in soil that remains evenly moist to damp. Divide as growth commences in spring or start from spring-sown seed. Pests and diseases are seldom serious.

CORTADERIA PAMPAS GRASS *Poaceae (Grass family)*

The South American *C. selloana* is perhaps the most imposing of all the ornamental grasses cultivated in gardens today. Its dense tussocks of arching leaves have a distinct architectural quality, while its showy white, cream, or pinkish flower plumes may reach 3 feet in length, atop sturdy stems. These are excellent for cutting; for drying, harvest when young to avoid shattering. In the landscape, pampas grass makes fine specimens or accent plants, or can be massed with spectacular results. It is wise to plant away from traffic areas, as the sharp leaf margins can cause injury. Pampas

Feather reed grass and Sedum x 'Autumn Joy' are two plants being promoted by advocates of the "New American Garden" style; both flower in late summer and early fall.

grass is monoecious, with male and female flowers on separate plants; don't be shy about asking for the much showier female plants! *C. selloana* needs plenty of space to show off its best form, but for smaller gardens the dwarf pampas grass *C. selloana* 'Pumila' is more suitable. It grows about 3-5 feet tall and is quite compact. Several other cultivars such as 'Sunningdale Silver', an outstanding white-plumed form, and pink pampas grass 'Rosea', with pink-tinged plumes, are on the market. Pampas grass prefers a position in full sun, but tolerates partial shade well, particularly in warmer parts of the country. Plant in spring in well-drained but slightly moist soil; growth is slowed in poor soil. Keep evenly moist by deep watering during dry weather. A light dressing of a complete fertilizer in early spring is recommended. Stock can be built up by dividing the plants in spring, but it is not an easy task; be sure to wear stout gloves. Seed-grown plants are variable, but interesting plants may appear. Since pampas grass is not reliably hardy north of Zone 8, special precautions need to be taken in colder climates. Except where winters are intensely cold, protection with a heavy mulch or layers of leaves covered with plastic should be sufficient. Elsewhere it may be prudent to plant in containers that can be brought into a cool, frost-free area for the winter; it is a daunting task to lift and bring huge plants inside annually. Grown as annuals, they will not reach the massive size that is typical of more established plants.

FESTUCA FESCUE *Poaceae (Grass family)*

Although this is a fairly large genus of grasses, mostly native to temperate regions, only a relative few are used as ornamentals, the bulk being valuable agriculturally. By far the most popular for the garden are blue fescue *F. glauca {F. ovina* var. *glauca}* and its cultivars. The species is very variable, and its nomenclature is quite confused; do not be deterred by different specific names in catalogs. Among the best are 'Elijah's Blue', which has soft blue foliage up to 8 inches tall, 'Sea Urchin', a silvery blue, up to 12 inches, and 'Azurit', with bright blue foliage 12-18 inches tall. The last two are often listed as cultivars of *F. cinerea*. The blue fescues are prized for their dense tufts of fine, blue leaves, which are more or less evergreen and tolerate the sea spray of coastal gardens well. They are often used as edging plants in flowerbeds and borders and in rock gardens as specimen plants or massed as a tough and impenetrable ground cover. Clumps may be planted out in spring or early fall in a sunny spot, although noontime shade is recommended in hot climates. Blue fescues prefer well-drained but evenly moist soils, but tolerate a wide range of soil types given good drainage; poor drainage encourages root rot. Supply extra water during dry times. As old clumps become overcrowded or die out in the center, they should be divided in spring or early fall. Use the young divisions to increase stock; seed-grown plants are not uniform and will have slight foliage variations. Deadhead to prevent self-seeding; cut back or comb out dead foliage as spring growth commences.

CALAMAGROSTIS X ACUTIFLORA 'KARL FOERSTER' (FEATHER REED GRASS) 5-6 feet tall, space 2-3 feet apart. Clumping grass with upright flower spikes that turn golden tan and persist into winter. Blooms late spring to early summer. Full sun. Zones 5-9.

CAREX MORROWII (JAPANESE SEDGE) 1½ feet tall, space 1-2 feet apart. Clumping or mounding plant with evergreen, flat ¼- to ½-inch-wide leaves; insignificant flowers. Blooms in spring. Full sun to shade, best in light shade. Zones 5-9.

CORTADERIA SELLOANA (PAMPAS GRASS) 5-12 feet tall, space 4-5 feet apart. Clump-forming; blue-green foliage with white or pink flowers in 1- to 3-foot-long fluffy plumes. Blooms in late summer. Full sun to partial shade. Zones 8-10.

FESTUCA GLAUCA (BLUE FESCUE) 6-18 inches tall, space 8-12 inches apart. Clump-forming; fine, narrow, silver-blue foliage, flowers not ornamental. Blooms in summer. Full sun in North, part-day shade in South and West. Zones 4-9.

HELICTOTRICHON SEMPERVIRENS (BLUE OAT GRASS) 12-14 inches tall, space 1½-3 feet apart. Mound-forming; narrow, light-blue foliage, persistent in winter; sparse flowers 6 inches above foliage. Blooms early to midsummer. Full sun. Zones 5-9.

IMPERATA CYLINDRICA 'RED BARON' (JAPANESE BLOOD GRASS) 1½-2 feet tall, space 10-12 inches apart. Slow-growing clump grass, leaves turn bright red in early summer through fall. Full sun to partial shade. Zones 6-9.

HELICTOTRICHON SEMPERVIRENS (BLUE OAT GRASS) 12-14 inches tall, space 1½-3 feet apart. Mound-forming; narrow, light-blue foliage, persistent in winter; sparse flowers 6 inches above foliage. Blooms early to midsummer. Full sun. Zones 5-9.

MISCANTHUS SINENSIS 'ZEBRINUS' (ZEBRA GRASS) 6-8 feet tall, space 3-4 feet apart. Loose-growing clump with horizontal yellow bands on green leaves, pale pink 8- to 10-inch-long flowers. Blooms in early fall. Zones 5-9.

HELICTOTRICHON BLUE OAT GRASS *Poaceae (Grass family)*

While many of the ornamental grasses are grown for their attractive and sometimes spectacular flower spikes, the blue oat grasses are prized for their spiky but delicate blue-green foliage and natural hummock-forming habit. More or less evergreen, the European *H. sempervirens* holds its blue leaves well through the cold months. It is ideal as an accent plant and should be sited so that its graceful architectural shape is not crowded, such as at the corners of borders. Planting is recommended in spring, in well-drained soil of average fertility. Improve drainage in soils that stay wet in winter, which promotes root rot, and avoid excess fertilizer. In areas of intense summer heat, blue oat grass benefits from part-day shade, but elsewhere a full-sun position is preferable. In early spring, comb out any yellow or dead leaves with your fingers rather than cutting back the whole clump; blue oat grass is very slow to grow back into its attractive mound shape. Under good growing conditions, division is seldom necessary, but if more stock is needed, spring is the best time to divide established plants. Otherwise plants may be started from seed in the spring.

IMPERATA CYLINDRICA VAR. RUBRA JAPANESE BLOOD GRASS *Poaceae (Grass Family)*

Japanese blood grass is a relatively new addition to the spectrum of ornamental grasses that can be found in most nurseries. It is listed most often in the nursery trade as *Imperata cylindrica* 'Red Baron', which is synonomous with *I.c.* var. rubra. It is a slow growing species that is unusual in that it is grown for its upright colorful foliage rather than for its flowers, which rarely appear. In the spring, its leaves emerge as medium green, but as the season progresses, the green foliage turns increasing red; by fall it is the "blood red" color of its common name. In late fall, the foliage ripens to a coppery tan, adding winter interest to the garden. Japanese blood grass prefers full sun, but will tolerate and even benefit from partial shade in the warmer sections of its range; shade will produce inferior color. Plant in soil that is well-drained but remains evenly moist and rich in organic matter. As with many other warm-season grasses, Japanese blood grass responds well to division in the spring rather than the fall. Cull out any plants that stay green rather than turn red in the fall for they are not only less attractive, but will also be invasive. NOTE: Some forms of this species are so invasive that they have been illegalized.

MISCANTHUS EULALIA *Poaceae (Grass family)*

This Asian genus includes many of the most spectacular ornamental grasses used in American gardens today. The most widely grown must be *M. sinensis,* eulalia grass, and its numerous cultivars, which vary in height, leaf patterns, habit, and flowering times. Which one to select depends not only on your own preference, but also on where they will grow and the function they fulfill. Many do not flower reliably in the Chicago area. Vase-shaped maiden grass *M. sinensis* 'Gracillimus' is popular as a specimen plant, but is also useful massed for a screen or hedge, while silver-variegated maiden grass 'Morning Light' [*M. s.* 'Morning Light', *M. s.* 'Gracillimus Variegata'] may be more suitable as a late-blooming specimen. The variegated eulalia *M. s.* 'Variegatus' has a loose but upright habit up to 7 feet tall with longitudinally striped leaves. It is striking planted with purple-leaved smokebush *Cotinus coggygria* 'Velvet Cloak' or other dark-leaved shrubs, as well as providing a winter foil for large junipers and other evergreens. Zebra grass *M. s.* 'Zebrinus' is unusual in having horizontal bands of yellow across each leaf. The banding does not show up until late spring or even midsummer, by which time the plant has attained about ⅓ its total height. This extremely vigorous plant benefits from staking. Its fluffy white flowers usually appear in September. Try zebra grass in containers. Porcupine grass *M. s.* 'Strictus' has similar banded leaves but is hardier and has a more upright habit. Giant Chinese silver grass, *M. floridulus {M. giganteus}*, may possibly reach 14 feet in height. It is ideal as an accent beside a boulder or with large shrubs in an extensive landscape, as well as being effective as a summer screen or a large-scale groundcover. Its foot-long reddish flower plumes mature to light tan in the fall. Eulalias are warm-weather grasses, so spring planting is advised for all but the warmest zones. Propagation by division is also recommended for spring, so that the new plants have sufficient time to become well rooted before cold weather. Many gardeners consider the eulalias to be most valuable during the winter, when their architectural forms cast beautiful shadows or are accented by falling snow. Leave them alone till they begin to look shabby and then cut them down, leaving a foot or so to protect the crown. (At the Chicago Botanic Garden, they are cut to the ground before spring to avoid damage to the leaf tips.) There are no serious pests or diseases, but rodents may overwinter in the old stems.

Zebra grass (*Miscanthus sinensis* 'Zebrinus').

PANICUM VIRGATUM SWITCH GRASS *Poaceae (Grass family)*

One of the original native grasses that made up the vast American prairies, switch grass and its cultivars have now become accepted as ornamental garden grasses. They are very versatile and appear as much at home as specimen plants in borders or beside pools as they do naturalized in meadows or mass plantings, where they provide valuable food for wildlife. The numerous narrow feathery spikes of attractive dark red to purple flowers spread widely as they mature atop sturdy stems to 7 feet tall. These and the leaves turn golden tan in the fall and persist well into the winter, making a striking contrast with berried shrubs such as cranberry bushes (*Viburnum trilobum, V. opulus*), and red chokeberry *Aronia arbutifolius*. Plant in spring or early fall in evenly moist soil of average fertility; rich soil encourages weak, rampant growth. It is not necessary to fertilize, but supply extra water during periods of drought. A position in full sun is best, although a little shade is acceptable. Plants may be raised from seed, or divide larger plants in spring or early fall. Several cultivars are readily available. Only 3-4 feet tall, red switch grass 'Haense Herms' is sought for its especially good reddish orange fall color. 'Heavy Metal' is taller; its very stiff, upright foliage is metallic blue, turning golden in the fall.

PENNISETUM FOUNTAIN GRASS *Poaceae (Grass family)*

Grown for their striking foxtaillike flower spikes, fountain grasses have become popular and easy-care additions to American gardens either as single specimen plants in the mixed border or masses in the larger landscape. One of the most ornamental is the Chinese fountain grass, *P. alopecuroides.* In the fall the foliage turns a lovely golden yellow and retains this color through much of the winter. It is especially attractive in combination with the fall-blooming asters and goldenrods and with berried shrubs such as chokecherry (*Aronia* species), winterberry (*Ilex verticillata),* and cranberry-bush (*Viburnum opulus)*. Its lower-growing cultivar 'Hamelin' blooms somewhat earlier, but resents hot, dry summers and is best in northern gardens. For warm climates select the Oriental fountain grass, *P. orientale,* which has blue-green leaves topped by pink foxtails when in bloom. Spring planting is recommended in a full-sun position, where the soil is well-drained, but slightly moist. However, the fountain grasses are tolerant of a wide range of soils, even those that tend to be dry and poor. Avoid fertilizing, but

This display of ornamental grasses at Longwood Gardens in Kennett Square, Pennsylania, indicates their range in size, color, and texture.

PANICUM VIRGATUM (SWITCH GRASS) 4-7 feet tall, space 2-3 feet apart. Clump- or mound-forming; feathery spikes of small red to purple flowers. Blooms mid to late summer. Full sun to partial shade. Zones 5-9.

PENNISETUM ALOPECUROIDES (FOUNTAIN GRASS) 2-3 feet tall, space 2½-4 feet apart. Clump-forming with 6-inch-long bottlebrushlike flowers; green foliage turns golden in fall. Blooms in late summer. Full sun to light shade. Zones 5-9.

PHALARIS ARUNDINACEA VAR. PICTA (RIBBON GRASS) 1½-2 feet tall, space 1-2 feet apart. Fast-spreading ground cover; alternately striped green and white leaves. Blooms early summer. Zones 4-9.

SACCHARUM RAVENNAE (RAVENNA GRASS) 10-14 feet tall, space 4-5 feet apart. 3- to 5-feet-long leaves, 2-feet-long flower spikes on 10- to 14-feet-tall sturdy spikes. Blooms late summer. Full sun. Zones 5-9.

water may be needed during drought. To build stock, divide established plants in spring or start from seed. Older plants may need division every 10 years or so to retain vigor. Self-seeding can be a nuisance in good soil.

PHALARIS RIBBON GRASS *Poaceae (Grass family)*

The ribbon grass usually grown as an ornamental is *P. arundinacea* var. *picta,* commonly called gardener's garters. It has earned its reputation as being extremely invasive, to the point that many gardeners are shy of planting it. However, if it is controlled properly it can be an excellent accent or container plant and is very effective massed along a fence, wall, or on a property line. It serves effectively as a weed-proof ground cover and is undeniably an asset in otherwise difficult places. Some gardeners plant the clumps in sunken containers to corral the roots. Planting in full sun, in dry, poor soil helps to curb its roving tendencies; rich, moist soil and fertilizer encourage the aggressive roots to run. Ribbon grass tolerates a wide range of soils and will even grow in shallow water. Where summers are hot, part-day shade protects the variegated leaves from burning. Set out new plants in spring or early fall, a foot or so apart if used as a ground cover. To propagate, divide established plants in spring. The young, longitudinally striped leaves of ribbon grass are striking in late sping, but often flop as they mature. If cut back to about 4-6 inches in early summer and kept watered, the plants will usually put out a second flush of neat growth. Two cultivars are gaining in popularity as they are much less aggressive. Garter's dwarf ribbon grass *P. a.* var. *picta* 'Garter's Dwarf' is compact, growing only to 12-15 inches; *P. a.* var. *picta* 'Feesey's Variety' has pink-flushed spring growth to about 3 feet tall. It spreads only slowly and is far superior.

SACCHARUM RAVENNAE [ERIANTHUS RAVENNAE] RAVENNA GRASS, PLUME GRASS *Poaceae (Grass family)*

A close relative of sugarcane, ravenna grass is one of the largest and most imposing of the ornamental grasses; a well-grown plant will form dense clumps of foliage topped by 2-foot-long flower spikes borne on 10- to 14-foot stems. Its massive proportions make it a useful screening plant, but in extensive areas, such as golf courses and parks, it is unmatched as a specimen plant. In early fall the white-striped V-shaped leaves color up, turning orange to tan and then golden and remaining so for most of the winter. The bold flower spikes are valuable for cutting both fresh dried; for drying, harvest when they are at their peak, since the flowers will shatter if cut too late. Spring planting is recommended in the North, but in milder climates both spring and early fall are successful. Choose an open, sunny position, away from high winds, which shatter the flower spikes. Even light shade encourages weak growth, which flops as it reaches its full height. Well-drained soil is essential, but for best results it should remain evenly moist even during periods of drought. Cut down the old clumps before young new growth starts in spring and propagate by division at the same time. Seed may be sown in spring or fall. Ravenna grass is seldom attacked by pests or diseases.

OTHER PERENNIALS

Many other perennial plants exist that merit attention; space considerations did not allow the inclusion of all the consulting gardeners favorites. Here are just a few:

Acanthus mollis (Bear's-breech) forms mounds of arching, long-stalked, shiny dark green leaves. full sun to partial shade; Zones 6-10.

Alyssum (Madwort) a sprawling, semiprostrate plant, is most useful in rock gardens. Full sun, Zones 3-9.

Anaphalis (Pearly everlasting) produces white button-like flowers that are excellent for dryings, and silvery or woolly-white foliage. Full sun, Zones 3-9.

Anchusa azurea (Italian bugloss) has a somewhat ungainly habit and intensely blue flowers. Full sun, Zones 3-10.

Bellis perennis (English daisy, bachelor's buttons), excellent for edging or as a companion for spring bulbs, produces daisy-like flowers in white, pinks, or red. Full sun to partial shade. Zones 3-10.

Catananche (Cupid's dart) forms neat clumps of slender gray green foliage with single flowers; excellent as cut flower. Full sun; Zones 4-10.

Cypripedium (Lady's slipper) Though difficult to establish and maintain, this American native is prized for its beauty; it is now are, and should not be purchased from nurseries that collect it from the wild.

Doronicum (Leopard's bane) One of the earliest daisies, leopard's bane produces bright yellow flowers and low mounds of fresh green foliage. Partial shade. Zones 4-9.

Erigeron (Fleabane) produces daisylike flowers with narrow rays around yellow disks. Full sun, zones 4-10.

Eryngium yuccifolium (Rattlesnake master) Long-flowering plants with tight, spiky round flowerheads in silver, steely blue or metallic purple. Full sun, zones 3-10.

Gentiana (Gentian) Many gentians are suitable for rock gardens; some like *G. asclepiadea, G. lutea,* and *G. scabra,* are larger and not as temperamental, producing blue, yellow, or white flowers in summer to early fall. Full sun to partial shade. Zones 5-9.

Gillenia trifoliata (Indian Physic) This erect, branching plant produces starry white or pinkish flowers in summer. Full sun to partial shade. Zones 4-8.

Hesperis matronalis (Dame's Rocket) An old-fashioned, fragrant plant, Dame's rocket is a subshrubby plant that produces many small flowers in loose racemes. Full sun to partial shade. Zones 3-9.

Incarvillea (Hardy Gloxinia) Large, showy flowers and odd-pinnate leaves make this a good addition to the summer border. Full sun. Zones 5-10.

Linaria (Toadflax) This easy-care plant has yellow or purple flowers that resemble snapdragons. Full sun. Zones 4-10.

Linum (Flax) These pretty but short-lived perennials have funnel-shaped flowers that last only a few days. Full sun, Zones 5-9.

Mertensia (Bluebells) Virginia Bluebell (M. virginica) is widely grown, but other species (m. ciliata, chiming bells, M. martimia, northern shorewort) also produce lovely flowers. Most need full sun, M. ciliata requires partial to full shade. Zones 5-9.

Patrinia villosa This long-blooming perennial produces clusters of feathery flowers. Full sun to partial shade. Zones 5-9.

Phlomis russeliana This unusual-looking plant produces hooded yellow flowers. Full sun. Zones 8-10.

Physalis alkekengi (Chinese lantern plant) A novelty, grown for its bright orange papery lanterns, often used dried in winter arrrangements. Full sun to partial shade. Zones 3-10.

Polemonium Caeruleum (Jacob's ladder) Beginning in early spring and lasting through midsummer, Jacob's ladder is covered with pale blue flowers. Full to partial shade. Zones 3-9.

Potentilla (Cinquefoil) Reliable and easy to care for, cinquefoils produce bright flowers ranging in color from white to yellow to pink to orange. Some species are low-growing, others are shrubby. Full sun, Zones 5-9.

Sanguisorba (Burnet) The bottlebrush flowers of burnets, which come in white and pink, provide texture and height in summer and early fall garden. Full sun to partial shade. Zones 3-9.

Senecio (Groundsel) This large genus includes many ornamental plants, including S. cinerea (Sea Ragwort), which tolerates seaside conditions. Full sun, zones 8-10.

Tanacetum vulgare (Common tansy) Though somewhat invasive, tansy's large clumps of ferny green foliage and bright yellow buttonlike flowers are valued in the perennial garden. Full sun. Zones 3-9.

Trillium (Wake-robin) These wildflowers need moist, rich soil, and produce pretty white, green, or purple flowers. Most species need partial shade. Zones 5-9.

Previous pages: The garden of Lynden
B. Miller, the public garden designer
who has transformed many public
spaces in New York City with perennials and shrubs. Lynden B. Miller
restored and redesigned the Irwin
Perennial Garden at The New York
Botanical Garden; in the garden itself
and in the photographs in this book,
you can see many of her ideas carried
out. This chapter on garden design
was taken from discussions with Ms.
Miller; she gave her thoughts on garden design, distilled from over twenty
years work in her own garden and in
other New York City garden, for the
benefit of the home gardener.

Let's assume that you have recently moved into a new house and can't wait to
"get the yard fixed." Most of the same procedures apply even if there is
already some sort of garden. I recommend seeing at least one full season
around, or one full year, making careful notes, sketches, and taking photographs, before doing any major renovating. Don't start out haphazardly and
buy plants that catch your eye at the local nursery–a little preliminary planning is in order. Your own life-style affects several important decisions. Do you
want a real garden or just an area around your house that requires little more
than mowing, raking, or sweeping? If you want a garden, why and for what
purpose? Will tending it be a therapeutic, leisure-time activity or will you pay
someone else to look after it? If the latter, does this fit into your budget?
Should it be strictly low on maintenance or will you enjoy tending it? Will
this outdoor living space be used for entertaining, for children's play, for relax-
ing, or for a combination of these and other activities? Who lives in the
house? A family with small children or older children who need even more
space to play, a rambunctious family pet, a career couple who entertain in the
evening and on weekends, an older parent who has difficulty with steps or
who loves gardening but would be able to cultivate raised beds more easily?
Do you need space for a vegetable or cutting garden? All these questions and
others should be addressed at the outset. Later on you will be glad this was
done.

In this small plot, a double border of
perennials–including deep red *Monarda*
and steely blue *Echinops*–is contained
within a stone wall. Good use of
verticals and unusual colors highlight
this garden.

An informal entryway garden softens an imposing building.

PLANNING ON PAPER

Having made some of these decisions, try to plan your garden out on paper as best you can, to scales. Figure out how much space you have and then decide on the scale. For the whole garden letting ⅛ inch equal 1 foot is useful, or for a single bed ¼ inch equaling 1 foot may be better. Graph paper is very useful. Everyone does plans a little differently; don't get discouraged if it doesn't look like a work of art, as long as it's functional. If you are fortunate to have a horticultural society, cooperative extension, or botanical garden, such as The New York Botanical Garden, within reach, by all means take a couple of courses to learn how to put a plan on paper and to read it. You may be surprised how easy it is, and may even want to continue to learn more about landscaping. Mark in the permanent structures first—the house, pool, decks and walls, paths, and any others that are more or less fixed. Then mark in arches, trellises and fences, benches, and others that are less permanent, as well as major trees, shrubs, and flowerbeds or borders. If there is nothing on the site, take a look at the plan and try to visualize some of these things to facilitate traffic flow, providing places for play, for reading or meditation, for entertaining, and

The New York Botanical Garden Perennial Garden contains sections with cool colors–pink loosestrife and purple smokebush, shown in the photograph on the right–and hot colors–bright yellow *Achillea* and fiery red *Crocosmia*–shown on the opposite page. In both cases, colors are blended with the use of silver or gray plants like *Artemisia* or *Stachys*.

so on. As you do this be mindful of the wider landscape or borrowed landscape beyond your own property. This includes views to be framed, eyesores to be camouflaged, neighbors to screen for your privacy and theirs. How does your property fit into the surrounding area? By this time, the plan will start to look quite structured. This will be the framework on which you will build the garden. Remember that the hardscape will be there all year round, so it's important to make the design as pleasing as possible, before the concrete has dried.

GARDEN TYPES

The next step is deciding the type of garden you want. Should it be formal or informal? This should reflect your taste, the architectural style of the house and perhaps of the neighborhood. A formal house demands a formal garden. But in some parts of the country it is fashionable to have a Japanese-style garden. This is fine in some places, but may look a little self-conscious alongside a traditional New England-style farmhouse. We can adapt all the wonderful things we learn from Japanese gardens, such as their emphasis on foliage, without reproducing them intact. A manmade rock garden can be stunning in a garden set among rocky hills, but may look too contrived in a totally flat landscape. What about a cottage garden? Is fragrance important to you? It could be especially pleasing if you entertain frequently; if your parties are at

night you may like to make an evening fragrance garden, or have major features such as specimen trees, fountains, or sculptures spotlighted. This can be
dramatic seen from inside the house as well. If you have enough space you can
create different gardens for all these things. Visit a large botanical garden and
get ideas from their demonstration gardens. The bottom line is does it look
good to you? However politically correct it may be, if it doesn't please you,
rethink it until it does.

THE RIGHT SITE

Choose the site carefully for your perennial garden. Will it get sun all day, part of the day, or not very much at all? Is the shade cast by tall buildings or evergreen trees, or is it dappled shade, as found under deciduous trees such as birches or dogwoods? Are the trees shallow-rooted, such as maples, or deep-rooted, such as oaks or ashes? Does the soil drain freely or does it remain wet several hours after rain? It is advisable to get the soil tested by your local cooperative extension office or agricultural school to determine the fertility level. Having decided on the location of your perennial garden, it's time to get down to the process of designing it. Will it be a border backed by a wall or hedge such as yew, *Taxus*, or Japanese holly, *Ilex crenata,* or will it be an island bed with access all round? What color is the wall? Will it be framed and set off by a lawn or perhaps a pathway? If it is a hard surface, choose the material. Bluestone and flagstone are both attractive, or perhaps gravel is more in order. This will kick around, so it should be set in soil or concrete or confined with a metal edging, Belgian blocks, or bricks. Woodland paths of bark or sawdust are appropriate since they maintain the peace and silence of the woods. The color of the material is important; if it is gray, for example, then gray-leaved plants along the front of the bed will not show up and must be placed farther back to make an impact. It is nice to allow the foremost plants to billow over the edge of the garden to soften it.

PROVIDING STRUCTURE

The most successful perennial gardens include small trees, evergreens, and shrubs to provide the "bones" of the garden. All gardens need some formality to structure them, even if the planting within them is very loose and informal.

Shrubs provide structure to perennial gardens, both as backdrops and as accents within the border. *Below:* A small rounded *Berberis* 'Crimson Pygmy' and a taller purple smokebush.

Plant the bones first; they will be visible all year round and should decorate the garden as much during the depths of winter as during the growing season. In a border the larger shrubs will be placed toward the back in a loose meandering form, but if you walk on both sides of a bed, make a backbone of shrubs down the middle. Group them so that you get different heights and some rounded shapes and some upright, thin ones. Choose the shrubs for their foliage shapes, textures, and colors as well. Try blue greens against yellow greens against purples. And don't forget winter barks against evergreens. If backed by a wall, the color of the shrubs must be compatible with it, and your choice of shrubs will reflect this. The smaller shrubs are similarly grouped and, of course, evergreens of different sizes are included. The size and number of shrubs will depend on the size of the bed. If possible, a border should be at least 12 feet wide with shrubs toward the back, but an island bed might be 15 feet or so wide. Island beds need some geometric reasoning, following a land contour or mirroring another feature of the garden, rather than suddenly being plopped down in the middle of nowhere. Don't give up if you have only a few feet in width, perhaps alongside the house or fence. Then remember to keep the planting very simple, probably only two or three kinds of plants that will carry it for most of the year. If the border is backed by a hedge or wall, allow an 18-inch maintenance path between it and the plantings. This allows room for the hedge roots as well. Narrower beds and borders need a system of stepping-stones among the plantings to facilitate maintenance, such as weeding, deadheading, and staking. Before anything is planted, improve the soil by working in as much organic material as possible–rotted manure, shredded leaves, compost, or whatever is available. Make the soil as good as you possibly can. The better the soil, the stronger your plants will grow.

After the shrubs are planned or, even better, in place, then and only then is it time to select perennials, although you may have made some early decisions on the plan, or lists of some of your favorites. Expect to plant most perennials in groups of no fewer than three and more likely fives or sevens if the bed is large. Only a few large plants such as Oriental poppies and *Miscanthus* grasses are used singly as specimens. It goes without saying that the plants you choose must thrive under the sun/shade and soil conditions of the site. Refer to the Plant Selector chapter for this information. The garden should be good-looking over a long period of time, particularly where space is limited, and each and every plant must earn its keep. In order to attain this, consider the foliage of the plants first. The flowers of most perennials come and go fairly quickly–they are the icing on the cake, so to speak–but we look at the cake all year long. Some plants such as hostas, lady's mantle, Siberian bugloss, and many ornamental grasses such as *Helictotrichon* and *Molini* are grown primarily as foliage plants, notwithstanding their attractive, but short-lived flowers. Try to contrast foliage shapes, sizes, textures, and colors to compose a pleasing picture. Ferns or astilbes with hostas are a traditional shade combination, for example. Remember that these plants are also compatible culturally. In a sunny spot the solid fleshy leaves of *Sedum* 'Autumn Joy' contrast well with

Foliage is more important than flowers in a perennial garden; flowers usually last no more than a few weeks, while foliage often provides a season-long display of color, texture, and shape. When choosing plants, consider their foliage as well as their flowers. Some, such as deep red *Heuchera* 'Palace Purple' (*above*) bear insignificant flowers, but their foliage makes up for it.

A perennial garden that relies on blooming flowers for its only interest misses some attractive effects–and can be enjoyed for a much shorter time period–in comparison to one that takes other stages of the plant into account. On the right, spent aster blossoms are an attractive foil to *Sedum* and *Artemisia*, well after they shone as blossoms. On the opposite page, The New York Botanical Garden fall border is interesting even in winter, when ornamental grasses and spent stalks of asters and sedums are covered with snow. For more information about planning for winter interest, see page 212.

ornamental grasses or Siberian iris. Contrast the flower habit as well; upright foxgloves, hollyhocks, and delphiniums bring height to a planting. Without enough verticals to play off the horizontal shapes, the overall effect is flat. Sometimes tepees of long stakes or metal tripods are used to support vines to give the effect of height and to bring structure to the garden. Apart from cultural compatibility, your own taste and imagination are the only limits to your design. Some parts of the garden may have large areas where flowers are not as important as just covering the ground and keeping the weeds down. Many perennials serve admirably as low-maintenance, ground-cover plants, and large sweeps of them can be planted closer than usual to speed colonization. Beware, however. The aggressive properties so desirable in ground covers may become a true nuisance if the plants escape their bounds.

COLOR

Although you might want to have a colorful garden all through the season, this is seldom practical, particularly without years of experience. It is less frustrating and frequently much more rewarding to design for flower color for only one or two times during the season. You hear of spring gardens, or fall gardens, when the best display is on view. This is preferable to having just a few flowers trickling throughout the year. Between bursts of color, well-designed gardens depend on long-term foliage effects from the perennials and, of course, the shrubs and evergreens. Consider your own taste in color. Some of us prefer soft cool colors, while others are more at home with the hot side of the spectrum. Use blues and grays to cool down hot combinations, and perhaps hot pink to enliven pastel lavenders, blues, and pinks. White can be a useful link or may pop out too strongly; it is great with other pale colors in an

evening garden. Orange is difficult to use for many of us, but try it using lots
of blue as a foil. If your goal is a monochromatic garden, you will find that
you do need other colors to set it off. For example, the famous White Garden
at Sissinghurst in England, though indeed predominantly white, also includes
grays and silver, pale yellows, and cream.

MIXING PLANTS

There is nothing sacred about an all or only perennial garden. Often they are
mixed successfully with roses, herbs, or vegetables. Annuals, biennials, and
bulbs have their place in the decoration of a young garden until the budget
allows more permanent plantings; they'll extend the blooming time or bright-
en things up when the perennials are in a lull. Plug them in wherever you
can; tuck in lots of small bulbs, such as glory of the snow, snowdrops, and
squills, at the feet of shrubs or group ten or a dozen or more showy tulips
between them, perhaps underplanted with biennial forget-me-nots, English
daisies, or pansies. When they become shabby after flowering all these can be
removed and replaced with later-blooming annuals. Be careful about using
bulbs that remain unsightly for a long period after flowering, such as daffodils
and narcissus. These are more of a liability than an asset in a formal spot, but
are ideal in a naturalized or meadow garden, with shrubs or perhaps combined with later-blooming perennials, such as daylilies, whose new growth
will quickly hide the tattered leaves.

Above all, don't be afraid to experiment. No garden is ever finished, and as
you grow and gain experience, your tastes will change and so will your garden. That's all part of the fun. Work in it and nurture it, and you will turn
your yard into a garden.

I want to work in the garden—weeding, pruning, planting, and doing things that I enjoy. I want the room and the opportunity to experiment with many different kinds of perennials, ornamental grasses, shrubs—even trees. I want a spring garden that doesn't resemble the summer garden, and a fall garden that is different from either. . . . The rub is that I would like all this—and more—without creating a monster by whom I am enslaved and without arriving at utter chaos.

Improbable as it sounds, my gardening life has been devoted to a search for form. The ideal form would be flexible enough to permit experiment without producing confusion and disciplined enough to satisfy a yearning for purpose and pattern without sacrificing variety.
FROM *A PATCHWORK GARDEN*, BY SYDNEY EDDISON

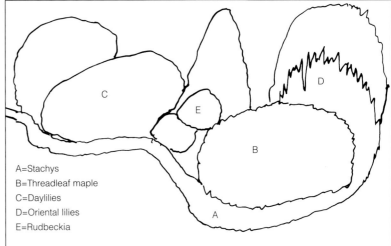

A=Stachys
B=Threadleaf maple
C=Daylilies
D=Oriental lilies
E=Rudbeckia

Garden writer Sydney Eddison's garden in Connecticut represents a careful combination of informality and discipline. Accent shrubs placed throughout the garden—including conifers and an anchoring dwarf threadleaf maple—provide a base for an ever-changing mass of flowers and foliage plants, including hostas, daylilies, lilies, and ornamental grasses in midsummer. An edging of stachys and *Sempervivum tectorum* (hens-and-chicks) presents a neat line that, from a distance, looks like a river bordering the garden. Eddison experiments with plants throughout the season, giving each at least 3 years to prove itself.

A=*Salvia farinacea*
B=*Physostegia*
C=*Salvia leucantha*
D=*Punica*

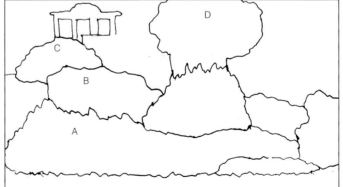

The Shakespeare Garden at Huntington Botanical Gardens in San Marino, California, makes use of vertical perennials in different heights to create an almost geometric regularity. The spiky *Salvia farinacea* and *Physostegia* are softened by the gently mounded *Salvia leucantha*.

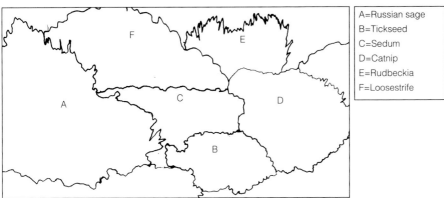

A=Russian sage
B=Tickseed
C=Sedum
D=Catnip
E=Rudbeckia
F=Loosestrife

This perennial border at Longwood Gardens in Kennett Square, Pennsylvania uses a variety of easy to grow perennials that are adaptable to a wide range of climates and are attractive over a long season. Even the plants that are not in flower, like sedum, are attractive in their foliage stage. The ornamental grasses in the background will remain in flower through the fall.

With experience, most gardeners develop their own techniques for tending their gardens; trial and error eliminates the procedures that are overcomplicated or unnecessary for a particular site and confirms those that work well. Personal style will also dictate the way a gardener works, choosing labor-intensive or time-saving methods according to his or her personal needs. But there are some basic techniques that all gardeners need to know, practices that will help assure dependable success.

CHOOSING THE SITE

The first step in choosing a site for a perennial garden or border is carefully examining the entire existing plot. Is there shade, and if so what kind and how much? Is the site sunny, and if so how much sun is there and at what time of day? Does the area drain well, and if not, how wet is it and what can be done about it? Is the area flat or sloping, and if sloping to what degree? Is the soil deep or shallow, poor or rich, sandy or clayey? All these factors should be considered before you start the garden. All existing plants on the site should be accounted for by incorporating them into the plan where they are (building the garden around them), or planning for their removal. Unwanted trees and shrubs can be relocated or removed entirely, but doing so can be time and energy consuming as well as costly.

Such naturally occurring features as water or rock outcroppings will limit the selection of plants that can be used, although these features can be rerouted or removed at some cost; with some extra thought and planning, these features can become interesting and integral parts of the garden. Sites that are flat to slightly sloping are the easiest candidates for perennials, but some perennials, such as daylilies and lilyturf, can be used with good effect on slopes up to 45 degrees.

Shade or Sun Shade or sun is a basic consideration because far more species of perennials require sun than shade. If well done, a shaded garden can be lovely and satisfying, and although it will not present the riotous masses of

Sun filtering through a small tree creates partial shade in this garden.

color found in a sun garden, it will have a character all its own. Shade gardens are subtle and delicate, cool, green, quiet, and inviting. In the shaded garden, the harmonious nuances of foliage and flower color are quietly blended into a symphonic whole that appeals strongly to the senses, which are so often jaded by too much exposure to the overpowering brilliance of the full-sun garden. Because it often utilizes a natural location, the shaded garden is easier and less expensive to install than the sun garden; trees, shrubs, water, and rock are assets rather than liabilities. Maintenance is less, for weeds do not flourish in the shade, and less watering is required.

Shade can be categorized into three types: deep shade, partial shade, and light shade. Deep shade is the condition when plants receive no direct sunlight, and the light intensity is low. This type of shade results from having a heavy canopy of trees that allows no sun to reach the ground. Year-round shade, such as that from evergreens, will further reduce the selection of plants that can be used in this type of garden. Such conifers as pine, spruce, and fir will also provide a shallow root system that will compete with the perennials and further reduce plant selection. All-year shade from a wall or fence can also prohibit sun from reaching the surface of the ground, but the light intensity may be strong enough to create a greater selection of plants.

Partial shade is the condition that occurs when the plants receive direct sun for part of the day. It is important to note that the time of day, season, and area of the country will influence this type of shade. Morning or late day sun will be weaker and less intense than sun during the midday to early afternoon hours, for even sun-loving roses can perform well in only 5-6 hours of direct sun provided it comes during these times. The sun in the spring or fall is less intense than during the summer months, and in many northern areas plants will be able to tolerate more direct sun at the same time of day (because of decreased intensity) than sections of the South and West. In the South many perennials that are typically known as sun plants will benefit from shade during the midday in summer.

Light shade—or dappled sunlight, as it is sometimes referred to—is the condition that arises when plants receive no direct sunlight, but the light intensity is high or is the result of sun filtering through a light canopy of branches from deciduous trees. This allows a dappling of sunlight to reach the foliage of the plants, yet the sunlight moves as the branches sway in the breeze or as the sun moves in the sky. Although sun will reach the foliage, it will not be intense enough or stay in one place long enough to harm even the most shade-loving plants. This is by far the most desirable type of shade, for it allows the greatest number of species to be successful.

Sun gardens are best described as those gardens that receive at least 5-6 hours of direct sun during the times when sun intensity is strongest; the types of plants that can be grown under these conditions prosper because of these conditions.

When considering whether to have a sun or shade garden, it is of the

VIEWPOINT
PERENNIALS FOR DEEP SHADE

In deep shade, we plant ground covers such as *Epimedium, Lamiastrum, Lamium*, ginger, pachysandra, and ivy. as well as hostas and ferns.
KIM JOHNSON, OLD WESTBURY GARDEN, NEW YORK

Pulmonaria species and cultivars do well in deep shade; so does *Polystichum acrostichoides*.
SUSAN NOLDE, BROOKSIDE GARDENS, MARYLAND

We use many species of aloe, sanseveria, hearts and flowers (*Aptenia cordifolia*), many species of *Kalanchoe*, species of *Heuchera* and *Aquilegia*.
MARY IRISH, DESERT BOTANICAL GARDEN

Lamiastrum is a great ground cover for deeply shaded areas.
ROBERT BOWDEN, ATLANTA

Shade is not a major issue for us; our concern is usually finding plants that can withstand strong sun. We find that even daylilies do well in fairly heavy shade if their roots are kept well-mulched with compost.
DONALD BUMA, BOTANICA, WICHITA

The following plants tolerate deep shade: *Trillium, Mertensia, Hosta, Geranium maculatum, Brunnera, Helleborus, Asarum, Liriope, Pachysandra*, and *Anemenolla thalictroides*. We also use shrubs, such as *Cotoneaster acutiflora, Ribes alpinum, Hamamelis, Hydrangea arborescens*, and *Viburnum trilobum* and *V. opulus*.
GALEN GATES, CHICAGO BOTANIC GARDEN

To determine whether your drainage is adequate, dig a hole large enough to hold a gallon pot. Fill the hole with water, and see how long it takes to drain.

There are 3 basic soil types: heavy, clay soil has little space between the soil particles and usually does not drain well. Sandy soil has a lot of space between the particles and some-times cannot hold organic matter. Loam, shown at right, is the best com-bination of the two.

utmost importance to remember that making a sun garden is relatively easy (though removing large trees and shrubs can take time, and requires a chainsaw); but producing a deep, light, or partial shade garden takes more time. Shade trees and shrubs of a size that can be purchased reasonably from local nurseries will not provide sufficient shade for many years.

Soil Just as shade or sun can be a limiting factor in the selection of perenni-als, soil and drainage are factors in determining which perennials can be grown. Before building the garden, dig a few widely spaced 18-inch-deep test holes. These will give you a soil profile, showing the depth of the top-soil, its makeup, and the makeup of the subsoil.

For most perennials, the topsoil should be 8-10 inches deep and well drained, but for some, like peony and bearded iris, 12-24 inches of well-drained soil are not unreasonable and will actually be preferred. The condi-tion of the soil will have to be remedied before planting if the topsoil is not at least 8-10 inches deep, or if the drainage is poor because of a hardpan layer of subsoil.

The preferred method of amending and preparing soil to be planted with perennials is by "double-digging," which consists of digging down to a depth of 2 spades while incorporating organic material, sometimes coarse sand. This is a backbreaking and time-consuming task, and if possible it should be accomplished using a back-hoe–unless, of course, you need the exercise and have the time.

An extremely attractive alternative to double-digging is single-digging, which sounds like–and is–half the work. Single-digging will provide enough soil preparation except for those gardens where there is a shallow hardpan or a drainage problem. It can be accomplished by digging to the depth of one spade or by rototilling to a depth of 8-10 inches and incorpo-rating organic material into the soil. Never add more than 2 inches of organic material to the soil at one time, for larger quantities are hard to mix into the soil–the soil and organic material will have a layer-cake look and will not mix well. If necessary or desired, more organic material can be added in subsequent diggings or rototillings.

If the soil in your garden does not meet your requirements, it can be amended or replaced. A soil test, which can be done at your local nursery or county extension office, will indicate what your soil needs. Amending or replacing poor soil is most easily done before starting a garden, but it can also be accomplished in existing gardens. Though time-consuming and labor-intensive, this process will contribute greatly to the health and success of your garden.

1. Carefully remove existing plants.

2. Place plants on burlap or other material so that they can be moved easily, and remove to a protected spot.

3. Remove the old soil, 1-2 spades deep.

4. Amend the removed soil with fertilizer, compost, or other necessary amendments, and mix well.

5. Replace plants and water generously but carefully.

FORMULA FOR ESTIMATING NUMBERS OF PLANTS

STEP 1 Determine the number of square feet in the area to be planted.

STEP 2 Determine the number of square inches in the area to be planted. This can be accomplished by multiplying the number of square feet by 144 (the number of square inches in 1 square foot).

STEP 3 Determine the number of square inches a mature plant will cover. This can be accomplished by multiplying the suggested spacing between plants by itself.

STEP 4 Divide the number of square inches required for 1 plant (Step 3) into the number of square inches in the plan (Step 2). The answer will be the total number of plants needed for that plot.

EXAMPLE

STEP 1 The area to be planted has been determined to be 18 square feet.

STEP 2 18 square feet x 144 = 2,592 square inches.

STEP 3 Japanese painted fern (*Athyrium niponicum* 'Pictum') should be spaced 12-18 inches apart (for faster coverage plant 12 inches apart; for average speed in coverage plant 15 inches apart; and if cost is tight plant 18 inches apart). If using the mid spacing multiply 15 inches by 15 inches = 225 square inches for 1 plant.

STEP 4 Divide Step 3 (225 square inches) into Step 2 (2,592 square inches). The result is that 11.4 or 12 (we have yet to find a way to plant .4 of a plant) Japanese painted ferns will be needed for that area.

It is important to use organic material to improve all types of soils, for it will add drainage to heavy soils and fluff up sandy or poor soils and help them retain moisture. Cow, steer, or horse manure, leaf mold, well-decomposed sawdust, peat moss, or any type of compost will give good results.

Whenever possible, after preparing the soil for planting and especially before putting in a new bed or garden, let the soil settle or age for a few months before planting. A new garden prepared in the fall should, if possible, be planted in the spring, and a garden prepared in the summer should be planted in the fall. I prefer fall preparation and spring planting for two reasons: digging is easier in the fall because of the cooler weather, and doing so gives me the whole winter (at a time when gardening is low and gardeners get cabin fever) to look through catalogs for the perennials I want to purchase.

Fertilizer Another important consideration in soil preparation is soil fertility. Before fertilizer is applied to the soil a soil test should be taken to determine the fertility of the soil and the pH. Most perennials perform best in soils that are slightly acid to slightly alkaline, although some benefit from an acid or alkaline soil. The pH is measured on a scale of 0-14, with 7 being neutral, 0-6.9 being acid, and 7.1-14 being alkaline. A soil test will give you instructions on how to raise the pH if your soil is too acid or how to lower your pH if the soil is too alkaline. The soil test will also give recommendations as to how much of a specific fertilizer should be added per square foot to bring the fertility of the soil up to balance.

Most fertilizers have varying proportions of the three major elements needed by plants: nitrogen, phosphorus, and potash or potassium. Complete fertilizers, such as 5-10-5 or 10-6-4, contain a percentage of all three of these elements, while fertilizers such as superphosphate (0-46-0) are incomplete because they do not contain a percentage of all three elements.

Perennials need very little nitrogen, and if overused it can cause weak spindly growth and large leaves rather than flowers. In most soils, it can be omitted by using 0-20-20 or reduced by using 5-10-5 at planting time, for the most important element to add at planting time is the middle number (phosphorus), which helps build strong roots, is important in cell division and growth, and is necessary for the production of flowers and strong stems. Unlike nitrogen, phosphorus does not move freely through the soil and should be mixed into all of the soil and not just the top layer. Potash (potassium) aids plants in resisting certain diseases and in the translocation of carbohydrates.

Spacing Preparing the soil in advance (in the fall for spring planting, for instance) will provide time in which to prepare a plan and determine how many plants of each type will be needed to fill each area. Having a plan before purchasing plants is always a good idea.

Perennials are usually planted in irregular groups and not in geometric shapes, so it will be necessary to either overlay the plan with graph paper

Which of these plants would you buy? The one on the far left appears most vigorous and healthy, and probably is. Other signs to look for when when purchasing plants for the perennial garden:
• Plants with the most flowers will probably continue to flower well.
• Plants should be established beyond the seedling stage and have developed into good, sturdy individuals–a minimum pot size of 3 inches is recommended.
• If the plant is a rooted cutting, it should have been pinched when young, which creates bushy and full growth, with more than a single stem.
• Foliage should be turgid (full, slightly swollen) and solid green.
• Leaves should be upright and undamaged.
• No infestation or damage by insects or disease should be evident. Pick the plant up for a close inspection.
• A potted plant should have a sturdy root system. Some buyers knock the plant out of the pot to be sure a healthy root system has been established. Often the top growth is an indicator of a healthy root system.
• Many yellow leaves at the base of a plant or roots growing out of the bottom of the pot are often an indication that the plant is pot-bound.

or to prepare a grid to calculate the number of plants (see pages 170-71 for information on preparing a plan). The four-step formula at left is an accurate way to proceed.

This formula should be used for each of the plots to be planted and when accomplished will give you a list of plants and how many are needed. At this point plants can be purchased or ordered for planting.

PLANTING Three main factors influence when to plant perennials. First and foremost are the plant's cultural requirements. For example, some perennials like bearded iris are best when planted 1-2 months after they flower, for this is the time when they produce new roots. Second, and almost as important, is the region in which you live, for the gardener's spring (planting time, not calendar spring) comes earlier in the South than in the North. In the coldest areas of the North it is better to plant in the spring, for fall plantings might not have time to establish themselves if winter comes early. On the other hand, it may be preferable to plant perennials in the fall in the South, for spring planting might be stressed by the onset on an early, hot dry summer. The third factor is simply the availability of plants, for many nurseries may have only certain plants in the spring or will ship only bare-rooted perennials, such as peonies, in the fall.

Most perennials can be easily planted in the spring or early fall from either containers or bare-rooted stock. It is preferable to plant bare-rooted stock in the spring while they are dormant, just starting growth, or in the early fall, for although the foliage may be going dormant the root system will still be active well into the fall to early winter in some areas. Container-grown material can be planted with excellent success in the

1. Add soil amendments as necessary—compost, leaf mold, peat moss, etc. Shovel necessary amendments on top of bed to be prepared.

2. Turn over soil, 1 shovel deep, incorporating amendments and breaking up any clods of soil. If you can, do this 2 or even 3 times. Soil should become loose and friable.

3. Using a steel rake, smooth and level surface of bed. Remove any stones, debris, or clods of earth.

4. Walk down the bed, firming up the earth; this prevents the soil from settling unevenly.

5. Rake smooth again, checking one more time for rocks. Smooth and grade the surface.

6. Dig the hole. Hole should be deep enough so that top of crown is even with surface of soil.

1. Carefully remove plant from container. If roots are pot-bound, tease them out a bit.

2. If necessary, add fertilizer, such as super phosphate, while preparing soil.

3. Place plant in hole. The crown should be level with the surface of the soil. A plant that is placed too deeply may develop crown rot; a plant that is not covered may become stressed from exposure.

4. With your feet, firm up soil under plant, pushing in earth that was removed.

5. With your hands, smooth out the area under the plant, removing hand- and footprints.

6. Water gently, but fully. Check plant daily several days after planting and make sure soil remains moist.

· **VIEWPOINT**

MULCHES

Both aesthetics and function enter
into choosing mulches. Ideally, a
mulch should be both organic and
visually appealing as you view the
bed. Attractive mulches are particularly important in early spring, when
much of the ground is visible. I prefer
uniform hardwood bark chips or
cedar mulch for larger beds because
of longevity. For smaller beds, a fine
leaf mold or compost may be preferable, depending on desired texture,
ease of application (it does not last as
long), and cost.
GALEN GATES,
CHICAGO BOTANIC GARDEN

The single most common mulch here
is inorganic, crushed granite called
decomposed granite. It cools roots
and soils, retards evaporation, holds
down weeds, does not encourage too
much moisture and therefore reduces
root and crown rot, and looks wonderful here in the desert. When the color
is chosen well, it blends with the surrounding area and looks like native
desert soil. Its only disadvantage is
that it adds to organic material.
MARY IRISH,
DESERT BOTANICAL GARDEN

Pine fines are our first choice. We also
use shredded wood chips, which are
practical for us because we have a lot
of them.
SUSAN NOLDE,
BROOKSIDE GARDENS

We always recommend organic
mulches–wood chips or composts.
RICHARD ISAACSON, MINNESOTA
LANDSCAPE ARBORETUM

Shredded and/or composted leaf
mulch is easy for us to get, inexpensive, and, because of its dark color,
looks good in the garden. Composted
horse manure, run through a shred-
der, is also excellent.
KIM JOHNSON and NELSON
STERNER, OLD WESTBURY GARDENS

spring, early fall, or even in the heat of summer, but those planted in summer will require more care and may establish slower than if planted in
spring or early fall.

Tough perennials like daylilies or lilyturf can be successfully planted in
the spring, summer, or fall. These bare-rooted perennials can even be
planted when they are in flower and with a little aftercare will recover
almost immediately. Knowing the conditions for the specific plant will
increase the gardener's success rate.

When planting container perennials it is important to keep them at the
same depth as they were in the container, but bare-rooted plants do not
have the same guidelines. They should be planted to the depth where the
old stems and the crown of the plant meet. Peonies and bearded iris are
two of the exceptions to this rule; specific requirements for these and other
plants that do not follow the general rule can be found in Chapter 2 of this
book.

If the soil that has been prepared for the perennials was recently roto-
tilled or dug and has not had a season to settle, it is best to "walk it down"
before planting. This does not mean stomping, and it should never be done
when the soil is wet (which ruins the texture of the soil by removing air
spaces): simply walk over the area in your normal stride until you have
covered the whole area, then rake to get it somewhat level and to remove
debris, such as large stones, roots, or any other material that does not
belong in the soil. Don't worry: if the soil isn't wet, and if it has been prepared with enough organic material, walking it down will not compact it.

Make the hole for the plant larger than the root area of the plant; this
will give the roots room to expand. And spread the roots outward and
downward; this enables the plant to establish itself quickly without chok-
ing or girdling itself by wrapping it roots around one another. Since water
moves through soil in an up and down movement, spread-out roots–since
they cover more area–will be able to acquire more water and nutrients. If
you find that the roots of a container-grown plant have become pot-bound,
tease the roots out before planting. Otherwise, they might not be able to
break free of this girdling.

When you have placed the plant at the proper depth and spread out the
roots, fill the hole with soil. Be sure to firm the soil around the roots to
remove any large air pockets in the soil and to give the roots good contact
with the soil.

The final step is to water the plant well, remembering that you cannot
overwater a plant with just one watering and that a shallow watering will
leave many air pockets.

MAINTENANCE

MULCHING Mulching involves covering the surface of the soil with either
organic or inorganic materials. Although there are many good reasons to
mulch perennials, all mulching can be divided into the two distinct types
of summer and winter mulching.

Summer Mulching Calling it summer mulching is actually misleading, for this type of mulching should be performed in the spring after new growth appears or in the late spring for plants that need warm soils to start growing in the spring. Nevertheless, there are six main reasons to summer mulch:

1. To discourage weeds, which compete with perennials for light, water, and nutrients and are unsightly as well.

2. To keep the soil evenly moist, which gives the roots a better environment by regulating the soil temperature. When soil becomes dry it heats up. Dry soil is very warm, and wet soil is cool; soil that is mulched will stay moist for a longer period, and this will keep water available to the roots. Another related benefit is that water loss from evaporation is lower in cooler soil than in warm soil.

3. To conserve water by keeping the soil moist, which allows for better penetration of both rain or irrigation; this is more efficient and eliminates much of the run-off that is not only wasteful but can erode the soil.

4. To gradually add some nutrients to the soil–but only if organic mulches are used and left to break down.

5. To keep the foliage of the plants free from soil, which can be splashed up from heavy rains or when the soil is irrigated. Foliage covered with soil is less effective at producing food though photosynthesis and is more likely to rot.

6. To give the garden a pleasing appearance (many mulches are decorative) while reducing the labor involved in weeding or frequent watering.

Summer mulches can be organic or inorganic, but most perennials perform better with organic mulches. Organic mulches decay and add nutrients to the soil, while inorganic mulches do not decay and thus do not add nutrients to the soil.

Stones, gravel, pea gravel, or pebbles can be used with good effect in desert gardens where warm soil is not a detriment and in rock or alpine gardens where a permanent, poor-nutrient mulch is beneficial (but not for perennials). Plastic or landscape fiber mulches are beneficial for keeping down weeds and conserving moisture, but they are better-suited to vegetable gardens or to other temporary crop areas than to perennials.

There are many good organic mulches; leaf compost, pine needles, pine-bark nuggets, buckwheat hulls, and licorice root are only a few. It is best to avoid fresh wood chips, for these must be supplemented with a dressing of a nitrogen-rich fertilizer in order to keep the microorganisms (nitrogen-fixing bacteria) from using the nitrogen in the soil. Peat moss can be used as a mulch but should be avoided, for when dry even a 1- to 2-inch layer of peat can become an almost waterproof layer, and it will take a lot of rain or irrigation to penetrate it. The type of mulch used may be determined by what material is available and by price. Many mulches, such as licorice root, are expensive or hard to get, while others, such as pine needles, can be relatively inexpensive or can be collected locally.

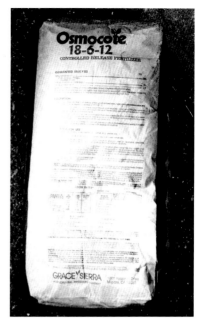

Most fertilizers list levels of Nitrogen (N), Phosphorus (P), and Potassium (K) in that order; an 18-6-12 fertilizer would be 18% nitrogen, 6% phosphorus, and 12% potassium. It is important to read the entire fertilizer bag; often information on the bag will effect whether or how you use a particular fertilizer. If you have questions, ask before you buy or call the manufacturer.

Place grow-through hoops on peonies before they begin to grow; raise them as the peonies expand.

The depth of the mulch varies with the type. Most mulches should be applied to a depth of 1-2 inches, but some should be used to depths of 3-4 inches. It is important to talk to the supplier or nurseryman about the type of mulch before applying it, for some commercially available mulches–such as spent hops–may ferment and harm some types of perennials.

Winter Mulching Winter mulching is a temporary covering of loose material, such as evergreen conifer branches, salt hay, or dry leaves. Winter mulches serve purposes much different from those of summer mulches.

Some perennials retain their leaves throughout the winter, and winter mulches can protect these from drying winds and the burning that can occur when the ground is frozen and the sun is strong. Another and per-haps more important reason to mulch in winter is to keep the ground uni-formly frozen. Alternate freezing and thawing can damage the roots of older plants or heave young or shallow-rooted plants out of the ground.

Use materials that are loose and permit air circulation on those perenni-als that retain leaves in winter. Failure to do so could cause rot. Winter mulch should be removed in the early spring when the perennials start to grow. It is important to uncover the plants a little at a time in order to acclimatize them, much the same as when a houseplant is brought outside from indoors. It is best not to expose them to the full sun at once, but to gradually remove the covering and expose them to the sun over a period of time. Remove the mulch covering over a period of ten days to two weeks and, if possible, do so on rainy or overcast days.

Do not apply winter mulch before the ground is frozen, for this may insulate the plants enough to cause premature growth and can provide a home for rodents with a ready food supply–your plants.

STAKING Although there are many perennials that need little care and can be thought of as low-maintenance plants, there are those that require much care in order to stay at their best. Many of the more vigorous or floriferous types need to be staked or pinched to prevent them from being broken by the wind or by the weight of their own flowers.

The best stakes to use are those that are never obvious–and those that are never used at all because other procedures make them unnecessary. Perennials such as the taller late-summer-flowering asters can be pinched in the late spring to early summer to about half their height at that time. This will not only reduce the final height of the plant but will also produce bushier plants that may not require staking.

When it is necessary to use stakes to support perennials, different species have to be staked differently. Peonies benefit from stakes that are actually hoops of wire on metals legs; these keep the stems upright and support the heaviest of the flowers. Many of these hoops have cross wires in a checkerboard pattern that gives the peonies more support than plain hoop supports. These supports should be used early in the spring when the peonies are starting to grow. Place them with the hoops at ground level or as close to the new growth as possible; and as the plant stems grow through and expand, the hoops can be raised with it. It is not wise to try to place the hoops on the peonies after they have grown, for this can damage the new growth.

Perennials such as ornamental grasses and many of the late-summer plants in the aster family also benefit from hoop-type staking. Plants such as foxglove (*Digitalis*) or delphinium which produce flowers in tall spikes should be staked using thin green bamboo-type stakes, fastened to the stems of the plants with green string, twist-ties, green plastic ribbon, or raffia. As a general rule, the tying materials that are softest or most pliable are preferred because they will not usually damage or constrict the stems. It is important to loop the tying material loosely around the plant stem then tightly around the stake; tying tightly around the plant stem may lead to damage.

Vigorous or floppy species of perennials can be supported by a method called brush or pea staking. Twiggy branches can be inserted into the ground to support even the floppiest of mums and should be inserted fairly early in the season, which will give the plant time to grow over the twigs and support itself. The stake should not be more than ⅔ the eventual height of the plant that it is supporting when inserted, so knowing the habit of the plant to be staked is important.

Bushy plants can be staked with wooden or bamboo stakes and string to confine the plant in a "cage" or "web." This should be used only when dealing with dense clumping types of perennials or when bushier perennials can be used in front of these cages to screen them. No matter what types of stakes are used, they should always support the plants without being conspicuous and without changing the natural growing habit of the plants.

DEADHEADING One of the first rules that should be taught to gardeners is to remove spent flowers as soon as possible; this procedure is called deadheading. The exceptions to this rule are for those perennials that have ornamental seedheads that are attractive either in fruit or during the winter or those for which seeds are wanted for propagation.

There are many advantages to deadheading perennials. The most vigorous plants, if deadheaded, will not self-sow and overrun the less invasive perennials. In addition, seeding of certain perennials will not be true to color of the parent and can be disappointing. Many perennials such as larkspur will rebloom if pruned back just past the faded flowers, but only if the deadheading is not delayed for too long. Allowing a plant that would normally rebloom to set seed, which is the reason that it flowers in the fist place, completes the plant's reproduction cycle, and no additional flowers are needed or produced. If deadheading removes the seed, the plant may rebloom to set new seed.

Deadheading also will help produce stronger plants for seed production

Frequent deadheading is one of the first rules a gardener should learn. Remove spent flowers as soon as possible; cut back stalks when flowering is done.

Controlled irrigation saves water and protects plants.

Weeding is critical to a garden's success; it prevents unwanted plants from competing with the ones you wish to thrive.

can stress plants, resulting in fewer blooms the following year. Plants such as daylilies or bearded iris will put their strength into producing stronger root systems or next year's flowers if not allowed to set seed.

Last, but certainly not least: Most perennials are aesthetically more pleasing when not in seed; plants that have gone to seed can give the garden a tired appearance. Vigilant deadheading maintains a neat, healthy, and fresh look.

WEEDING Although weeding is not much fun, it is important to the health of your garden. Weeds compete with other plants for nutrients, water, and sunshine; they need to be removed continually. Hand-weeding–going through the beds regularly and pulling any weeds you see–is the best approach. Try to get to the weeds before they flower and go to seed and multiply ten- or a hundred-fold. In a short time, you'll be able to recognize weed seedlings by just their first pair of leaves. If you are working with a very large area, you can hoe weeds, although with a hoe, you run the risk of damaging the fine roots of adjacent plants. The best time to hoe weeds is on a hot, sunny day; the hoed weeds will wilt and die quickly. If you hoe on a cool, damp day, a lot of the hoed weeds will reroot themselves and keep on growing.

IRRIGATING Many perennials require a little extra water. You can irrigate by hand with a hose, which is very time-consuming, or you can set up various sprayers or sprinklers to cover an entire area. The advantage to overhead irrigation systems is that they cover a large amount of space quickly; the disadvantage is that they waste a lot of water. Overhead irrigation should be done on sunny days, and completed early in the day so that the plants can dry before nightfall, reducing the risk of disease caused by wet foliage. Soaker and drip irrigation use less water, but are more expensive to install and make it necessary to exercise extreme care when digging in the garden to divide or move plants. (See page 74 for viewpoints on irrigation systems.) Don't irrigate so the water just penetrates the first inch of soil; irrigate so the soil is moist to a depth of perhaps 6 inches. Plants send their roots down as deeply as water is available, so deep watering will produce better-anchored plants that are less susceptible to wilting when the soil dries out (which it does from the surface first).

PROPAGATION

At some point in their lives, most perennials should be propagated. There are three main reasons for the propagation of perennials: To keep the plants young and vigorous; to keep overly vigorous plants in bounds; and to increase the number of plants without buying more. All methods of propagation can be grouped into two categories: sexual (or seed) production, and asexual (or vegetative). Sexual reproduction results in the production of new plants from seed while asexual reproduction is defined as reproduction using part of the parent plant–stems, roots, buds, etc.

Sexual (Seed) Reproduction Many perennials, especially those that have not been hybridized, can be grown from seed. Lady's mantle (*Alchemilla mollis*) and purple coneflower (*Echinacea purpurea*) are just two examples of perennials that

1. Collect seeds after they have completely ripened.

2. Store them in a clean envelope; mark the envelope with the identification of the seeds and the date on which they were collected.

3. Place seeds in soil or other planting medium. Place an identification marker in the pot.

4. Cover seeds with soil or planting medium; depth of covering should be the same thickness as size of seeds. Very fine seeds can be left uncovered.

5. Water thoroughly but gently.

6. Most seeds will germinate in a few weeks at a temperature of about 60-75° F.

HYBRIDIZING DAYLILIES

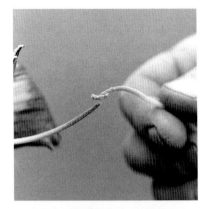

1. Remove the anther from the pollinating daylily, and place on the stigma of the receiving daylily. **2.** Identify the names of both daylilies on a tag. **3.** If the procedure works, the pollinated daylily will develop seeds, which can be collected and sown.

can easily be increased in this inexpensive manner.

When sowing seeds indoors or outdoors, the rule of thumb is to cover the seeds with about the same amount of soil or planting medium as the seeds are thick. Extra-fine or small seeds should not be covered at all. After sowing, water the seed containers or ground in which seeds have been sown gently, so as not to wash away the seeds. If the seeds are in containers, this can be accomplished by placing the seed container in a tray of water that is slightly shallower than the container and letting the water percolate up from the bottom. Outdoors, it is preferable to use a fine watering hose or water breaker, that, when attached to a watering can or hose, gently disburses the flow of water. It is also important to keep the seed containers out of the direct sun and to cover them with clear plastic or glass to help keep the soil evenly moist until germination takes place. Most seeds will germinate in a few weeks at a temperature of about 60-75° F. Some perennials such as butterfly weed (*Asclepias tuberosa*) do not like to be disturbed and are hard to transplant; these should always be sown in individual pots or outside in the area in which they are to be grown. When the seedlings germinate, move the pots into the sun or under growth lights. Light from most windows will not be sufficient and will lead to weak, leggy seedlings. When the seedlings show their first set of true leaves, move them from community pots into individual pots. In a few weeks these transplanted seedlings can be transferred into a cold frame or other protected area for the summer. In the early fall, they can either be left in the cold frame or transplanted into their position in the garden. It is important to protect these young plants for at least the first winter (see winter mulch, page 195).

Asexual (Vegetative) Reproduction In most cases, it is preferable to propagate perennials by vegetative means rather than by seed. Seed-produced perennial plants are more or less genetically different from their parents, and although many species do not show these differences, seedlings of hybrids or cultivated forms will in most cases result in offspring that are not identical to the parent. Perennials that are propagated by vegetative means will, except in a very few cases, result in offspring identical to the parent.

Vegetative propagation of perennials can be accomplished in many ways; cuttings and division are the two most frequently used and generally the most successful methods.

Cuttings Reproducing plants by using pieces of plants is probably the easiest and most popular means of propagating perennials. Chysanthemums, sedums, and many other bush, low-growing perennials can be increased efficiently and easily through cuttings.

Tip cuttings are 3- to 4-inch sections of leafy stems taken from nonflowering side shoots that are healthy, semi-firm, and have 3-4 nodes. These sections should be cut just below the bottom leaf node with a sharp knife, razor blade, or shears. The cut section should be dipped in water, then in a rooting hormone before being inserted into the rooting medium. A rooting hormone specific to herbaceous perennials can be purchased in most nurseries. Success can

1. Prepare a flat with proper medium.

2. Using a pencil eraser or other device, make a hole in the planting medium.

3. Select a strong, healthy shoot.

4. With a sharp knife, make a diagonal cutting 2-3 inches long.

5. Insert cutting into prepared hole.

6. When a strong root system has developed, transfer to individual pots.

often be achieved without use of the hormone with many types of vigorous perennials.

Rooting mediums can be quite varied; gardeners have used washed builder's sand, soil, vermiculite, perlite, peat, sphagnum moss, combinations of these materials, and plain water. Many of these materials, including soil and water, hamper root development and aftercare and should not be used. Equal parts of peat moss and sand or perlite can be easily mixed and will be more than adequate for most perennial cuttings; for succulent types such as sedums, which hold a good deal of moisture, a higher percentage of sand should be used to ensure proper drainage.

The medium should be moist and packed firmly before the cuttings are inserted, which will give the cuttings a firm foothold. Make a small hole in the medium with the eraser end of a pencil, a small piece of plant stake, or your finger, then press the medium firmly toward the base of the cutting. It is very important to have good contact between the base of the cutting and the medium or the cutting will dry out and die.

After the cuttings are inserted, they should be watered well, and the container they are in should be placed in an area that can provide humidity. A plastic bag with a few airholes or an empty fish tank can provide an excellent rooting chamber. After several weeks, check the cuttings to see if they are rooted sufficiently to be transplanted into individual pots. This can be accomplished by gently tugging on the cuttings; or lift one cutting out of the medium; if it does not have sufficient roots, it can be replaced in the medium and watered.

Some perennials such as bleeding hearts (*Dicentra*) can be reproduced by root cuttings, which consist of 2- to 3-inch pieces of their fleshy roots. Take the cuttings when they are not in active growth, and place them in equal parts of peat, sand, and perlite. In a few weeks, the cuttings will have a few new sets of leaves and can be transplanted into individual containers and then into the garden or cold frame.

Perennials propagated from either type of cutting should be protected the first winter (see winter mulching, page 192).

Division For most gardeners, division is both the easiest and quickest way to reproduce perennials. In the broadest of definitions, division is the splitting of one plant into two or more plants with each part having roots and stems or roots and a portion of a crown that contains buds that will become stems.

Some perennials such as chrysanthemums, which have the tendency to be overly vigorous, need to be divided on a regular basis to keep them in good health and to keep them from overwhelming other weaker or less invasive plants; perennials such as peonies may not need to be divided for many years.

Although most perennials can be successfully divided in the spring or early fall, a very loose general rule states that plants that flower in the early spring be divided in the fall and plants that flower in the fall are divided in the spring. Although both spring and fall are both acceptable times for dividing, there are people who prefer the early fall. In spring, gardeners have more

When dividing irises, cut away all diseased or dead matter; let roots dry in the sun for several hours before replanting.

1. This large clump of daylilies is ready to be divided.

2. The entire clump can be lifted out with a spade or digging fork.

3. Another method is to use a spading fork to separate the daylilies.

4. The easiest method is to use two forks, with their prongs placed between each other.

5. Divide the roots.

6. After reducing foliage, replant each division at the proper spacing; photo above shows peonies being replanted. Peonies, and other tuberous-rooted perennials resent being redug, and should not be divided often.

When dividing peonies and other tuberous-rooted perennials, keep in mind that 3-5 buds or "eyes" are needed for a flowering-size plant.

tasks to complete than they do in the fall, and, more important, it is easier and less damaging to most perennials to be divided in the fall. In the spring, division should take place as the plant emerges into leaf; lifting and damaging the foliage can set the plant back slightly, for it has to replace the foliage while making roots. Unexpected hot weather can also stress a plant. In the early fall, the foliage of most perennials will have started to go dormant and the plant will spend its energy to produce roots rather than foliage.

In the colder northern areas, it is preferable to divide plants in the spring or very early fall in order to give them time to establish root systems before winter. These plants should also be protected for at least the first winter.

There are perennials that have a more specific timetable for division. Peonies should be divided only in the fall, and it is preferable to divide bearded irises 1½-2 months after they flower. Daylilies can be divided in the spring, fall, or even in the summer while they are in flower.

Although some perennials can be divided with a sharp spade without being lifted from the ground, it is almost always better to lift the plant before dividing. Not only will it make the dividing easier, it will also give you a chance to rework the soil before replacing the plants.

Perennials can grouped into three main division types according to their roots: tuberous, rhizomatous, and fibrous.

Tuberous-rooted perennials, such as herbaceous peonies, should be carefully lifted in the fall and washed so that buds are clearly visible. The tuberous root system should be sliced with a sharp knife from the crown downward, keeping in mind that 3-5 buds or "eyes" are needed for a flowering-size plant. Discard weak, diseased sections or those that have fewer than 3-5 buds unless you want to keep 1 or 2 eyed sections that will take much longer to establish. Most of the tuberous-rooted perennials resent being dug and disturbed, and unless it is absolutely necessary they should not be divided.

Rhizomatous-rooted perennials, such as bearded iris, are easily lifted, for their root systems are at or just below the surface of the soil. After lifting the plant, remove most of the soil by gently shaking the rhizomes so that they are clearly visible. If any soil remains on the rhizomes, you can wash it off with water. The rhizomes should be checked for damage, insect pests, or diseases at this time and then, with the aid of a sharp knife, cut off the old growth, leaving the new healthy divisions. In the case of iris, the foliage and old roots should be reduced at this time. (See bearded iris, page 95.) Most other rhizomatous perennials should be planted as soon as they are divided.

Fibrous- or fleshy-rooted perennials Plants such as phlox with fibrous root systems, or those such as hostas or daylilies with fleshy root systems, can form tremendously interwoven crowns and root systems, and although they can be lifted and divided with the aid of a sharp spade or knife, they are best and more easily divided with the use of spading forks. After lifting the clump, some of the soil can be either shaken or washed off the roots. Turn the clump on its side and insert one of the spading forks fully into the root system just below ground level. The second fork should then be inserted with its prongs between the prongs of the first fork. By grasping the handles of the forks and gently pulling them apart, the clump can be easily divided with a minimum of effort and the least possible damage to the plant. This process can be repeated if smaller or more divisions are desired.

PESTS AND DISEASES

The use of the term pests and diseases can be misleading, for although we may think of pests as those members of the animal or plant kingdom that cause damage to plants we do not normally include most of the microorganisms in this definition. We normally consider pests as creatures—ranging from ants and beetles to deer and woodchucks—but weeds can also be put into this definition, as well as diseases such as bacteria, fungi, and viruses. In any case, we can categorize anything or anyone that causes damage to plants as pests and diseases.

Powdery mildew

It is safe to assume that there is no way to rid the garden of all pests and diseases, but it is possible to prevent or control the level of pests and to keep them at an acceptable level.

The first step in insect control is always prevention, and prevention starts with good sanitation. Many pests such as slugs thrive in gardens that are unkempt for they hide and lay their eggs under flowerpots, weeds, wood, and wherever there is trash. Keeping the garden clean and free from weeds and trash effectively reduces the number of pests by reducing breeding and hiding spots. Removing dead or diseased foliage in the fall will have the same effect and will also reduce the number of pests for some of these pests lay eggs that overwinter on the food source—your perennials.

Diatomaceous earth

Other insects such as whitefly are usually considered greenhouse pests but can and will prosper in the garden relatively quickly if allowed. In most cases, whitefly will be brought into the garden from infected plants, but by carefully inspecting plants that are purchased and buying pest-free plants they can be kept out of the garden.

Soft-bodied insects such as aphids, caterpillars, and slugs can be kept controlled with the use of diatomaceous earth, which is made from the ground skeletons of small fossilized animals. When spread around the plants, it forms a sharp barrier that will cut the bodies of the insects and cause them to die from dehydration. Diatomaceous earth can be expensive, but is easily available from nurseries or from swimming pool suppliers (it is used in swimming pool filters as well).

You can reduce some pests and diseases by selecting resistant species or cultivars, particularly if you know a problem is rampant in your area. Planting mildew-susceptible plants in areas that have excellent air circulation and thinning out some of the stems from crowded mature plants (which will increase air circulation) will also reduce the amount of disease.

In smaller gardens, it is possible to control certain insects by hand-picking or crushing them while wearing cotton gloves so as not to damage the plant. Slugs are easy to pick off, on a damp summer night, and aphids can

COMPOST

In forests and prairies, swamps and backyards, an amazing process is continuously taking place. Plant parts and animal leavings rot or decompose with the help of fungi, bacteria, and other microorganisms. Earthworms and an assortment of insects do their part digesting and mixing the plant and animal matter together. The result is a marvelous, rich, and crumbly layer of organic matter we call compost.

BENEFITS OF COMPOST Compost encourages the growth of earthworms and other beneficial organisms whose activities help plants grow strong and healthy. It provides nutrients and improves the soil. Wet clay soils drain better and sandy soils hold more moisture if amended with compost.

HOW TO MAKE COMPOST A compost pile keeps organic matter handy for garden use and, as an added advantage, keeps the material from filling up overburdened landfills. To make your own compost, start with a layer of chopped leaves, grass clippings, and kitchen waste like banana peels, eggshells, old lettuce leaves, apple cores, coffee grounds, and whatever else is available. Keep adding materials until you have a 6-inch layer, then cover it with a 3- to 6-inch layer of soil, manure, or finished compost.

Alternate 6-inch layers of organic matter and 2- to 3-inch layers of soil or manure until the pile is about 3 feet tall. A pile that is 3 feet tall by 3 feet square will generate enough heat during decomposition to sterilize the compost. This makes it useful as potting soil, topdressing for lawns, or soil-improving additives.

COMPOST CARE Keep your compost pile in a semishaded area to keep it from drying out too much. But if your compost pile is near a tree, turn it frequently to make sure tree roots don't grow into it. Make an indentation in the top of the pile to hold water and sprinkle the pile with a garden hose when it looks dry. Keep the compost moist, but not wet. Beneficial organisms cannot survive in soggy conditions.

USING COMPOST When your compost is ready, it can be mixed into the soil before planting, or applied to the surface of the soil as a soil-enriching mulch.

QUICK COMPOST If you need compost in a hurry, speed up the process by turning the pile with a pitchfork once a week for a month. Mixing the compost allows oxygen into the center of the pile, where it encourages the growth of bacteria and fungi. A pile that is turned regularly will become finished compost in 4-8 months.

MAKING A COMPOST BIN As illustrated below, many elaborate compost bins are sold. Some of these have devices for turning the compost and for removing it from the bin. Although these store-bought bins don't do the compost pile any harm, they are really not necessary. An enclosure made from chicken wire or from 5 wood pallets (one on the bottom, and four wired together for the sides) does the job just as well.

WHAT TO COMPOST

- kitchen waste
- lawn clippings (in thin layers so they do not mat down)
- chopped leaves (large leaves take a long time to break down)
- shredded branches
- garden plants
- shredded paper
- weeds (but be sure to use before they go to seed or weeds may sprout in the garden)
- straw or hay

WHAT NOT TO COMPOST

- orange and other citrus peels
- meat scraps, fatty trash (to avoid rodents and animals)
- excessive wood ashes

be easily crushed by hand. Shallow trays of stale beer will attract and kill slugs. Aphids can be syringed off perennials with a heavy stream of water that can be controlled by placing your thumb over the end of a hose, and a light, frequent syringing will also help control red spider mites, which do not like water.

If and when it becomes necessary to use chemicals to control a high infestation of insects, it is strongly advised to consult the agricultural agent in your area for recommendations as to what effective chemicals can be used for the targeted insect, with the least toxicity to humans, animals, plants, and the environment. For information about organic pest control, see page 210.

Some perennials recommended by Mary Irish of the Desert Botanical Garden in Phoenix:

Baileya multiradata: A low plant with bright yellow flowers, requiring moderate to low water.

Calylophus hartweggii is a fairly new plant to the area, outstanding as a ground cover or low perennial. It has bright clear yellow flowers and needs moderate water.

Hesperaloe parviflora, a longtime desert favorite, is characterized by stiff green leaves.

Salvia greggii, which bears profuse pink blooms, is very drought tolerant.

Agave macroacantha, a small but striking plant with grayish-blue leaves and black spine; it needs partial shade, moderate water in summer.

Agave parryi, a medium size agave has wide leaves that end in acute points in symmetrical rosettes; it is very cold-tolerant, and thrives in full sun or partial shade.

Dalea greggii, a popular ground cover, has tiny compound leaves, and intense blue flowers in summer. It needs moderate water during establishment, low water thereafter, and does well in full sun or partial shade.

Encelia farinosa, a signature native of the area, is a nearly woody perennial with yellow ray flowers that bloom from January to May, and sometimes during summer rains or fall.

PERENNIALS IN DRY CLIMATES

The American Southwest is an ideal place to garden, but gardening practices there are significantly different from elsewhere in the country. There are many excellent perennials that bloom in every season; unlike other regions, perennials in the Southwest can produce continuous color. It is not only wise and thrifty but also lovely and natural to use desert perennials in the Southwest. They perform better, bloom longer, take less water, have greater tolerance for the few pests that exist in the region, and are readily adapted to soil chemistry and climatic conditions. Native plants are already well-suited to the rigorous conditions of desert gardening, have a wide variety of form and color for use in the garden, support a wide variety of wildlife, and give the entire urban area a visual and aesthetic tie to the surrounding desert.

Most perennials—and other plants—are most successfully planted in the fall. This allows the establishment of an ample root system and less transplant shock and water loss; as a result, the final plant is more able to withstand the rigors of its first summer.

Perennials that are desert-adapted usually do not need large amounts of soil amendments when planted. Some mulch or compost—up to 25 percent of the backfill—is sufficient. Hole are typically dug a bit wider than than deep, both for drainage and to accommodate spreading root systems.

Mulching is an excellent practice. It reduces weeds, cools the soil in the root zone thereby allowing greater soil moisture retention, and of course, slowly releases organic matter. Decomposed granite, an inorganic, crushed mulch is often used; it blends well with the surrounding area, holds down weeds, cools roots and soils, retards evaporation, and keeps roots and crowns from becoming too wet; however it does not add organic material to the soil.

Most desert gardeners use some artificial irrigation. Some gardeners recommend using two irrigation systems: an overhead sprinkler, turned to its lowest volume, and a hand-held hose. The sprinkler delivers the amount of water needed by the least thirsty of the plants; you will be able to control which plants get more water with the hose. Daylilies, which sometimes suffer from dehydration get an extra dose, while *Echinacaea* get the minimum. Flooding a crop can do just as much damage as keeping it too dry. Take no advice about how much water their plant needs; personal observation of one's own site is the only way to judge. At the Desert Botanical Garden, overhead and drip irrigation are used—overhead irrigation for the large wildflower beds, and drip irrigation because it waters plants thoroughly, uses less water, and delivers water where and when the plants need it most.

PERENNIALS IN COLD CLIMATES

Gardeners who live in cold climates have a vast assortment of perennials to choose from. There are many plants that actually need cooler weather to thrive; delphinium for example, is much more successful in areas where summer evenings are cool. By carefully choosing cultivars and caring for them properly, a varied and long-lived garden can be created.

If you are growing perennials in a cold region, it is best to buy your plants in that region, or to swap with friends; local sources naturally breed more cold-hardy versions of most plants.

Locating the garden in a sheltered area will help some marginally hardy plants survive. Of course, the sunniest spot should be chosen, but try to find an area that is protected by a wall or large trees, creating a "microclimate" within it—hilltops, valleys, and open areas will usually be the coolest, areas protected by trees and walls will be the warmest. But don't allow your protective device to block out all sunlight. Exposure to southern currents is advantageous as well, and these should not be blocked out.

A variety of devices has been developed to help the cold-climate gardener. Black plastic mulch is very effective at warming the soil at the beginning of the season, and it reduces weeds if left on all summer. But if you find it unslightly—and it is—other mulches will work almost as well. Protective devices—row covers, hot caps, cloches, and shade—protect new seedlings in the even of an unexpected cold snap.

To help tender perennials survive the winter, apply a heavy mulch such as bark chips, straw or pinestraw or lay branches of christmas trees over the garden after the ground freezes. Remove as soon as the threat of frost is over.

Some tender plants can be potted up and brought indoors in winter; begonias and mums, for example, benefit from a winter vacation inside. However, these plants sometimes have trouble adapting to a too-quick change from life in the ground to life in an indoor container. To help them get over this double shock, leave them outdoors for a few days after they have been potted, then transfer them to a transitional area such as a patio or terrace.

A plant will have less trouble adapting to cold if it is healthy in other respects; northern gardeners should pay particular attention to soil maintenance, monitor insect infestations, and provide adequate water.

Perennials for winter interest

Why have a garden that looks like a graveyard in winter? Many perennials are evergreen, bloom in winter, or have attractive dried foliage or seeds which greatly enhance the winter landscape. Plant them in locations you will pass in winter, or where you can view them from inside the house—winter flowers are particularly nice when seen from a kitchen window on cold winter mornings. Try to locate grasses where dried foliage and seedheads will be backlit by the low angle of the winter sun.

Winter flowering perennials
Helleborus niger, H. foetidus, H. orientalis

Evergreen plants
Polystichum acrosticoides
Polystichum polyblepharum (in the South; in Maryland foliage usually lasts until December)
Dryopteris erythrosora
Dryopteris marginalis
Carex morrowii 'Aureo-variegata'
Carex pendula
Arum italicum 'Pictum', 'Dr. Comstock'
Helleborus species
Iris foetidissima

Plants with dried interest
Sedum x 'Autumn Joy'
Miscanthus species and cultivars
Pennisetum alopecuroides (var. *purpurascens* holds up best, but is invasive)
Calamagrostis x *acutiflora* 'Stricta'
Panicum virgatum 'Heavy Metal'
Eupatorium x 'Gateway'
Coreopsis verticillata 'Moonbeam'
Astilbe species and hybrids
Matcecccia struthiopteris

Bulbs
Ganthus elwesii, G. nivalis
Crocus speciosus, C. tomisinianus
Narcissus 'Rijnveld's Early Sensation' can bloom as early as January in Maryland

SUSAN NOLDE, BROOKSIDE GARDENS

PERENNIALS FOR THE ROCK GARDEN
For spring
Alyssum murale (Yellow-tuft)
Campanula poscharskyana
(Bellflower)
Coreopsis auriculata 'Nana'
(Tickseed)
Dianthus gratianopolinus 'Tiny
Rubies' (Cheddar pink)
Euphorbia myrsinites (Spurge)
Pulsatilla vulgaris (Pasque
flower)
For summer and fall
Campanula rotundifolia
(Bluebell)
Centaurea montana (Mountain
bluet)
Helianthemum nummularium
(Sun rose)
Hemerocallis 'Happy Returns'
(Daylily)
Iberis sempervirens (Candytuft)
Liatris cylindracea (Blazing star)
Limonium platyphyllum (*L. latifoli-
um*) (Sea lavender)
Veronica alpina 'Alba' (Speedwell)
V. spicata ssp. *incana* (Woolly
speedwell)
V. prostrata (Harebell
Hungarian speedwell)

Below: The rock garden at The New York
Botanical Garden.

PERENNIALS IN ROCK GARDENS

Making a rock garden is not simply mounding soil and spreading rocks on top. A good rock garden is created much as a painter paints a picture or a flower arranger combines a bouquet—with creativity and at least a little technical knowledge. The purpose of most rock gardens is to emulate the dramatic beauty of natural rock outcroppings, splashed with the textures and flowers of nature's alpines. Few gardeners restrict their choice of perennials for the rock garden to true alpines; any plant that fits the proportions of the garden and is not invasive can be used. Small, low growing plants are most often used to fill the numerous nooks and crannies in the rocks.

Placement of a rock garden requires some planning. Site selection should be governed by topography, incorporating any existing rock. It is best to work with an existing or created slope, which brings the rock into better view. If the slope is steep, take special care to make sure the rocks are anchored and stable. Choose a site that receives full sun or partial shade; a southeast exposure is best. The soil must be graded and amended so that water will percolate through it rather than wash over it. Ideal pH is 6.2-6.8; add lime if pH is too low, and add leaf mold if it too high. If subsoil comes to the surface while you are regrading, you will need more soil additives or topsoil. Sculpt the soil into the desired shape. If you move a lot of the soil in the process, it is likely to settle. Wait for several days for the settling to occur, then work in your soil amendments with a digging fork or rototiller.

Native rock is not only less expensive than imported, it also looks more natural. Limestone is a superb rock because it porous and retains moisture that encourages plant growth. (If you have limestone in your rock garden, you should check the soil periodically for high pH.) Granite is so hard that few plants can grow on it. Study natural rock outcroppings for inspiration on placing additional rock. Place the rock so that it is visible from the main viewing area. Select focal points or areas by deciding where a person will stand when looking at the garden, then arrange the rock so that it is visually balanced within each focal point, between focal points, and with the garden as a whole. Bury the rocks enough to make them look as though they belong there; if they are shallow, they will appear to have been set on top of the soil A good rule of thumb is to cover ½ to ⅔ of each rock with both soil and plants. Begin placing the rock at the highest point and work downward, making sure the rocks won't wobble or give way when you step on them. You will need access to the rocks for weeding and harvesting, so consider natural stepping stones or meandering paths throughout the garden.

Plan your rock garden to contain some fairly large spaces where you can plant a low ground cover such as cheddar pinks. Fill in the spaces between the rocks with slow-growing small perennials, usually 1-3 plants for each space. You do not need the large number of plants you would use in perennial border. As you gain expertise in rock gardening, you will find that this specialty is a challenging and rewarding way to garden.

PERENNIALS IN CONTAINERS

There are many good reasons to grow perennials in containers. Planting in a container allows you to choose your own soil, and so to grow plants that will not thrive in the soil of your region. Containerized plants add a lovely touch to terraces, decks, and patios. Some invasive plants remained "contained" only if planted in a container. A smaller containerized plant can be brought indoors in winter, allowing you to grow plants that are not cold hardy in your zone. And the containers themselves lend an architectural note to the garden.

Any container will work, so long as it provides drainage through a hole in its bottom. Avoid containers that will crack (such as clay) if you live in a cold region. Before planting, place a few pottery shards over the hole, and cover with an inch or two of gravel; this keeps the hole from becoming clogged. Soil for containers should be light but rich; amend with generous amounts of compost, and add some perlite or vermiculite. Fill the container with this mixture so that the top of the plant will rest about two inches below the rim of the container.

For best results, purchase containerized plants for your own containers. Tease their roots slightly before placing in the new container; if the roots are potbound, cut them with a knife. Place the plant in the container and cover with topsoil; tamp down the soil to remove any air pockets.

Containerized plants need some extra care; their roots cannot seek nutrients throughout the garden, so you must be sure to provide sufficient fertilizer and water. If the plant becomes too large for the pot, remove it to a larger pot, or divide it. You can grow plants that are not hardy in your zone if you place them in a sheltered area and make sure they are not subjected to drying winds.

This spectacular terrace garden, high above Manhattan, employs an ingenious system of containers on wheels. The gardener moves whichever plant is in bloom to the forefront, creating a constant display of lush color. This photograph, taken in the early fall, shows mums, Montauk daisies, and pink asters.

ORGANIC GARDENING

Few gardeners today are unaware of the devastating effect pesticides and other chemicals used in the past have had on our environment. Rachel Carson's searing exploration of the subject, *Silent Spring* (1962), exposed the "needless havoc" wrought by products designed to promote healthy plants. Not only were the chemicals poisoning our environment, they were also killing the natural predators of the pests we were seeking to destroy, making it impossible for nature to come to its own defense.

In the past few decades a vast and successful effort has been made to find new ways to garden without using harmful chemicals. The approach is directed at the soil and at the measures taken to control pests.

The soil is built up through the addition of organic materials, especially compost. The addition of compost, homemade or store-bought, and other organic material such as peat moss, green cover crops, and bone meal makes the soil so fertile and productive that petrochemicals are not needed.

Pest problems are handled through a practice called Integrated Pest Management (IPM), developed by the Council on Environmental Quality. IPM is defined as "maximum use of naturally occurring pest controls, including weather, disease agents, predators, and parasitoids. In addition, IPM utilizes various biological, physical, chemical controls and habitat modification techniques. Artificial controls are imposed only as required to keep a pest from surpassing tolerable population as determined from accurate assessments of the pest damage potential and the ecological, sociological, and economic costs of the control measures." In other words, gardeners must make reasonable assessments of how much damage a particular pest will do. If the pest is just munching on foliage, let it be. If controls must be taken, nonharmful ones should be tried first. Only in extreme cases is chemical warfare waged–and then in the most nonharmful ways possible.

The weapons in the IPM arsenal include:

• Careful monitoring to identify problems before they become widespread.

• Beneficial insects, such as ladybugs, praying mantises, and some nematodes, which feed on garden pests. Some of these reside naturally in your garden; others can be bought and placed there.

• Bacteria such as Bt (*Bacillus thuringiensis*) that attack garden pests. These bacteria can be bought by the pound and dusted on the plants; strains have been discovered that breed and attack many common pests.

• Insecticides such as rotenone, pyrethrum, and sabadilla and insecticidal soaps.

• Pest-repellent plants such as marigolds, which repel bean beetles and nematodes, and garlic, which repels whitefly.

• Hand-picking pests off foliage wherever they are seen in small numbers.

See pages 201 for more information about pest control.

ENABLING GARDENS

Being forced to stop gardening is one of the worst fates that can befall a gardener, but the inability to get down on one's hands and knees owing to arthritis, a bad back, a heart problem, the need to use a wheelchair—or the normal aches, pains, and fatigues of advancing age—is no reason to stop gardening. By using a few different gardening techniques, modifying tools, following new criteria in the selection of plants, and tapping into the many resources available for information and help, no one should ever have to stop gardening.

Begin by thoroughly and frankly assessing your situation.
•How much time can you devote to gardening?
•Do you need crutches, a cane, or wheelchair to get around?
•Can you get up and down from the ground without assistance?
•How much sun or heat is wise for you?
•Can you bend at the waist easily?
•Is your coordination impaired? balance? vision? ability to hold tools?

Consult your doctor, occupational or physical therapist, and most importantly speak to a horticultural therapist.

Horticultural therapists are specially trained in applying horticulture in therapeutic programs for people with disabilities and older adults. They have developed specialized gardening tools and techniques that make gardening easier for every situation.

Once you've decided how much you can and want to do, the garden can be planned. For example, people with relatively severe mobility impairments should have firm, level surfaces an easy distance from the house and should use containers or raised beds to bring soil up to a comfortable working height—usually somewhere around 2 feet high with a maximum width of 30 inches if worked from one side and 60 inches if both sides of the container or bed are accessible. People with more mobility can work with easily worked, light soils mounded to 8-10 inches above grade and should use lightweight, long-handled tools. Smaller containers can be hung within easy reach on poles or fences, and an overhead structure can be used to support hanging baskets on ropes and pulleys so the baskets can be lowered for care and then replaced to an out-of-reach position.

Important considerations when planning the garden layout include:
•Start small: keep it manageable
•Use or create light, easily worked soils so less force is required to work them either by hand or with tools
•Keep all equipment and tools in accessible places
•Arrange for a nearby water source—soaker hose or drip irrigation, perhaps—to minimize the difficulties in watering
•Use mulches to cut down on weeding

SOME SOURCES
American Horticultural
Therapy Association
 362A Christopher Avenue,
Gaithersburg, Maryland 20879
800-634-1603

Canadian Horticultural Therapy
Association
c/o Royal Botanical Garden
PO Box 399, Hamilton,
Ontario, Canada, L8N 3H8
416-529-7618

GROWING PERENNIALS IN THE SOUTH

Soil preparation and lack of water are the two most important factors in growing perennials in the South. Water rationing is becoming commonplace, and many southern gardeners are using plants that can withstand the searing summer heat of the South and are also highly decorative. Drought-resistant perennials need not look like weeds; *Baptisia, Echinacaea, Iberis, Nepeta, Oenothera, Rudbeckia,* and *Waldstenia* are all able to withstand hot, dry conditions, and are beautiful as well.

Water-holding capacity and temperatures go hand-in-hand. Along the various coasts and in nearly all of Florida, sand allows water and nutrients to flow through the root zone at a rapid rate. Adding a rich organic matter to the soil during planting will encourage strong root development. In the mid South, red clay is a particular problem. Washed sands of various types will encourage the flow of water away form the root zone. Most important is to water thoroughly. A deep thorough watering encourages deep roots, which can withstand drought conditions better than the shallow roots that are caused by frequent sprinkling. Watering should be done in the late afternoon to replenish the plant's water supply and to allow the leaf surface to dry before sundown, which significantly reduces disease.

The perennial garden at Callaway Gardens, Pine Mountain, Georgia, includes many perennials that thrive in the North (Shasta daisies, purple coneflowers), as well as some that are tender in colder regions (lantana, salvias).

Good housekeeping in southern gardens is the best way to maintain healthy plants. To ensure adequate air circulation, and reduce disease, space properly when planting, taking into account the ultimate size of the plant. With many plants, including the forever powdery-mildew-ridden phlox, simply removing ⅓ of the stems will produce larger flowers and allows for greater air penetration to the interior of the plant, reducing disease formation.

The South is the perfect climate for extending the zones of many plants. Many plants that don't like the cold can be grown in the South if a proper place can be found to give them winter protection; the same is true for those that don't like heat. *Actinidia kolomita* (hardy kiwi) would survive in the searing heat of southern mornings if provided with afternoon shade.

It is commonly thought that peonies can't be grown in the South. However, some of them do thrive. Proper selection is the secret. Among those that can be grown in the South are 'Festiva Maxima', 'Kansas', and 'Monsieur Jule Elie' (early season cultivars), and 'Felix Supreme', 'Fibrio Gold', 'Gay Paree', and and 'Sea Shell' (midseason varieties). Because the spring is so short-lived in the South, late-season peonies are blasted with high temperatures and often fail to blossom.

Perhaps the biggest problem with growing perennials in the South is nighttime temperatures. For years, many people thought that some plants did poorly in the South because they needed cold temperatures in winter. Actually, it is the summer nighttime temperatures that are the culprit. Cool-temperature plants like delphiniums are difficult to grow in the South because nights simply don't get cool enough; plants like delphiniums and most foxgloves are best treated as annuals. They will do well in spring, languish in summer, and rebloom again with limited vigor in the fall. The plant will put on a poor show the following spring; it is best to remove it, saving seeds to start the following spring.

acidic soil–Soil with a pH below 7.0; most perennials do best in soils from 6.0 to 7.0.

alkaline soil–Soil with a pH above 7.0.

annual–A plant that lives for only one year or one growing season.

anther–Part of a plant's stamen that bears pollen grains.

aphid–Insect that sucks the juices from a plant's tissue.

axil–Angle formed by a leaf-stalk, flower-stalk, or branch with the stem or another branch.

biennial–A plant that lives for two years or growing seasons, producing leaves the first season and flowers and seeds the second.

blackspot–Fungus disease that produces black spots on leaves, which then yellow and fall off.

blast–Blighting or sudden death of young buds, flower clusters, or fruits.

botrytis–Tiny fungus that causes many destructive blights.

bract–A small, modified leaf, with or without a stem.

B t–*Bacillus thuringiensis,* a bacteria that attacks and kills many common garden pests; can be bought by the pound.

bud–Unexpanded leaf, stem, or flower that will develop at a later time.

bulb–Encased leaf or flower bud, as an onion or tulip.

bulbil–Small bulblike bud produced in the axil of a leaf or flower.

calyx–All the sepals, the outer parts of a flower.

carpel–One of the seed-bearing units of a pistil or ovary.

chlorophyll–Green coloring matter in plants, essential to photosynthesis.

clay soil–Soil composed of many very fine particles, sticky when wet but hard when dry; water and air have a hard time moving through clay soil.

cold frame–A low frame or box on the ground with a light-transmitting cover that protects young plants from frost and helps transplants harden off.

compost–Decomposed plant material that adds nutrients to the soil and improves soil composition.

corolla–The inner set of a flower's petals; the petals as a whole.

corymb–Flat-topped or convex grouping of flowers.

crown–The section of a plant where stem and root meet; the topmost part of a root system, from which the leaves and shoots emerge.

cultivar–A variety of a plant that has been created by human intervention rather than naturally.

cultivate–Stir the soil surface to eliminate the weeds, aerate the soil, and promote water absorption.

cutting–Part of a plant (stem, leaf, root) cut off and then rooted to form a new plant.

cyme–A fairly flat-topped, often branched cluster of flowers.

deadhead–Remove old flowers to prevent seedpods from forming and improve the plant's appearance.

deciduous–Shedding leaves or other plant parts each year.

die back–Process by which a plant appears to die back to the ground during its dormant period; the plant begins growing again in the spring.

diploid–Having two sets of chromosomes.

division–Method of propagating by separating parts from a plant to produce new plants.

dormant oil spray–Light oil spray applied while a plant is dormant (in an inactive state) to suffocate pests.

drainage–The ability of the soil to move water so the roots of the plant don't become waterlogged, and so nutrients move through the soil.

evergreen–Having leaves year-round.

fertilizer–Any material that supplies nutrients to plants.

filament–Structure that supports the anther; filament and anther together make up the stamen.

friable–Term for soil that easily breaks apart or crumbles when handled.

frond–Leafy portion of a fern.

germination–The beginning of plant growth from a seed.

heaving–Lifting action exerted on plants by soil as it alternately freezes and thaws; can lift a plant entirely out of the ground or tear roots away from the crown.

herbaceous–Dying to the ground; not woody.

humus–Decayed organic matter, black and crumbly, that improves soil texture and moisture retention.

hybrid–A plant created by crossbreeding two or more different plants.

inflorescence–The arrangement of flowers on a plant, as spikes or umbels.

insecticide–A product that kills insects.

lace bug–Insect with broad, lacy wings that sucks sap from plants.

leaf miner–Small insect that lives and feeds inside a leaf.

loam–The best garden soil, a balanced mix of silt, sand, and clay.

manure–Livestock dung used as an organic fertilizer, rich in nitrogen.

mildew–Fungal disease that produces white dust or downy tufts on leaves.

mulch–Any material spread on the soil surface to conserve moisture, check weed growth, and protect the plant from excessive heat or cold.

nematode–Microscopic wormlike animal that may be harmful or beneficial to plants.

neutral soil–Soil with a pH of 7.0.

nitrogen–One of the three most important plant nutrients, needed for production of leaves and stems.

node–Place where the leaf is attached to the stem of a plant.

nutrients–Elements in the soil absorbed by plants for growth.

open-pollinated–Pollinated by the wind or animals, not by human manipulation.

organic gardening–Practice of gardening without the use of synthetic chemicals.

organic matter–Part of the soil that consists of decayed or decaying plant and animal matter (humus).

ovary–Bulbous part of the pistil that contains the ovules, which contain eggs that will become seeds when fertilized.

panicle–Grouped flowers.

peat or peat moss–Decayed remains of ancient plants, added to soil to increase the soil's ability to absorb and hold moisture.

peduncle–The stalk of an individual flower or inflorescence.

perennial–A plant that lives for more than two growing seasons.

perlite–Volcanic glass used in seed-starting and growing mediums.

pesticide–A product that kills garden pests.

petal–Part of a flower's corolla, next layer after the sepals; often colorful.

petiole–Leaf stem or stalk.

pH–A measure of the acidity or alkalinity of the soil, on a scale of 1 (extremely acid) to 14 (extremely alkaline), with 7.0 being neutral. Herbs grow best at a pH of 7.0 or slightly higher.

phosphorus–One of the three most important plant nutrients; good organic sources are bonemeal and powdered rock phosphate.

photosynthesis–Process by which plants capture energy from the sun and convert it into compounds that fuel growth and life.

pinch–Snip back new growth, to keep plants compact and encourage bushiness.

pistil–Innermost part of a flower, the female reproductive organ; consists of the stigma, style, and ovary.

pollination–The movement of pollen from one flower to another, necessary for fertilization and therefore fruit production.

potassium–One of the three most important plant nutrients; good organic sources are greensand and small amounts of wood ashes.

pot-bound (also root-bound)–Condition of a pot-grown seedling or plant whose root ball is thickly matted and contains little soil.

prune–Remove dead or living plant parts, to improve the plant's form or increase fruit or flower production.

pyrethrum–Insecticide made from chrysanthemums.

raceme–Long flower cluster, with flowers opening from the bottom first.

ray–One of the marginal flowers of the head in a composite plant.

receptacle–The end of the flower stalk which bears the flowers of a head.

rhizome–Underground stem, thick and fleshy and usually creeping.

rosette–Dense cluster of leaves on a very short stem.

rotenone–Biological insecticide.

rust–Fungal disease that produces rust.

sabadilla–Insecticide made from a Mexican plant of the lily family.

sachet–Small bag filled with herbs and spices used to scent clothing and linens.

sandy soil–Soil with a high percentage of sand, or large soil particles; water travels through sandy soil very easily, so nutrients leach out quickly.

scape–Leafless flowering stem that arises from the ground.

seedling–A young plant, especially one grown from seed.

sepals–Outermost part of the flower, part of the calyx.

set (fruit)–Develop fruit or seeds after pollination.

set out–Plant a seedling in the garden.

slug–Slimy, short, worm-shaped creature that eats leaves.

soil test–Analysis of the soil to determine its pH and available nutrients.

species–Related strains of a plant that occur naturally.

spider mites–Insects that rasp chlorophyll off of broadleafed plants.

spike–Elongated flower cluster.

spore–Microscopic reproductive body of a fern, corresponding to a seed.

stamen–The pollen-bearing, or male organ, of a flower; consists of filament and anther.

stem–Plant tissue that supports leaves and connects leaves with roots.

stigma–Tip of the pistil; it receives the pollen.

stolon–Slender, trailing stem that roots at the nodes.

style–Slender stalk of a pistil that connects the stigma and ovary.

subshrub–Partly shrubby plant, with persistent but not hard-wooded stems.

succulent–Plant with juicy, water-storing stems or leaves.

sucker–Leafy shoot at a stem junction.

taproot–Main root that grows downward.

tepal–One of six similar floral segments on a daylily.

tetraploid–Having four sets of chromosomes.

thrips–Insect that rasps chlorophyll off of broadleafed plants.

till–Cultivate the soil, especially with a mechanical tiller.

trace elements–Soil compounds essential to plant growth and development but present and needed in only very small amounts.

transplant–Move a plant to another location; also, the plant so moved.

triploid–Having three sets of chromosomes.

true leaves–The leaves that appear after the first, or seed, set of leaves.

tuber–A short, naturally swollen underground stem.

umbel–Flat-topped, umbrella-like flower cluster.

vermiculite–Lightweight, highly water-absorbent mineral used in seed-starting and growing mediums.

virus–A ultramicroscopic disease-causing organism.

whiteflies–Tiny flies that suck a plant's juices; often look like a cloud of smoke.

woody–Having bark-covered stems that do not die to the ground at the end of the growing season.

NOTE: The inclusion of a nursery in this list does not indicate a recommendation, and many other fine nurseries are not included.

Kurt Bluemel, Inc.
2740 Greene Lane
Baldwin, MD 21013
410-557-7229
Fax 410-557-9785
Grasses and sedges

Bluestone Perennials
7231 Middle Ridge
Madison, Ohio 44057
800-852-5243
Fax 216-428-7198

Busse Gardens
13579 10th Street
Cokato, MN 55321-9426
800-544-3192
Fax 612-286-2654

Burch Estate
650 Dodds Lane
Gladwyne, PA 19035
215-649-8944
Fax 215-649-0468

Canyon Creek Nursery
3527 Dry Creek Road
Oroville, CA 95965
916-533-2166
Uncommon perennials

Carroll Gardens
444 East Main Street
PO Box 310
Westminster, MD 21157
1-800-638-6334

Cordon Bleu Farms
PO Box 2017
San Marcos, CA 92079-2017
Daylilies

The Crownsville Nursery
PO Box 797
Crownsville, MD 21032

Foliage Gardens
2003 128th Avenue
Bellevue, WA 98005
206-747-2998
Hardy ferns

Gardens of the Blue Ridge
PO Box 10
Pineola, NC 28622
Nursery-propagated wildflowers

Heronwood Nursery
7530 288th Street
Kingston, WA 98346
Uncommon perennials

Hillside Gardens
515 Litchfield Road
PO Box 614
Norfolk, CT 06058
203-542-5345
Does not ship

Holbrook Farm and Nursery
115 Lance Road
PO Box 368
Fletcher, NC 28732-0368
704-891-7790
Fax 704-871-1505

Klehm Nursery
4210 N. Duncan Road
Champaign, IL 61821
800-553-3715
Fax 217-373-8403
Wholesale and retail, peonies, hostas, daylilies

Matterhorn Nursery
227 Summit Park Road
Spring Valley, NY 10977
914-354-5986
Fax 914-354-4749

Mileagers Gardens
4348 Douglas Avenue
Racine, WI 53402-2498
800-669-9956

Niche Gardens
1111 Dawson Road
Chapel Hill, NC 27516
919-967-0078
Uncommon perennials

North Creek Perennials
Route 2, Box 33
Landenberg, PA 19350
215-255-0100
Wholesale perennials

Oakes Daylilies
8204 Monday Road
Corryton, TN 37721
615-687-3770

Plant Delights Nursery
9241 Sauls Road
Raleigh, NC 27603
919-772-4794
Uncommon perennials, hostas

Savoys Greenhouses and Gardens
5300 Whiting Avenue
Edina, MN 55435
612-941-8755
Hostas

Schreiner's Iris
3625 Quinaby Road
Salem, OR 97303-9720
800-525-2367

Siskiyou Rare Plant Nursery
2825 Cummings Road
Medford, OR 97501-1524
503-772-6846
Rock garden and rare plants

Sunny Border Nurseries, Inc.
1709 Kensington Road
PO Box 86
Kensington, CT 06037
203-828-0321
Fax 203-828-9318
Wholesale only

H.R. Talmage & Sons
Horticultural Goddess
36 Sound Avenue
Riverhead, New York 11901
516-727-0124
(Shipping upon request)

Andre Viette Farm and Nursery
Rte 1, Box 16
Fishersville, VA 22939
703-949-2315
Fax 703-943-0782

Wayside Gardens
Hodges, SC 29695-0001
1-800-845-1124

We-Du Nurseries
Rte 5, Box 724
Marion, NC 28752
704-738-8300
Uncommon perennials

Weston Nurseries
Rte 135
PO Box 186
Hopkinton, MA 01748-0186
508-435-3414
Fax 508-435-3274
Will only ship wholesale orders

White Flower Farm
PO Box 50
Litchfield, CT 06759-0050
203-496-9600
Fax 203-496-1418

PERIODICALS

The Avant Gardener
PO Box 489
New York, NY 10028

Flower and Garden Magazine
4251 Pennsylvania Avenue
Kansas City, MO 64111

Horticulture
300 Mass Avenue
Boston, MA 02115

Organic Gardening and Farming
Organic Park
Emmaus, PA 18049

ORGANIZATIONS

American Hemerocallis Society
1454 Rebel Drive
Jackson, MS 39211

American Hosta Society
3103 Heatherhill Drive SE
Huntsville, AL 35802

American Iris Society
6528 Beachy Avenue
Wichita, KS 67206

American Penstemon Society
1569 Holland Court
Lakewood, CO 80226

American Peony Society
250 Interlaken Road
Hopkins, MN 55343

American Primrose Society
6730 Mercer Way
Mercer Island, WA 98040

American Rock Garden Society
15 Fairmead Road
Darien, CT 06820

Canadian Chrysanthemum and Dahlia
Society
83 Aramaman Drive
Agincourt ONT M1T 2PM

International Geranium Society
4610 Druid Street
Los Angeles, CA 90032

National Chrysanthemum Society, Inc.
5012 Kingston Drive
Annandale, VA 22003

The New England Wild Flower Society
Garden-in-the Woods
Hemenway Road
Framingham, MA 01701

The Perennial Plant Association
Department of Horticulture
Ohio State University
2001 Fyffe Court
Columbus, Ohio 43210

NOTE: Bold entries indicate illustrations

INDEX

CONTRIBUTORS

Dr. Linda McMahan
The Berry Botanic Garden
11505 S. W. Summerville Avenue
Portland, Oregon 97219

Donald Buma
Botanica, The Wichita Gardens
701 North Amidon
Wichita, Kansas 67203

Susan Nolde
Brookside Gardens
1500 Glenallen Avenue
Wheaton, Maryland 20902

Galen Gates
Chicago Botanic Garden
PO Box 400
Chicago, Illinois 60022-0400

James Heinrich
Denver Botanic Garden
909 York Street
Denver, Colorado 80206

Mary Irish
Desert Botanical Garden
1201 N. Galvin Parkway
Phoenix, Arizona 85008

Kathy Musial
Huntington Botanical Gardens
1151 Oxford Road
San Marino, California 91108

Richard Isaacson
Minnesota Landscape Arboretum
3675 Arboretum Drive
Chanhassen, Minnesota 55317

Kim Johnson and Nelson Sterner
Old Westbury Gardens
PO Box 430
Old Westbury, New York 11568

PHOTO CREDITS

All photographs ©Albert Squillace with the following exceptions:

©Ruth Clausen: 48BR, 103BR, 124, 138TL
©Ken Druse: 65, 268
©Galen Gates: 678TR, 75TL, 111BL, 150BL, 157TR
©Dency Kane: 27BR, 30BL, 39, 55, 67BL, 79TL, 94TR, 119, 122TR, 138BR, 140TL, 153BR
©Sylvia Martin: 184, 201T, 202, 212
©Elvin McDonald: 29TL, TR, 37TR, 52, 53BL, 61BL, 62TR, BL, 68, 69TR, 100TR, 100TL, TR, BL, 101, 121BL, 132BR, 201B
©Jerry Pavia: 173
©Photo/NATS: ©Ann Reilly: 67BL, 89BR, 126BL, 162BL, ©Les Saucier: 142BL. ©David Stone: 153BL
©Michael Ruggiero: 37BL, 53BL, 93, 108BL, 132BL, 137TR
©David Schilling: 169
©Sylvia and Stephen Sharnoff: 28, 30BR, 102
©John Smith: 143TR
©John Trager: 103TR, 178
©Chani Yammer: 158TL, 161, 179

llustrations on endpapers and on pages 16-17 by Delores Bego; illustration on page 23 courtesy of The United States Department of Agriculture; all other illustrations by Eric Marshall

T=Top; B=Bottom; R=Right; L=Left

LEAF SHAPES

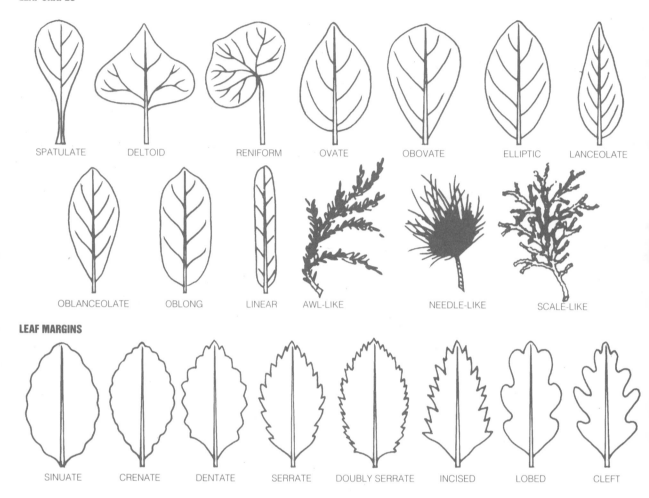

SPATULATE DELTOID RENIFORM OVATE OBOVATE ELLIPTIC LANCEOLATE

OBLANCEOLATE OBLONG LINEAR AWL-LIKE NEEDLE-LIKE SCALE-LIKE

LEAF MARGINS

SINUATE CRENATE DENTATE SERRATE DOUBLY SERRATE INCISED LOBED CLEFT

LEAF ARRANGEMENTS AND STRUCTURES

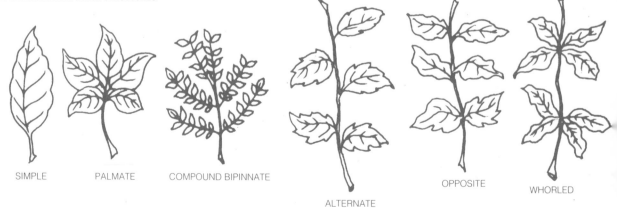

SIMPLE PALMATE COMPOUND BIPINNATE OPPOSITE WHORLED

ALTERNATE